America's Choice

A Nation Under God or Without God?

Tad R. Callister

First Edition
ISBN 13: 978-1-4621-4580-5

Published by CFI, an imprint of Cedar Fort, Inc.
2373 W. 700 S., Suite 100, Springville, UT 84663
Distributed by Cedar Fort, Inc., www.cedarfort.com

CONTENTS

ACKNOWLEDGMENTS

While I have received helpful suggestions from many in the creation of this book, I want to first and foremost thank my wife, Kathy, who has patiently reviewed numerous drafts, entertained multiple discussions, and given me compassionate but candid and needed comments. I also want to thank my children and grandchildren, many of whom have given valuable input.

Ted Barnes and Brian Hansbrow have also been invaluable resources as they have spent hours of time editing, formatting, and verifying numerous footnotes.

I also want to thank the many others who have graciously given of their time and provided me with many helpful insights—intellectually, historically, and spiritually—that were needed to refine, improve, and market this book. These include Kelly Bakes, Craig and Melissa Ballard, Dean and Susie Becker, Mark Boehlen, Douglas Callister, Mark Callister, Jim Cowley, Larry and Linda Cox, Lew and Barbara Cramer, Jack and Dolores Dickson, Devin and Julie Durrant, Don and Diane Hallstrom, Clark Hinckley, Richard Hinckley, James and Sarah Jones, Laura Kirton, Devin Knighton (and his BYU graduate class), Max Molgard, Brent and Marcia Neilson, Curtis Oscarson, Don Peay, Mel and Linda Reeves, Ted and Lora Stewart, Lance Wickman, James Welch, Kenneth Woolley.

My thanks also goes to those at Fulton Books who have made this possible: Gina Devin for opening the door with Fulton Books, Shannon Kuno for her meticulous and cheerful oversight of the entire publishing process, and others, such as editors, design artists, etc., who should be thanked.

INTRODUCTION

This book examines evidence of God's hand in the discovery, establishment, and preservation of America as confirmed by many of our Founding Fathers and national leaders. It challenges the accuracy of revisionist historians that demean Columbus and other national heroes, often without appropriate use of primary sources. It discusses the divine calling of the Founding Fathers and their belief that (1) the effectiveness of the Declaration of Independence and Constitution is dependent on the morality of the people, (2) that morality requires religion, and (3) that religion's purpose is to learn and live God's will.

This book describes how God's will can best be discovered in interpreting the Constitution (originalism vs. the living document method). In addition, it explores God's will on matters such as the exercise of religion in the public sector, abortion, same-sex relations, zero population growth, and capitalism v. socialism. It also addresses the ultimate solution to our country's ills—namely a return to family, moral values, and God—and the need for statesmen rather than politicians to help remedy our country's ailments.

Within this book, I quote some who are considered conservative in political matters and others who are considered moderate or liberal. I hope the reader will not accept or dismiss a person's words solely because of his or her political leanings but instead will focus on the historical accuracy, rationale, and spirit of each message. Such an approach seems to be the hallmark of an honest, mature, and enlightened learner. When all is said and done, my intent has been to find and disclose the truth wherever my research has taken me—in other words, to let the chips fall where they may, regardless of competing social norms or political ideology. Hopefully, this approach has led to a work that is fair, truthful, and uplifting, recognizing that at times it may be unsettling to the reader's current belief structure.

CHAPTER 1

What Role Has God Played in America's Origin and Destiny?

America—a Remarkable Country

The United States of America is a most remarkable country. How many other countries have defeated their enemies in war and then immediately given them aid and resources to rehabilitate them, not as vassals of the victor but as independent countries that retain their national identity and sovereignty? Japan and Germany are classic examples. They were our bitter enemies in World War II, having taken scores of American lives, yet in victory we did not enslave their people or expropriate their land or resources. To the contrary, we invested billions of dollars in those countries to restore their economies and transform them into local democracies. America's goal was not expansionism but liberty for all.

What other government and people have provided such staggering amounts of humanitarian aid for other nations in need? What other country has the equivalent in churches, service organizations, and other charities that freely give time, money, and needed resources to those who are disadvantaged?[1] What other nation has produced such astonishing advances in science that have propelled our civilization to heights never before attained? And what other nation has more liberties or has done more to promote human rights on a worldwide basis?[2] Suffice it to say, America—imperfect as it may be—is still a shining bastion of goodness, freedom, and progress.

David McCullough, best-selling author and highly respected historian, wrote of our nation's greatness: "It's said that everything has changed. But everything has not changed. This is plain truth. We are still the strongest, most productive, wealthiest, the most creative, the most ingenious, the most generous nation in the world, with the greatest freedoms of any nation in the world, of any nation in all time."[3] What a tribute to America from one of the finest historians of our day.

Nikki Haley, daughter of immigrant parents and a former United States Ambassador to the United Nations with a worldwide perspective borne from conversations with many world leaders, wrote a concurring opinion in a recent book: "America is, hands down, the best country in the world."[4] She then concluded with this significant statement: "And remember: Even on our worst days, we are blessed to live in America."[5] Hopefully, we will never lose sight of that fact or take this country for granted.

Criticism of America

Despite America's remarkable ideals and achievements, some have sought to focus on its faults. But such an approach leads one to ask, "If the United States is so fault-ridden, as some claim, why do millions throughout the world seek to immigrate here, more than any other country? And why are the numbers who leave its shores so negligible?" No doubt, you, like me, have met dozens, perhaps hundreds, who have immigrated here. On the other hand, how many do you know who have permanently left here? I can't name a single soul who has done so. Why is that?

Because America is still the beacon of light on the hill—the most magnificent republic (often referred to as a democracy in this book)[6] the world has ever known. It offers economic opportunities, relief from oppression, freedom of speech, religious freedom, and other democratic benefits sought by those whose countries do not provide the same. No wonder there is a mass rush to its entrance gate while its exit gate is seldom, if ever, opened.

Nonetheless, some are severely critical of America and argue that our nation's history is blighted, for example, with its early and unfair treatment of Native Americans, the existence of slavery, and, for many years, unequal rights for women. That is fair criticism, but it is only half the equation. Just as people are imperfect, likewise nations are imperfect. The Founding Fathers understood this and accordingly put into place the finest democracy ever known to man—a system that possesses a self-correcting mechanism, that allows for adjustment and improvement via Constitutional amendments as determined by the will of the people, a system that proposes to "form a more perfect union." As a consequence, at least partial restitution was made for the Native Americans through Affirmative Action and the creation of federal bureaus to assist with education and health.

Slavery was ended and Affirmative Action granted for many Black Americans, and many additional rights given to women. All this is a witness to the genius and workability of the democratic system crafted by our Founding Fathers. Some people still believe, however, that further restitution for these groups and other historically underprivileged groups is due, and if true, our democracy allows that discussion to continue and further remedies to be made if the electorate concurs.

Our Constitutional form of government is a brilliant pragmatic system that over time is designed to eliminate injustices and maximize opportunities for the life, liberty, and pursuit of happiness for all—a testament to America's greatness.

Washington confirmed this truth: "Democratic States must always feel before they can see;—it is this that makes their Governments slow, but the people will be right at last."[7] President Harry S. Truman concurred, "The people have often made mistakes, but given time and the facts, they will make the correction."[8] Our history is living proof of their observations. While our nation falls short of perfection, we have a system, thanks to our Founding Fathers, that has allowed us to make many corrections over time and thus make steady progress in that pursuit.

It is easy and tempting to be a political Monday-morning quarterback—to find fault with those in the past while remaining oblivious to our own current shortcomings. Who knows but what future generations, with the benefit of hindsight, will condemn our generation for taking innocent lives by legalizing and funding abortions, for the recurring breakdown in marriages and families, for the increase in fornication and adultery, for the expansion in drug usage, and for the explosion in pornography, abuse, suicides, and crime, but on the other hand forget the substantial advances we have made in reducing discrimination, poverty, and illiteracy. Hopefully, future generations will do more than condemn us. Hopefully, they will learn from the past and be grateful for a Constitution that provides an inspired system whereby we can build on our strengths and rectify our shortcomings.

David McCullough addressed the current criticism of America: "Let's stop the mindless destruction of historic America… In my experience, the more one learns of that founding generation of Americans—and I mean the real flesh-and-blood human beings, not the myths—the larger they become, the more one wonders what we've lost, or are in grave danger of losing."[9] Perhaps President John F. Kennedy had a perspective that should be adopted by us all: "I can assure you that we love our country, not for what it was, though it has always been great—not for what it is, though of this we are deeply proud—but for what it someday can and, through the efforts of us all, some day will be."[10] What a wonderful message—America is great, and it always has been, but let's work together to make it even better.

What Is America's Origin and Destiny?

As will be discussed in subsequent chapters, history presents compelling evidence that this country was divinely discovered and established and will be divinely guided so long as we worship God. Rudyard Kipling penned these lines about the British Empire that seem equally needed by America:

> The tumult and the shouting dies
> The Captain and the Kings depart
> Still stands Thine ancient sacrifice

An humble and a contritie heart.
Lord God of Hosts be with us yet
Lest we forget—lest we forget"[11]

So that we will not forget God and our Founding Fathers who were so instrumental in the birth and establishment of our nation, we have Independence Day, Thanksgiving, Christmas, Presidents' Day, Memorial Day, Veterans' Day, the crosses at Arlington National Cemetery, the Tomb of the Unknown Soldier, the Washington Monument, the Lincoln and Jefferson Memorials, our national flag and anthem, and many other reminders. These holidays and symbols are a reminder of the heroes who laid the groundwork of this great nation, the ideals for which it stands, and most importantly, God's influence in helping make these ideals a reality.

Author Gerald Lund shared an account of a climbing instructor, Alan Czenkusch, who ran a mountain-climbing school in Colorado. By way of background, Lund explained that mountain climbers like Czenkusch rely on a safety system called belaying, in which one climber anchors the rope and himself to the mountain so he can hold his partner should he fall. Lund then quoted from the account:

"Belaying has brought Czenkusch his best and worst moments in climbing. Czenkusch once fell from a high precipice, yanking out three mechanical supports and pulling his belayer off a ledge. He was stopped, upside down, 10 feet from the ground when his spread-eagled belayer arrested the fall with the strength of his outstretched arms.

"'Don saved my life,' says Czenkusch. 'How do you respond to a guy like that? Give him a used climbing rope for a Christmas present? No, you remember him. You always remember him.'"[12]

What a simple but poignant thought. How, then, do we respond to the Founding Fathers and the God of heaven who gave us the life and liberties we so abundantly enjoy? We remember them, honor them, and do all within our power to further the principles upon which they built this nation. In this way, we show our gratitude to them. With the passage of time, it is so easy to take for granted their sacrifices, focus on their weaknesses, and in the process become ungrateful. In truth, they put their lives, their fortunes, and their reputations on the line for us.

Nonetheless, there exists a current crusade by some to denigrate and diminish our national heroes and the God-given values for which they stood by unduly focusing on their imperfections rather than their achievements, by attempting to maximize every flaw and minimize every strength. In addition, they seek to eliminate or alter some of our national holidays and symbols. For example, some propose changing Columbus Day to Indigenous Peoples' Day or Exploration Day, removing the crosses from Arlington National Cemetery and other public places, eliminating the Pledge of Allegiance from public schools or at least removing the words *under God* and replacing the phrase *Merry Christmas* with *Happy Holidays*. In each of these examples, the consequences would compromise the heroes we honor or cause us to forget and put aside the values on which this country was founded. And in the process, these critics would convert us from a God-fearing nation to a Godless society—from a nation under God to a nation without God.

America's Origin and Destiny: Secular or Divine?

What then is the origin and destiny of America? Is it secular or divine? Answers to the following questions may provide some insights:

- Does America have a divine role to play in God's plan for humanity, or is it just one more secular nation among many?
- Was America discovered and established by chance or by divine design?
- Were the Founding Fathers raised up by God, or are they a rare collection of brilliant minds serendipitously born at the same time and in the same locale?
- Must the Constitution have a moral people to fulfill its purpose? If so, who determines morality?
- Has God spoken on any of the critical moral issues that confront our nation such as the role of religion in the pub-

lic sector, abortion, same-sex marriage, population control, and socialism? And if so, what has He said?

- What role, if any, should God play in the future of America?

The purpose of this book is to explore the answers to those questions and what effect those answers should have on our conduct. Accordingly, the following chapters discuss the extent to which God has been involved in the discovery, establishment, and preservation of America, why He is so concerned with the destiny of this country, His will on critical moral issues, and why we desperately need His help to preserve and maximize our freedoms.

---

[1] Arthur Brooks, in his extensive study on charity, came to this conclusion: "It is clear that the stereotype of stingy Americans just doesn't hold up. The American government is not the only giver. When we look at the overall charity of Americans, we see that by international standards we are an extraordinarily generous nation" (*Who Really Cares*, 121). Nikki Haley, former US Ambassador to the United Nations, concurred: "Don't let anyone tell you America isn't generous in our support of suffering people around the world. It's a false and ungrateful statement. For decades, right up through today, America remains by far the most generous country in the world" (*With All Due Respect*, 235).

[2] Haley observed: "The United States does more for human rights, both inside and outside of the United Nations, than any other country in the world. It's not even close" (*With All Due Respect*, 225).

[3] McCullough, *The American Spirit*, 92.

[4] Haley, *With All Due Respect*, 247.

[5] Haley, *With All Due Respect*, 248. Ben Carson expressed a similar sentiment: "God has opened many doors of opportunity throughout my lifetime, but I believe the greatest of those doors was allowing me to be born in the United States of America" (*America the Beautiful*, 180).

[6] Actually, the United States of America is a republic, not a democracy, but the term *democracy* has been so frequently and commonly used to describe our form of government that the term is liberally used throughout this book. James Madison clarified the difference between a democracy and a republic as follows: "In a democracy, the people meet and exercise the government in person; in a republic, they assemble and administer it by their representatives and agents. A democracy, consequently, must be confined to a small spot. A republic may be extended over a large region" (*Federalist Papers*, no. 14, 42).

7 Washington, "From George Washington to Lafayette," founders.archives.gov; emphasis in original.
8 Meacham, *The Soul of America*, 255.
9 McCullough, *The American Spirit*, 41, 47.
10 Kennedy, "Address at a Luncheon Meeting of the National Industrial Conference Board," presidency.ucsb.edu.
11 Kipling, "Recessional," 57.
12 Lund, *The Grace and Mercy of Jesus Christ*, 48.

CHAPTER 2

The Discovery of America—Was Columbus Inspired of God?

Was Columbus an Instrument in God's Hands?

To determine the extent of God's hand in America, we need to go back to its discovery and what role was played by Christopher Columbus in that effort. Was Columbus driven primarily by secular motives, or was he inspired and led by God? And what difference does it make?

What Was Columbus's Motive?

For many years, Columbus sought financing and royal permission for his desired voyage to no avail. After rejecting Columbus's request three times, Queen Isabella of Spain finally gave her approval. Even though the voyage would have profound financial benefits for Spain, Columbus was under no misapprehension about the purpose of his voyage. He knew it was much more than a secular quest. He knew it was an integral part of God's divine master plan. He was not alone in this understanding. Gonzalo Fernandez de Oviedo, Spain's royal historian, referred to the king and queen's "faithful service to Jesus Christ and their fervent desire for the spread of His holy faith." He then added, "It was for this purpose that the Lord brought Christopher Columbus to their notice."[1]

Some historians suggest that Columbus was principally driven to discover a new trade route to the "Indies" by a desire for fame or power or wealth. He was indeed a mortal man, and no doubt some of these passions were motivating factors.[2] Some argue that he could not have been inspired by God, pointing to evidence that he was ineffective as a colonizer and mistreated some of the native inhabitants of the Americas. Such conclusions, however, are difficult to support when all the known historical facts are taken in their totality and in context, and when "presentism" (interpreting past events in terms of modern-day values) is excluded from the equation.

While fame and fortune may have contributed to Columbus's interest in exploration, his main motivation, according to Pulitzer Prize-winning biographer Samuel Eliot Morison, was his belief that he was an instrument in God's hands: "For God is with men who for a good cause put their trust in Him. Men may doubt this, but there can be no doubt that the faith of Columbus was genuine and sincere, and that his frequent communion with forces unseen was a vital element in his achievement… *This conviction that God destined him to be an instrument for spreading the faith was far more potent than the desire to win glory, wealth and worldly honors, to which he was certainly far from indifferent.*"[3]

Not only did Columbus desire to spread Christianity among the natives whom he encountered, but he also sought gold and wealth for a very specific purpose—to finance a crusade that would conquer Jerusalem and rebuild the temple. In his own words, Columbus said: "I urge your Highnesses to spend all the profits of this my enterprise on the conquest of Jerusalem."[4] Being a devoutly religious man, Columbus believed this conquest and the rebuilding of the temple was necessary in order to prepare the way for the Second Coming of Christ.

God Works through Imperfect Men

At some point, this key historical question must be addressed: "Was Columbus divinely inspired or were his voyages nothing more than secular quests?" Columbus certainly had his weaknesses, but if God could use only perfect men to advance His work, He would be left empty-handed. To illustrate, suppose I were to tell you these four historical facts about a New Testament character and nothing more: first, Jesus said to him, "Get thee behind me, Satan" (Matt. 16:23).[5] Second, the Lord reprimanded him as follows: "O thou of little faith" (Matt. 14:31). Third, in a fit of rage, this man cut off the ear of the high priest's servant (see John 18:10). And fourth, this man denied knowing the Savior on three occasions, even though he walked with Him daily (see John 18:27). If that were all you knew or focused upon, would you deem this man a servant of God or a reprobate? A saint or a sinner? This man, of course, was Peter, Christ's chief apostle. Would his imperfections cause you to reject or abandon Christianity? Or would you say that his imperfections were only a small part of the total man? Would you put those events in context of his entire life so as not to lose proper perspective? If we focus only upon Peter's weaknesses, we will have missed the real man, his mark and his mission—the man who left his fishing nets to follow Jesus, the man who saw heavenly angels, the man who was a mighty preacher of righteousness, the man who healed the infirm and even raised the dead, and the man who gave his life for his testimony of Jesus Christ.

The same rationale that applies to Peter also applies to other historical figures. George Washington and Thomas Jefferson made enormous contributions to the founding of this nation, yet they were slaveholders. Martin Luther King Jr. played a pivotal role in advancing racial equality for which he should be commended, yet it is no secret he engaged in serious moral transgressions.[6] Sometimes we are blinded by our political prejudices. We see only the good in those who agree with our philosophy of life and only the bad in those who have opposing views. But the world is not so tidy, not so compartmentalized.

To illustrate this point, I share an observation made by my wife, Kathy: "In the Louvre Museum in Paris, France, there is a majestic marble statue commonly referred to as *Winged Victory*. A Greek sculpture from the 2nd century BC, it is one of the most famous statues in the world. Towering at the top of a sweeping staircase near the entrance to the museum, it is breathtaking at first sight. Even though severely damaged—missing her head, arms, and feet—with her gracefully outstretched wings and robes, seemingly fluttering in the wind, she is stunningly beautiful." We have a replica of that statue in our home. Imperfect as it may be, it is nonetheless one of the masterpieces of all time. How shortsighted and tragic it would be if people focused only on that which is missing and failed to see the glorious work of art which remains.

Similarly, there are some who focus only on the weaknesses in the life of Columbus, but if this is their prime focus and they fail to put those weaknesses in the context of his entire life, then they too will miss the real man, his mark, and his inspired mission. Fortunately, God uses imperfect men and women to advance His purposes. The critic sees only warts and blemishes. God sees the beauty and strengths, and then He uses them to further His cause.[7] And so it was with Columbus.

To deny his essential and God-inspired role in events which ultimately made possible the birth and founding of the United States of America is to suffer from a severe case of historical myopia.

The Revisionist View of Columbus

For purposes of this book, the term *revisionist historians* refers to those historians who would rather promote their own prejudices and perspective of history than actual facts as reflected in primary sources (meaning original sources created during the historical time under discussion). In addition, revisionists often demean or vilify those historical figures with whom they disagree in an attempt to diminish their influence. Such a technique was used by the critics of the Savior who "mocked him" (Luke 22:63) and falsely referred to Him as "a man gluttonous, and a winebibber" (Matt. 11:19), a "malefactor" (John 18:30), a blasphemer (see John 10:33), and a traitor (see Luke 23:2).

Primary sources for learning the history of Columbus include such records as Columbus's journal and letters, a biography by his son Ferdinand Columbus, an investigative report by his bitter enemy Francisco de Bobadilla, and writings from contemporary historians such as Peter Martyr of Angleria, Bartolome de las Casas, and Andrés

Bernáldez. As I read about the life of Columbus, I realized that Columbus, like the rest of us, was certainly imperfect. However, I was surprised and disappointed at the many times revisionists quoted passages out of context, cited other revisionists without reference to primary sources, or simply failed to quote primary sources that disproved or weakened their position. Lest there be any question, a partial truth presented as the whole truth is an untruth, and there is no doubt but that many revisionists have engaged in partial truths. Following are but a few examples of such partial truths, each of which is designed to demean Columbus and his God-inspired mission.

Columbus did not introduce slavery into the New World.

Perhaps one of Columbus's greatest alleged sins is that he enslaved certain of the natives that he conquered in war. Historically, for centuries, the conquered often became the slaves of the victor. Slavery was not an invention of Columbus. In fact, some native tribes had slaves of their own, contrary to the false impression spread by revisionists that Columbus introduced slavery into the New World.[8] For example, historian Peter Martyr d'Anghiera recorded that the eldest son of Comogre (a native chief) presented seventy slaves to Spanish leaders as a gift.[9] He also noted, "When the Spaniards left his village, [Chief Taocha] not only furnished them guides, but also slaves who were prisoners of war."[10] This is not to excuse slavery but to put it in perspective at the time of Columbus, a perspective often ignored by the revisionists.

Columbus wanted to convert any slaves to Christianity to bless their lives.

Furthermore, one needs to understand the context in which Columbus sent some slaves to Spain. King Guacanagari was a native chief who helped Columbus when the *Santa Maria* shipwrecked and who later sought the help of Columbus to defeat an enemy tribe of cannibals who were destroying his own tribe. Columbus did assist in this request and sent the captured cannibals as slaves to Spain.

Regarding these slaves, Columbus wrote to the monarchs: "We send by these two vessels some of these cannibal men and women, as well as some children, both male and female. Their Highnesses can order them to be placed under the care of the most competent persons to teach them the language." Columbus then explained his motive for sending these slaves: "that they may one day be led to abandon their barbarous custom of eating their fellow-creatures. By learning the Spanish language in Spain, they will much earlier receive baptism and ensure the salvation of their souls; moreover, it will be a great happiness to the Indians who do not practice the above-mentioned cruel custom [cannibalism], when they see that we have seized and led captive those who injure them, whom they dread so much, that their name alone fills them with horror."[11]

Columbus also said of the slaves that he sent to Spain that he "intended to reclaim" them and then "return them to their lands so they would instruct others."[12] This, of course, does not justify the slave trade, but it helps us understand the motives behind Columbus's actions—to help civilize and save a people, some of whom practiced cannibalism. This is an important insight completely neglected by the revisionists who want only to paint Columbus in a negative light. Likewise, it is important to understand that Columbus, who the revisionists accuse as a slave trader, never personally owned a slave, either in the Indies or in Spain.[13] In other words, any natives sent to Spain were not for the personal benefit of Columbus but for what he thought might be the ultimate education and conversion of these natives to Christianity.

Columbus wanted to make friends, not enemies of the natives.

It is true that Columbus did kill some natives, but this was largely in response to the death of thirty-nine Spaniards (killed by these same natives) that Columbus had left behind to govern the island of Hispaniola. As to this event, Las Casas, a contemporary of Columbus and historian, wrote: "Truly, I would not dare blame the admiral's intention, for I knew him well and all I know his intentions were good."[14] This is consistent with Columbus's own self-admission: "I know, assuredly, that the errors which I may have fallen into, have been done without the intention to do wrong."[15]

This also seems consistent with the observation of Carol Delaney, emeritus professor of Stanford University and a lead historian on the life of Columbus, who indicated that Columbus wanted to make friends, not enemies of the natives. In a conversation with Delaney, Alton Pelowski noted that "the popular view today is that Columbus is responsible for countless atrocities against the native peoples." Pelowski asked her if she felt "this is a fair assessment." Delaney, after having reviewed all the available evidence on the subject and being as well-informed or perhaps better than any other on the subject, responded with impartiality: "*No, not at all.* The late twentieth century brought a lot of critique about him from the perspective of the natives, and Columbus has become a symbol for everything that went wrong. But the more I read of his own writings and that of his contemporaries, *my understanding of him totally changed.* His relations with the natives tended to be benign. He liked the natives and found them to be very intelligent. *Christopher strictly told the crew not to do things like maraud [or] rape, and instead to treat the native people with respect. There are many examples in his writings where he gave instructions to this effect. Most of the time when injustices occurred, Columbus wasn't even there.*"[16]

On one occasion Columbus hanged two Spaniards for mistreating the natives. Delaney wrote: "These were men who had been punished for their rebellion and the hideous deeds they had committed against the Indians. Columbus intended their deaths to serve as an example not only to the rest of the colonists, but also to show the Indians that the rule of law also applied to his own men."[17] Why is it that the revisionists never report this event? Because it is contrary to their agenda claiming that Columbus mistreated the natives.

In my own reading of original sources, I came to the same conclusion as Delaney. Columbus pretty well summarized his attitude toward the natives in this diary entry: "I knew they were a people to be converted and won to our holy faith by love and friendship rather than by force."[18] Peter Martyr, a contemporary historian, confirmed this belief of Columbus: "*As he had never mistreated the natives*, the inhabitants [of Cuba], both men and women, gladly brought him gifts, displaying no fear."[19] One must ask, "Why is it that these trusted original sources—the personal diary of Columbus and the impartial testimonies of contemporary historians—are so frequently in opposition to the conclusions of the revisionist historians and seldom, if ever, quoted? And why is it that contrary to the allegations of the revisionists, Columbus was usually quick to punish those responsible when bad things were done to the natives?"[20]

Columbus is blamed for the acts of others even when he was not present.

There were atrocities committed by the Spaniards, but the vast majority of these occurred by the Spaniards whom Columbus left behind while he returned to Spain and by the two Spanish leaders who governed in his absence, namely, Francisco de Bobadilla and Frey Nicolás de Ovando y Cáceres.[21] Later, Columbus referred to Spaniards who mistreated the natives as "debauchees, profligates, thieves, seducers, ravishers, vagabonds,"[22] hardly descriptions of individuals whose conduct was approved by him. To the contrary, Columbus wanted the natives to be treated fairly. He wrote, "I do not think it would be well or desirable, on the part of your Highnesses, to take possession of it [gold] in the way of plunder; by fair dealing, scandal and disrepute will be avoided."[23] One must wonder why revisionist historians often omit these mitigating details as set forth in primary sources.

On one occasion, Columbus left fifty men under the supervision of Pedro Margarit to mine gold on the island of Cibao. He sent Margarit instructions that the Indians were to "receive no injury, suffer no harm, and that nothing is [to be] taken from them against their will; instead make them feel honored and protected so as to keep them from becoming perturbed."[24] Does this sound like a tyrant as asserted by the revisionists? As Carol Delaney noted, "What Columbus didn't know was that Margarit, and the men under his command, had gone on rampages, marauding the native villages and raping the women." These were actions for which the revisionists blame Columbus.[25] Delaney also said, "*They're [the critics] blaming Columbus for the things he didn't do... I just think he's been terribly maligned.*"[26]

In support of Delaney's foregoing observation, Las Casas, who meticulously detailed the brutality of the Spaniards, nonetheless, made this exculpatory observation about Columbus: "[T]he desolation of these Isles and Provinces [Hispaniola] took beginning...about the year 1504 [*after* Columbus's four voyages were completed and at a time when he had no administrative responsibilities in the New World], for before that time [when Columbus governed in part] very few of the Provinces situated in that Island were oppressed or spoiled with unjust Wars, or violated with general devastation as after they were."[27] What a defense of Columbus—not to be found in the writings of the revisionist historians.

Columbus's intentions were good. He wanted to enlist the natives, not destroy them.

Columbus is accused of widescale genocide, meaning mass killing of the natives he encountered. It is true that many Native Americans died from diseases transmitted by the Spaniards because they had little, if any, immunity. This was a tragic occurrence, but there is no historical evidence that this was intentional in any way. Columbus came to America to find wealth to be used in the retaking of Jerusalem in the name of Christianity and to convert the natives to Christianity, not to exterminate them. To suggest that Columbus purposely sought extinction is a fact nowhere to be found in history. Delaney made this significant observation about Columbus: "He surely did not intend to commit genocide, of which he has been accused. He wanted to enlist the...people on his side, not to destroy them."[28]

It is true there were diseases transmitted and subsequent loss of life, but countering that, the revisionists have failed to mention a very significant fact—the rise of the magnificent Hispanic race numbering in the multimillions. Who are these people? They are the descendants and beneficiaries of the fusion between the Spanish and native cultures, made possible in the Americas because of Columbus.

Revisionists misquote Columbus as endorsing rather than merely reporting sexual slavery.

An additional partial truth is that Columbus sanctioned and supervised the selling of native girls into sexual slavery. For support, the revisionists love to quote one sentence from a letter of Columbus: "For one woman they give a hundred castellanos, as for a farm; and this sort of trading is very common, and there are already a great number of merchants who go in search of girls; there are at this moment from nine or ten on sale; they fetch a good price, let their age be what it will." But revisionists quote this statement out of context. Columbus was reporting an event, not endorsing it. He was writing about atrocities committed by those who had now settled in the Indies. In fact, before making reference to the sex slavery mentioned above, Columbus wrote, "It would be well to send people from Spain, and only to send such as are well known, that the country may be peopled with honest men." After making reference to the women being sold into slavery, he observed, "I aver, that a great number of men have been to the Indies, who did not deserve baptism in the eyes of God or men, and who are now returning thither."[29] In other words, it seems Columbus was condemning, not condoning such actions.

As further evidence of his motives, Columbus tells of two native girls sent to his ship, about seven and eleven years of age, very immodestly dressed. Did he take advantage of them? Sell them? No. In his own words, "I gave them some articles to dress themselves out with, and directly sent them back to the shore."[30] In fact, we do not have one historical evidence of Columbus ever taking advantage of a native girl or woman.

Columbus brought the natives a much better way of life.

Some revisionists would have us believe that the natives with whom Columbus interacted were all peace-loving, free of major diseases, and living in harmony and happiness before Columbus "destroyed" all that.[31] The facts reveal, however, that many tribes were continually at war.[32] The British historian Hugh Thomas responded to this so-called noble savage myth by offering this insight about the native tribes: "Had it not been for the Spanish invasions, it is likely that the Caribs [a native tribe]would have destroyed the Tainos as the Tainos had destroyed the Ciboneys. Some have written of the ancient Caribbean as if it had been Elysium. But it was an Elysium with savagery in the wings."[33] Furthermore, the facts reveal that some of these natives were cannibals,[34] that some ate their own children,[35] that they were subject to major diseases,[36] that some possessed slaves as discussed above, that some performed human sacrifices,[37] and that some practiced witchcraft,[38] among other atrocities.[39] To suggest that Columbus destroyed their peaceful, civilized, and harmonious societies is pure fiction.

To the contrary, Columbus brought them a much better way of life—Christianity. That is why the Americas today are filled with Christian nations where cannibalism has been eradicated, slavery abolished, human sacrifices done away, major diseases minimized, life expectancies extended, poverty reduced, and education made available to most.[40] That is the true legacy of Columbus.[41] In many ways, he was the catalyst for Western civilization.

A Partial Truth When Told as the Whole Truth is an Untruth

As stated, a partial truth when told as the whole truth is an untruth, and unfortunately, the revisionists have propagated partial truths in exponential degrees. And in the process, they have used such partial truths to denigrate a man, admittedly imperfect, but nonetheless one who made a monumental contribution to the discovery and settlement of America and thus deserves to be honored by all Americans.

Perhaps one of the most impartial witnesses of Columbus was the contemporary historian Las Casas, who was concerned about the welfare and treatment of the indigenous natives and who was not afraid to point out Columbus's weaknesses. Nonetheless, taking Columbus's shortcomings into account, Las Casas summarized his life as follows: "I think Christopher Columbus was the most outstanding sailor in the world, versed like no other in the art of navigation, *for which divine Providence chose him to accomplish the most outstanding feat ever accomplished in the world until now.* Many is the time I have wished that God would again inspire me…to extol the indescribable service to God and to the whole world which Christopher Columbus rendered at the cost of such pain and dangers, such skill and expertise, when he so courageously discovered the New World."[42] What a compelling witness from a contemporary historian of God's hand in the life of Columbus and his significant contribution to the world.

Las Casas further wrote, "Truly this man had a good and Christian purpose."[43] Quotes such as these, however, are noticeably absent from the writings of the revisionists who seem to have an agenda at the cost of historical accuracy. I understand and agree with constructive criticism—that is fair and warranted—but the revisionists have become so one-sided, and in many cases historically inaccurate, that their credibility has become tenuous at best.

Las Casas was not naïve; he was keenly aware of the many false accusations against Columbus. He marveled why the king of Spain (after Queen Isabella died) was so unkind to Columbus, "one whose unparalleled services no other monarch ever received." He then gave this possible reason: "Perhaps he was unduly impressed by the arguments and false testimonies of the admiral's enemies and rivals,"[44] a common malady suffered by many revisionist historians today.

Historian Carol Delaney exposed another of the revisionists' fatal flaws—a resort to presentism, the superimposing of present-day values and cultural norms on previous generations: "The 'presentist' perspective that dominates the contemporary view, even among some academics, holds him responsible for consequences he did not intend, expect, or endorse. Judging Columbus from a contemporary perspective rather than from the values and practices of his own time misjudges his motivations and his accomplishment."[45]

If Columbus was an evil man, as some assert, one must wonder why he took no slaves for himself, why we have no record of him taking advantage of native women even though many Spanish sailors engaged in such conduct, why he did not personally hoard gold like those who succeeded him in administering the islands, and why he did not seek for uncontrolled power over a people who were inferior to him in military might. In addition, we must ask why we have so many firsthand accounts of him speaking well of the natives and treating them fairly, why his prime motivation for all his acts was the conversion of the natives to Christianity, and why, in his last will and testament, he donated money for a church and hospital for the benefit of the indigenous natives. Las Casas, a contemporary historian, as well as Morison and Delaney, modern-day historians, summarized Columbus's life in positive terms, not because they were blind to his weaknesses but because they were able to put them in proper perspective.

Columbus Was Inspired by the Holy Ghost

What then is the real story of Columbus? Historical references to Columbus as an instrument in God's hands are numerous. Nonetheless, some historians minimize these references or altogether avoid them, perhaps in an effort to demonstrate some intellectual superiority that doesn't fall victim to belief in divine things. Perhaps others want to promote their own creative view of history. And perhaps others can't resist the affliction of presentism. In any case, the facts are overwhelming in spite of one's ideological bent—God's hand was in the life of Columbus and his contribution in the ultimate discovery and settlement of America.

Clark Hinckley, who authored the book *Christopher Columbus: A Man Among the Gentiles*, wrote, "Most historians are comfortable writing about Columbus's skill as a mariner and his weaknesses as a colonial administrator but are considerably less comfortable writing about his deeply held religious beliefs and his scriptural insights, which portray a divine plan of history with Columbus as a central player."[46]

To bolster the assertion that Columbus was a divine agent, Hinckley further wrote, "This tendency to ignore or discount Columbus's most deeply religious and spiritual writings is evidenced in the history of the *Libro de las profecías*. It was written by Columbus during 1501 and 1502, with some additions as late as 1505. It... summarizes the thoughts and beliefs that were the driving forces of his life and provides support for those beliefs with citations from the Bible and a variety of other sources. Yet it has been largely ignored by scholars."[47]

In his *Libro de las profecías*, Columbus shared his conviction that God's hand was in the discovery of the Americas: "With a hand that could be felt, the Lord opened my mind to the fact that it would be possible to sail from here to the Indies, and opened my will to desire to accomplish the project. This was the fire that burned within me… *Who can doubt that this fire was not merely mine, but also of the Holy Spirit…urging me to press forward?*"[48]

Delno C. West and August Kling, who translated and gave commentary on *Libro de las profecías*, made this observation about the character of Columbus: "The documents surrounding the life of Christopher Columbus support the fact that he was the kind of person he claimed to be. His way of life and his dealings with all sorts and conditions of people, both in close relationships and in casual acquaintanceships, was generally consistent with that kind of profession of religious faith."[49]

On March 15, 1493, Columbus wrote the king and queen concerning his first voyage to the Indies: "Of this voyage I observe that it hath miraculously been shown…by the many signal miracles that He [God] hath shown on the voyage and for me…which I hope in Our Lord will be to the greater glory of Christianity, which to some slight extent already has occurred."[50]

In further corroboration of Columbus's divine mission, Hinckley wrote, "In a letter to the monarchs of Spain dated 7 July 1503, Columbus records hearing a divine voice declaring that 'since thou wast born, ever has He [God] had thee in His watchful care' and that when he had reached an age which pleased God, 'of the barriers of the Ocean Sea, which were closed with such mighty chains, He gave thee the key.'"[51] As confirmation to this, Las Casas, wrote, "God granted to this man [Columbus] the keys to this awesome sea, and would not that any other should unlock the darkness."[52]

One must keep in mind that Columbus was not only an avid student of geography with supreme mariner skills, but he was also a devoted student of the Bible. His claims of divine intervention were not the hollow claims of a stranger to God but were the heartfelt sentiments of someone who loved God and diligently studied His teachings. Columbus honestly believed his mission was to open pathways that would allow the gospel of Jesus Christ to be preached to all people. He repeatedly advocated and advanced that cause.

There can be no dispute about Columbus's religious nature. For all the sinister motives Columbus supposedly had, Las Casas made this observation: "He observed the fasts of the Church most faithfully; confessed and made communion many times; prayed at all of the required times like a churchman or member of a religious order, hated blasphemy and profane swearing."[53] Fernando, the son of Columbus, was in agreement: "[Columbus] was so observant of religious matters that when it came to fasting and saying all the canonical prayers, he might have been taken for a member of a religious order."[54] All this is compatible with his claim that he was inspired by the Holy Ghost.

Columbus Brings Christianity to the Americas

During Columbus's first voyage, he wrote to the king and queen of Spain about the native people: "May your Highnesses believe that in the whole world there cannot be a better or more gentle people. Your Highnesses should take much joy in that soon you will make them Christians and will have instructed them in the good customs of your realms, for neither better people nor land can there be."[55] Columbus was not a racist. To the contrary, he wanted to bring joy to these natives through Christianity.[56] Some may disagree with his methods, but it would be hard to argue with his motives.

Fernando, the son of Columbus, noted, "Just as it is said that St. Christopher [a Catholic saint] is said to have been so named for carrying Christ over the depths of the waters, with great danger… so the Admiral Christopher Columbus, requesting the aid of Christ, that He would favor him in the perils of his voyage, completed the journey to convert the *indios* into members and inhabitants of the triumphant church of heaven."[57]

Hinckley offered this succinct summary of the motivation behind the journeys of Columbus: "The key themes of the *Libro de las profecías* are clear and simple. They are that God had called Columbus and qualified him to open the gates of the Ocean Sea for the purposes of preaching the gospel to all nations and obtaining the gold necessary to finance a new crusade, retake Jerusalem, and rebuild the temple in preparation for the return of the Savior."[58]

Alejandro Bermudez, a Peruvian American, wrote this op-ed in the *Wall Street Journal* in support of what Columbus accomplished:

"As a Catholic, I particularly value Columbus for bringing the first of many missionaries who showed millions of people the path to salvation.

"Human sacrifice was not unusual in my home country, as in much of the Americas. In what is now Peru, children were sacrificed by the Incas… Those who hate Columbus and his legacy still must acknowledge that this indigenous practice vanished thanks to the advent of Christianity in our hemisphere.

"The notion that indigenous life was perfect and Western culture is the locus of all evil is…absurd."[59]

Those who believe that Columbus mistreated the natives should ponder this observation of the historian Samuel Eliot Morison concerning the last will and testament of Columbus: "This document [which contains instructions by Columbus concerning disposition of his property] proves not only the Admiral's loyalty to his native city, but his interest and faith in the future of the colony that he had founded. His heir is ordered to erect a church in Hispaniola [the island that was later divided into the states of Haiti and the Dominican Republic]…and a hospital 'as well planned as may be like those in Castile and Italy.' He must further 'maintain and support in Hispaniola four good Masters of Sacred Theology,' whose main object shall be to work for the conversion of the natives."[60] What a generous and loving expression of goodwill by Columbus on behalf of the people of Hispaniola!

Columbus Opened the Doors to the Settlement of America

People may debate Columbus's character. That is understandable. But there is little doubt that Columbus was inspired in his voyages and discoveries, as evidenced by multiple sources. And thus the question: "What was God's purpose in this?"

Certainly, one important reason was for Columbus to introduce Christianity to millions in the western hemisphere. But perhaps of equal or even greater import, Columbus opened the doors to a land that had been kept by God separate and apart from the superstitions, state-mandated religions, and regal dictators of Europe. The Lord needed a place that could spawn freedom of conscience, freedom of speech, and freedom of religion—a nation that would protect life, liberty, and the pursuit of happiness, a nation whose people would worship God and follow His will and thus be a light to the world. That nation would be the United States of America. Columbus made its founding possible as he was the first man to blaze the path across the seemingly impassible ocean that led to the Americas and their eventual European settlement.[61]

The significance of this discovery is contained in an unsubstantiated story about Columbus that nonetheless teaches an important principle. A courtier, jealous of Columbus as a foreigner, and in an effort to demean his achievements, asked Columbus if it were not possible that other men could have accomplished the same goal as he had done. As the story goes, "Columbus made no immediate reply, but, taking an egg, invited the company to make it stand on one end. Every one attempted it, but in vain; whereupon he struck it upon the table so as to break the end, and left it standing on the broken part; illustrating, in this simple manner, that when he had once shown the way to the New World, nothing was easier than to follow it."[62] And in truth, he did open the gate to the New World and its ultimate settlement.

Morison concluded his Pulitzer Prize-winning biography of Columbus with these words: "The whole history of the Americas stems from the Four Voyages of Columbus… Today a score of independent nations and dominions unite in homage to Christopher… who carried Christian civilization across the Ocean Sea."[63] Suffice it to say, Columbus was inspired by God to discover the New World and bring Christianity to its shores. In accordance with actual and not revisionist history, Columbus had the courage to follow God's promptings, the daring to cross the seemingly impassible ocean and discover the New World, and the righteous desire to share

Christianity with the natives. His discoveries led to a people that eventually abandoned slavery, cannibalism, and human sacrifices, and instead replaced it with religion, education, and a more refined civilization. What a colossal contribution to society!

Why Do We Need Heroes?

Was Columbus a hero? The word *hero* can have many different definitions depending on the context in which it is used. In one sense, it may be used to refer to a man or woman who was inspired by God and who made an extraordinary contribution to the discovery, establishment, preservation of this country, and the moral values for which it stands. Columbus had his weaknesses, but he was clearly inspired of God as attested to by him and other independent witnesses. He was instrumental in the discovery of this country, overcoming incredible odds and hardships in that pursuit. In addition, he introduced Christianity into the Americas, which eventually enhanced the way of life for Native Americans and became the basis for the moral code of the United States of America. In that sense, he was certainly a hero.

In a larger sense, heroes are anyone who brings out the best in us. More than a platitude—more than a moral principle—they constitute the real-life example of a man or woman who has the inherent power to unleash the divine potential within us, to lift us to new, even seemingly unattainable heights. Learning about heroes is much more than a history lesson, much more than an intellectual exercise or fact-finding mission. It causes a stirring of our heart and soul that refines and purifies our character. Heroes eliminate excuses and a victim mentality. They give us an enhanced vision of who we are and what we can become. And with that increased vision comes increased motivation.

Heroes help us know that a mere mortal with all his faults and weaknesses can rise above them and achieve greatness. They are what give us hope and strength to be better and carry on even in moments of despair or discouragement. Simply said, heroes inspire greatness in both individuals and nations. While there is some dispute whether or not Abraham Lincoln gave this quote, it nonetheless rings with truth: "Any nation that does not honor its heroes will not long endure."

Why then the concerted effort by some to denigrate our national heroes? Perhaps, some people try to tear others down in an effort to lift themselves up. If they can get rid of heroes and their moral values, they can better justify their own immoral behavior. Perhaps some want to get rid of our national heroes (most, if not all of whom were believers in God) so they can better advance their secular agenda. Perhaps others feel it is a sign of their intellectual brilliance to focus on a discovered or known weakness rather than one's obvious strengths. But whatever the reason, the emphasis on one's weaknesses to the exclusion of one's multiple strengths is nothing less than a historical misrepresentation—a form of revisionist history.

We have many heroes in American history who deserve our respect and admiration, such as Columbus and the Founding Fathers. Of course, these individuals were not perfect, but if we will focus on their incredible accomplishments—their efforts in the discovery and establishment of the greatest nation on earth—rather than their few weaknesses, and in addition avoid the trap of presentism, then we will discover heroes worthy of our emulation. Then we will have heroes whose lives will touch a responsive chord within us, heroes who can inspire us to be true patriots and more heroic in our own lives.

Honoring our nation's heroes and giving respect for the sacrifices they made breeds a positivism and patriotism that is wholesome and uplifting. President Bill Clinton demonstrated this spirit while participating in a documentary on the life of George Washington that highlighted his incredible contributions to the foundation of this nation: "Americans [have] no idea how indebted they are to him."[64] In other words, contrary to the conclusion of revisionist historians, Washington is a hero of immense proportions.

It is time for our long-held national heroes to be reenthroned and revered consistent with actual history, not revisionist history, hence the next chapter on our Founding Fathers.

---

1 In Cohen, *The Four Voyages of Christopher Columbus*, 35.

2 Delno C. West and August Kling wrote: "We cannot deny that the Admiral wanted a comfortable income for himself and his heirs, but the primary motivation in his quest for gold was spiritual. On many occasions, he clearly stated that any gold found should be used first and foremost to propagate the faith and to launch the final crusade to Jerusalem" (in *The Libro de las profecías*, 69).

3 Morison, *Admiral of the Ocean Sea*, 47; emphasis added.

4 Columbus, *The Diario of Christopher Columbus's First Voyage to America*, 1492–1493, 291.

5 All references to Bible passages in this book are from the King James Version unless otherwise noted.

6 See Abernathy, *And the Walls Came Tumbling Down*, 471–475; also see Morrow, "A Reckoning with Martin Luther King," wsj.com.

7 Saul, who later became Paul, is a case in point. He went about persecuting the Christians. Members of Christ's church knew him only for the evil that he had done. When Ananias, a disciple of Christ, was instructed by the Lord in a vision to seek out Saul and give him a blessing, he was understandably reluctant: "I have heard by many of this man, how much evil he hath done to thy saints" (Acts 9:13). But the Lord had a deeper and greater perspective into who Saul really was and who he could really become: "He is a chosen vessel unto me, to bear my name before the Gentiles and kings, and the children of Israel" (Acts 9:15). And what a powerful disciple he became.

8 For one example of this view, see Strong, "Slavery and Colonialism Make Up the True Legacy of Columbus."

9 See D'Anghera, *De Orbe Novo*, 1:220.

10 D'Anghera, *De Orbe Novo*, 1:298.

11 Columbus, *Select Letters*, 81–83.

12 In Rafael, *Christopher Columbus the Hero*, 136.

13 See "Columbus: Fact vs. Fiction," 3. Historian Carol Delaney added: "Columbus, who never owned slaves, is reviled and blamed for everything that went wrong in the Indies" (*Columbus and the Quest for Jerusalem*, 252).

14 In Rafael, *Christopher Columbus the Hero*, 220.

15 Columbus, *Select Letters*, 167.

16 Pelowski, "Why Columbus Sailed," kofc.org; emphasis added.

17 Delaney, *Columbus and the Quest for Jerusalem*, 181.

18 In Cohen, *The Four Voyages of Christopher Columbus*, 55.

19 Martyr, *De Orbe Novo, The First Decade*, Book III, 101; emphasis added.

20 See Stepman, "The Truth about Columbus," dailysignal.com.

21 Carol Delaney noted, "While recognizing Columbus's shortcomings in the administration of the colonies, Las Casas still claimed that Columbus was far better and fairer than either Bobadilla or Ovando or any of those who came later" (*Columbus and the Quest for Jerusalem*, 230).

[22] D'Anghera, *De Orbe Novo*, 142.

[23] Columbus, *Select Letters*, 198. On another occasion, Columbus forbade his men from taking advantage of the natives as they bartered one with another. Columbus then noted that he "gave them [the natives] many beautiful and acceptable articles which I had brought with me, taking nothing from them in return" (*Select Letters*, 8).

[24] In Delaney, *Columbus and the Quest for Jerusalem*, 145.

[25] Columbus sent Alonso de Hojeda to replace Margarit. But as noted by Delaney: "Columbus misjudged Hojeda's character. He would later learn that Hojeda used brutal tactics against the Indians to demonstrate the dire consequences of their attacks. For example, when Hojeda heard that a few Indians had robbed several Spaniards of some of their clothes, he cut off the ears of one of the natives and sent the chief and several others in chains to La Isabela... Columbus was angry over what Hojeda and his men had done, and he should have punished them, but he realized that would only infuriate them further and make insurrection more likely. So to demonstrate his authority, he made a show of preparing to execute the captives. When the Spaniards were distracted, he released them" (Delaney, *Columbus and the Quest for Jerusalem*, 146).

[26] In Jones, "Critics of Columbus Day Get History Wrong, Scholar Says," catholicnewsagency.com (emphasis added).

[27] Las Casas, A Brief Account of the Destruction of the Indies, 18.

[28] Delaney, *Columbus and the Quest for Jerusalem*, 237.

[29] Columbus, *Select Letters*, 157–58, 159–60.

[30] Columbus, *Select Letters*, 192.

[31] See Rafael, *Christopher Columbus the Hero*, 11.

[32] See d'Anghera, *De Orbe Novo*, 79, 222.

[33] Thomas, *Rivers of Gold*, 115.

[34] See d'Anghera, *De Orbe Novo*, 62–63, 72–74, 155, 315, 342, 401–2.

[35] Columbus, *Select Letters*, 31.

[36] See Rafael, *Christopher Columbus The Hero*, 119.

[37] See d'Anghera, *De Orbe Novo*, 387.

[38] See Rafael, *Christopher Columbus The Hero*, 80.

[39] See Rafael, *Christopher Columbus The Hero*, 11.

[40] Two of the more undeveloped countries in South America are Bolivia and Ecuador, yet UNESCO reports that Bolivia has an adult literacy rate of 92 percent and Ecuador has a rate of 93 percent (UNESCO eAtlas of Literacy, tellmaps.com). One can imagine what an improvement that is from the pre-Columbian literacy rates in these same countries. In addition, Bolivia has a life expectancy of 71.2 years while Ecuador has a life expectancy of 76.8 years (World Bank, "Life Expectancy at Birth," data.worldbank.org). A New York Times article summarizing the study of anthropologists, economists and paleopathologists concerning a seven-thousand-year study of the health of people in the western hemisphere concluded, "In the healthiest cultures in the 1,000

years before Columbus, a life span of no more than 35 years might be usual" (Wilford, "Don't Blame Columbus for All the Indians' Ills," nytimes.com). In other words, the life expectancy of Native Americans has more than doubled since the time of Columbus.

41 Perhaps the most potentially damaging evidence against Columbus is a forty-eight-page document discovered in a state archive in Spain in 2006 called *La caída de Cristóbal Colón*. It alleges that Columbus or his men were responsible for atrocities such as cutting off a man's nose and ears for stealing corn and parading a woman naked through the streets and eventually selling her off into slavery. If Columbus was personally responsible for any of these activities, then certainly it would be a black mark on his character. In fairness to Columbus, it is important to note that he spent years refuting these claims. In addition, such actions were often the acts of his men without his approval or the actions of other Spaniards while he was not present. Furthermore, the revisionists have neglected to mention that there is a major problem with this report. It was prepared by Francisco de Bobadilla, a bitter enemy of Columbus who "successfully usurped power from him in the West Indies" (Michael J. Knowles, "Historical Record Shows Christopher Columbus Actually Was a Great Man" dailywire.com). In fact, Columbus said of Bobadilla, "he made innumerable unjust and disgraceful charges against me" (*Select Letters*, 155). To give full credit to this report would be something like treating a history of the Jews by Adolf Hitler as an impartial work or a history of Jesus Christ by the Pharisees and Sadducees as an accurate historical picture of Christ's life. In support of this conclusion, Las Casas noted that Bobadilla told his men: "[T]ake as many advantages as you can [against the natives] since you don't know how long this will last" (*History of the Indies*, 79). Delaney then added: "By 'advantage' he meant for the men to take as much of the gold, women, and labor of the Indians as they could. Las Casas said the obvious: 'The Spaniards loved and adored him in exchange for such favors,' and because they were allowed to get away with murder, literally, they were not about to denounce Bobadilla." Instead, they were willing to denounce Columbus to gain the favor of Bobadilla. No wonder Delaney concluded: "Because there was no opportunity for Columbus to counter the accusations against him made by Bobadilla, the recently found report by Bobadilla, La caída de Cristóbal Colón, *is highly suspect*" (Columbus and the Quest for Jerusalem, 181–82, 206; emphasis added).

42 In Rafael, *Christopher Columbus The Hero*, 227–28.

43 In Morison, *Admiral of the Ocean Sea*, 516.

44 Las Casas, *History of the Indies*, 139.

45 Delaney, *Columbus and the Quest for Jerusalem*, 236. Delaney also commented, "Judging Columbus from a present-day ethical standard is not only anachronistic, it reduces his intentions to their [unintended] effects; that is, it mistakes the consequences for the motivations" (*Columbus and the Quest for Jerusalem*, xiii).

46 Hinckley, *Christopher Columbus*, 8.

[47] Hinckley, *Christopher Columbus*, 7–8.
[48] Columbus, *The Libro de las profecías*, 105.
[49] West and Kling, *The Libro de las profecías*, 42.
[50] In Morison, *Admiral of the Ocean Sea*, 352. On March 30, 1493, the king and queen, recognizing God's hand in the mission of Columbus, wrote to him: "We have seen your letters and we have taken much pleasure in learning whereof you write, and that God gave so good a result to your labors, and well guided you in what you commenced" (in Morison, *Admiral of the Ocean Sea*, 355).
[51] In Hinckley, *Christopher Columbus*, 24.
[52] Las Casas, *Historia de las Indias*, 1:471.
[53] Las Casas, *Historia de las Indias*, 1:44.
[54] Colón, *Historia del almirante*, 1:14.
[55] Columbus, *Diario*, 273.
[56] In fact, this was a continuous theme in the writings of Columbus. On one occasion, he prophesied, "Your Highnesses have won these great lands, which are another world, where Christianity will have so much enjoyment and our faith, in time, so much growth" (in Las Casas, *Historia*, 2:255).
[57] Colón, *Historia del Almirante*, 6.
[58] Hinckley, *Christopher Columbus*, 160.
[59] Bermudez, "Catholics against Columbus," A13.
[60] Morison, *Admiral of the Ocean Sea*, 514.
[61] As to the naming of America, Delaney observed: "It was an injustice that the continent would be named after Amerigo [Vespucci] rather than its discoverer [Columbus]" (*Christopher Columbus and the Quest for Jerusalem*, 234).
[62] Irving, *The Life and Voyages of Christopher Columbus*, 1:238.
[63] Morison, *Admiral of the Ocean Sea*, 671.
[64] In History Channel, *Washington*, season 1, episode 3, "Father of His Country."

CHAPTER 3

The Establishment of America—Secular or Divine?

God's Hand Is Everywhere

Once one recognizes that God's hand was in the discovery of America, the next questions arise: Was He also involved in the settlement of America? The raising of the Founding Fathers? The Revolutionary War? The Declaration of Independence and Constitution? Suffice it to say, God's guiding hand in America is everywhere to be found. He is not some peripheral force. Rather, He was and is the dominating, driving force in the discovery, establishment, and preservation of this nation.

The Settling of America to Fulfill God's Purposes

It is a well-established historical fact that many of the European settlers of North America came for religious reasons. In a Library of Congress exhibit titled "Religion and the Founding of the American Republic," the following observation was made: "Many of the British North American colonies that eventually formed the United States of America were settled in the seventeenth century by men and women who, in the face of European persecution, refused to compromise passionately held religious convictions and fled Europe. Some settlers who arrived in these areas came for secular motives—'to catch fish' as one New Englander put it—but the great majority left Europe to worship God in the way they believed to be correct. They enthusiastically supported the efforts of their leaders to create 'a city on a hill' or a 'holy experiment,' whose success would prove that God's plan for his churches could be successfully realized in the American wilderness." This same exhibit noted, "Beginning in 1630 as many as 20,000 Puritans emigrated to America from England to gain the liberty to worship God as they chose."[1]

The Founding Fathers were well aware of this religious motivation. Thomas Jefferson was one such example: "The poor Quakers were [fleeing] from persecution in England. They cast their eyes on these new countries as asylums of civil and religious freedom."[2]

Arthur Schlesinger, noted historian and Harvard professor, summed up the mass exodus from the Old World as follows: "From the beginning of the sixteenth century to the middle of the seventeenth the Old World had been rent with theological dissension, and the vast transatlantic continent offered a natural refuge for the persecuted minorities."[3] John Fiske, an American philosopher and historian, underscored the motivation for these migrations: "Their exodus [from Europe] was that of a chosen people who were at length to lay the everlasting foundations of God's kingdom upon earth."[4]

While no doubt many came to America in its early stages for wealth and other reasons, history repeatedly confirms that the majority came for religious purposes. In support of this, Alexis de Tocqueville, the great French political scientist, described the voyage of the Pilgrims as "the scattering of the seed of a great people which God with His own hands is planting on a predestined shore."[5] And why was God planting them on this predestined shore of America? The next events in the history of America give the answer.

The Founding Fathers—Coincidence or Providence?

Did the Founding Fathers coincidentally and conveniently appear on the scene at the same time, or were they raised up by God at a specific time for a specific purpose? F. W. Boreham, a Baptist minister and author, gave us some profound insights on how God directs and influences the destiny of nations:

> [In 1809] men were following, with bated breath, the march of Napoleon, and waiting with feverish impatience for latest news of the wars. And all the while in their own homes, babies were being born. But who could think about *babies*?
>
> Everybody was thinking about *battles*... In one year, lying midway between Trafalgar and Waterloo, there stole into the world a host of heroes! During that one year, 1809, Mr. [William] Gladstone was born in Liverpool; Alfred Tennyson at the Somersby rectory; and Oliver Wendell Holmes made his first appearance in Massachusetts. Abraham Lincoln drew his first breath at Old Kentucky. Music was enriched by the advent of Felix Mendelssohn in Hamburg. But nobody thought of babies. Everybody was thinking of battles. Yet...which of the battles of 1809 mattered more than the babies of 1809?
>
> "We fancy that God can only manage His world by big battalions abroad, when all the while He is doing it by beautiful babies at home. When a wrong wants righting, or a work wants doing, or a truth wants preaching, *or a continent wants opening*, God sends a baby into the world to do it.[6]

And thus, God provided for the events leading to the discovery of America with the birth of Columbus and for the establishment of this country with the births of the Founding Fathers, perhaps the most extraordinary group of men to be born at one time and in one place.

Norman Cousins, a political journalist and author, wrote, "It has often been asked how it was that within a short span of time on the east coast of the North American Continent there should have sprung up such a rare array of genius—men who seemed in virtual command of historical experience and who combined moral imagination with a flair for leadership."[7] Charles Krauthammer, Pulitzer Prize winner and syndicated columnist, made a similar observation: "Many things are miraculous about the Constitution. The first is that, somehow, on the edge of the civilized world 250 years ago there could have been a collection of such political geniuses as to have actually written it."[8] And the eighteenth-century British statesman William Pitt said of the Founding Fathers, "I must declare and avow, that in all my reading and observation...that for solidarity of reasoning, force of sagacity, and wisdom of conclusion, under such a complication of difficult circumstance, no nation, or body of men, can stand in preference to the general Congress at Philadelphia."[9]

Similar observations have been made by numerous historians who marveled at this incredible assembly of pragmatic and brilliant visionaries. Arthur M. Schlesinger referred to the Founding Fathers as "the most remarkable generation of public men in the history of the United States or perhaps of any other nation." He then added, "An explanation of the phenomenon lies beyond the wit of the historian."[10] Why? Because it was not coincidence but providence.

Historian Henry Steele Commager wrote that the Founding Fathers were "a galaxy of leaders who were quite literally incomparable. What explains this remarkable outpouring of political leadership, this fertility in the production of statesmen—a fertility unmatched since that day? Was it an historical accident?"[11] And yet another historian, Barbara W. Tuchman, noted, "It would be invaluable if we could know what produced this burst of talent from a base of only two and a half million inhabitants."[12]

But we do know what produced this burst of talent. It was not a series of random births or "a lucky concatenation of genes."[13] Rather, it was pursuant to God's master plan for America. The Bible tells us that God "hath determined the times before appointed [meaning when we would come to the earth] and the bounds of their habitation [meaning where we would be born]" (Acts 17:26). And so, it was with the Founding Fathers. God sent them at a specified time and to a specified place to fulfill their divinely appointed mission. No doubt the words of Mordecai to Queen Esther, who saved her people, are applicable here: "And who knoweth whether thou art come to the kingdom for such a time as this?" (Esther 4:14).

Ben Carson summed it up well when he said, "We must be careful not to allow those who like to rewrite history to silence the voices of those God-fearing visionaries who founded America."[14] In other words, they were men of God.

The Revolutionary War

The Founding Fathers were principal participants in the Revolutionary War. And in retrospect, who can honestly doubt the Lord's hand in that world-shaping event? One can almost visualize Washington's ragtag band of soldiers struggling for survival at Valley Forge. They were ill-trained, ill-equipped, and ill-paid. In fact, some would go not only months but years without pay or decent food or clothing.

David McCullough confirmed this sad state of affairs: "They were in rags—they were in worse than rags. The troops had no winter clothing. The stories of men leaving bloody footprints in the snow are true—that's not mythology."[15]

These patriots were badly outnumbered, shivering and starving, but there was a sense of divine purpose that transcended it all, that somehow gave them the stamina and will to carry on, to stick it out one more day, to find sustaining power in the will and vision of their inspired commander. It was as though Washington spoke Elisha's words: "Fear not, for they that be with us are more than they that be with them" (2 Kings 6:16). There was unquestionably a higher power that was the source of their motivation.

It was December 31, 1776. McCullough shares the dire circumstances of the war. The enlistments for Washington's entire army were expiring at year's end. This meant that the soldiers could leave the next day and return to their families, who were in desperate need of their help, some literally starving. Washington called a large portion of his troops before him and offered them an extra month's salary if they would reenlist for six months. This was a substantial bonus, particularly considering that almost all the soldiers' families were in perilous financial straits.

The drums then rolled, and all who would reenlist were invited to step forward. But not one responded. The drums continued to roll, and not a single soul stepped forward. One can imagine the heartbreak, the overwhelming sense of despondency that must have weighed upon Washington. In one day, he would be a commander without an army. The vision of independence must have seemed like a fleeting dream. Washington then started to ride away. But in that moment, it must have dawned upon him that there was a power—a motivational force far greater than that of money.

He returned to his troops and said, "My brave fellows, you have done all I asked you to do, and more than could be reasonably expected, but your country is at stake, your wives, your houses, and all that you hold dear. You have worn yourselves out with fatigues and hardships, but we know not how to spare you. If you will consent to stay one month longer, you will render that service to the cause of liberty, and to your country, which you can probably never do under any other circumstance."[16]

McCullough then writes, "Again the drums rolled. This time the men began stepping forward. Now that is an amazing scene, to say the least, and it's real. This wasn't some contrivance of a screenwriter."[17]

No wonder Nathanael Greene, one of Washington's generals, noted of the occasion, "God Almighty inclined their hearts to listen to the proposal and they engaged anew."[18] When money was insufficient, it was a higher power—God, family, and patriotism—that caused them to put their lives and fortunes on the line for an extended period. What heroes they were! Many remain nameless in the records of mortal history but forever will be bright stars in the heavenly annals of eternity.

Such a sense of divine purpose and devotion may cause one to reflect upon Shakespeare's lines in *Henry V*. The place was the fields of Agincourt in France. The hour of battle was at hand. The English were battle-weary and severely outnumbered, but what were odds to them who had a commander of invincible will and God to speed their charge? One then hears the prayer of their courageous commander, King Henry V, a prayer perhaps akin to Washington's petitions:

> O God of battles! steel my soldiers' hearts;
> Possess them not with fear; take from them now
> The sense of reckoning, if the opposed numbers
> Pluck their hearts from them.[19]

This interchange then takes place among King Henry's men:

> Of fighting men they have full threescore thousand.
> There's five to one,
> Besides, they are all fresh:

Another chimes in:

> God's arm strike with us![20]

And so God's arm would be with Washington and his often-outnumbered men at such places as Lexington, Concord, Brooklyn, Trenton, and Yorktown. The words of David, spoken as he confronted Goliath, seem so apropos: "The battle is the Lord's" (1 Sam. 17:47).

In recalling those hallowed days, George Washington spoke these farewell words to his army on November 2, 1783: "The disadvantageous circumstances on our part under which the war was undertaken, can never be forgotten. *The singular interpositions of Providence in our feeble condition were such, as could scarcely escape the attention of the most unobserving; while the unparalleled perseverance of the Armies…was little short of a standing miracle.*"[21] John Ferling, who wrote a comprehensive history of the Revolutionary War, was in accord with Washington's observation: "The forlorn conditions under which America's soldiers were made to live and campaign was a national disgrace. That the army did not implode in a frenzy of mutinies long before 1781 was little short of miraculous."[22]

On another occasion, Washington reaffirmed his feelings of divine intervention: "The man must be bad indeed who can look upon the events of the American Revolution without feeling the warmest gratitude towards the great Author of the Universe whose divine interposition was so frequently manifested in our behalf. And it is my earnest prayer that we may so conduct ourselves as to merit a continuance of those blessings with which we have hitherto been favored."[23]

Charles Bracelen Flood, a researcher of the Revolutionary War, noted that "there were at least sixty-seven desperate moments when Washington acknowledged that he would have suffered disaster had not the hand of God intervened."[24]

Certainly, one of those moments was at the Battle of Long Island, also known as the Battle of Brooklyn. Washington's army was outnumbered by about three to one. His men had their backs to the East River and were surrounded by the British forces who were slowly but steadily inching their way forward. It was one of those times when the better part of valor was to retreat and fight another day. But such a retreat would be impossible in plain sight of the British Army. A retreat would require Washington to evacuate his entire army, abandon their fortifications, cross a river a mile wide with a strong current, and do so with a British fleet waiting to intercept them at any time. But then Providence stepped in. David McCullough described the Continental Army's precarious state of affairs and the events that followed:

> Incredibly, yet again, circumstances—fate, luck, Providence, the hand of God, as would be said so often—intervened.
>
> Just at daybreak a heavy fog settled in over the whole of Brooklyn, concealing everything no less than had the night. It was a fog so thick, remembered a soldier, that one "could scarcely discern a man at six yards distance." Even with the sun up, the fog remained as dense as ever, while over on

> the New York side of the river (where the British army was camped) there was no fog at all.
>
> In a single night, 9,000 troops had escaped across the river. Not a life was lost.[25]

When the fog lifted, the British were stunned to discover that Washington and his entire army had escaped undetected. Some things are beyond luck and coincidence. This was no doubt one of them.

Thomas Jefferson wrote of those character traits of Washington that made him a unique instrument in God's hands: "He was, indeed, in every sense of the words, a wise, a good, and a great man… On the whole, his character was, in its mass, perfect, in nothing bad, in few points indifferent… His was the singular destiny and merit, of leading the armies of his country successfully through an arduous war, for the establishment of its independence…and of scrupulously obeying the laws through the whole of his career, civil and military, of which the history of the world furnishes no other example."[26] It was such a man of character that God sent to lead the Continental Army and be unanimously chosen as our nation's first president by those of all political persuasions, and who refused to take a salary in either capacity.

Washington was one of those rare men who could resist power, even when handed to him on a silver platter. He resisted the temptation to be America's first king and to serve a third term as our nation's president. He believed in the principle of government by the people and unselfishly devoted his life to that cause. No wonder that James Thomas Flexner, a renowned historian, referred to Washington as "the indispensable man" of the American Revolution.[27] Washington's birth was not a random happening, a chance occurrence. It was divinely orchestrated from above.

God had a mission for Washington and raised him up at the exact time and place he was needed to help lay the foundation of this divinely destined nation. And Washington knew it. As to the Revolutionary War, he wrote, "Disposed, at every suitable opportunity to acknowledge publicly our infinite obligations to the Supreme Ruler of the Universe for rescuing our Country from the brink of destruction; I cannot fail at this time to ascribe all the honor of our late successes to the same glorious Being."[28] Who would be so presumptuous to argue this point with Washington, who, as a firsthand witness and pivotal participant, repeatedly testified of God's hand in the Revolutionary War and establishment of America?

The Declaration of Independence—a Divinely Inspired Document

To revolt against the British Crown was treason of the highest order. Benjamin Franklin, sensing the seriousness of the time and the need for unity among all the signers of the Declaration of Independence, is reported to have quipped, "We must all hang together, or most assuredly we will all hang separately."[29]

The men who signed the Declaration of Independence were not just signing a nicely written proclamation with wonderful philosophical and moral ideas. They knew they may be signing their own death sentences. Benjamin Rush, one of the signers, wrote to John Adams, "Do you recollect the pensive and awful silence which pervaded the house when we were called up, one after another, to the table of the President of Congress, to subscribe what was believed by many at that time to be our own death warrants?"[30] They knew that if the little colonies of America did not prevail, they would likely be hanged as traitors to the cause. Yet they sensed a divine destiny in this country that compelled them to put their pen to perhaps the greatest declaration of freedom and individual rights the world has ever known. Before signing this inspired document, John Adams declared, "There's a Divinity which shapes our ends."[31]

The Declaration of Independence refers to God on four occasions. One of the best-known statements reads, "We hold these truths to be self-evident, that all men are created equal, that they are endowed by their Creator with certain unalienable Rights, that among these are Life, Liberty and the pursuit of Happiness." These were not rights granted by a king or government. These were rights granted by the loving and merciful Creator of us all.[32] They preexisted any government and therefore were independent of any state-created rights. President John F. Kennedy confirmed this truth: "The rights of man come not from the generosity of the state, but from the hand of God."[33] But why are they unalienable rights? Because God granted unto us these rights so that we might fulfill the measure of our creation and become more like Him (see Matthew 5:48). Without those rights, we are stymied in that pursuit.

The Declaration of Independence also acknowledges our "firm reliance on the Protection of Divine Providence." In other words, the principles and morals that govern our nation are founded on a firm belief in God and ongoing reliance on Him.

Thomas Jefferson, who drafted the Declaration of Independence, gave us these words, etched in marble on his memorial: "God who gave us life gave us liberty. Can the liberties of a nation be secure when we have removed a conviction that these liberties are the gift of God?"[34] It was these deeply held beliefs that inspired and guided Jefferson in his drafting of the Declaration of Independence.

Just one year before the Declaration of Independence was drafted, Alexander Hamilton wrote, "The sacred rights of mankind are not to be rummaged for, among old parchments, or musty records. They are written, as with a sun beam, in the whole volume of human nature, by the hand of divinity itself; and can never be erased or obscured by mortal power."[35] It was these divine rights that were incorporated into the Declaration of Independence.

The Founding Fathers understood two great principles underlying the formation of our government. First, that every man and woman has certain unalienable rights that are God-given, namely, life, liberty, and the pursuit of happiness. And second, that government has the duty to protect those rights, hence the Declaration of Independence and the Constitution. As straightforward and intuitively correct as those principles seem, they were not to be the basis for the French Revolution which followed the American Revolution by just thirteen years. The charter document for the French Revolution, written in 1791, provided that all rights spring from the state, not God. What a difference in underlying philosophies.

Shortly after the Revolutionary War, Washington became our first president. He would never forget the merciful hand of God in helping to establish our nation. In his first inaugural address, he so declared, "It would be peculiarly improper to omit in this first official Act, my fervent supplications to that Almighty Being who rules over the Universe... No people can be bound to acknowledge and adore the invisible hand, which conducts the Affairs of men, more than the People of the United States. *Every step, by which they have advanced to the character of an independent nation, seems to have been distinguished by some token of providential agency.*"[36] The Declaration of Independence was one of those providential steps.

The Constitution—Another Miracle

But other miracles would yet be needed. In midsummer, 1787, the Constitutional Convention was in disarray. Franklin stepped to the forefront. He reminded all present of the need for divine intervention:

> In this situation of this Assembly, groping as it were in the dark to find political truth...how has it happened, Sir, that we have not hitherto once thought of humbly applying to the Father of lights to illuminate our understandings? *In the beginning of the Contest with G. Britain, when we were sensible of danger we had daily prayer in this room for the divine protection. Our prayers, Sir were heard, and they were graciously answered... And have we now forgotten that powerful friend? Or do we imagine that we no longer need his assistance?* I have lived, Sir, a long time, and the longer I live, the more convincing proofs I see of this truth—that God governs in the affairs of men... *I therefore beg leave to move—that henceforth prayers imploring the assistance of Heaven, and its blessings on our deliberations, be held in this Assembly every morning before we proceed to business.*"[37]

While historical evidence suggests the motion was probably not acted upon, because as some have suggested there were no funds for a paid minister, Franklin's reference to daily prayer held in that same room during the beginning of the Revolutionary War, and the need for prayer again during the Constitutional Convention helped rivet everyone's mind on the need for God in their Herculean task ahead.[38]

In speaking about the process by which the Constitution was achieved, Franklin further wrote, "I must own I have so much faith in the general government of the world by Providence, that I can hardly conceive a transaction of said momentous importance to the welfare of millions now existing, and to exist in the posterity of a great nation, should be suffered to pass without being in some degree influenced, guided, and governed by that omnipotent, omnipresent, and beneficent Ruler, in whom all inferior spirits live, and move, and have their being."[39]

James Madison, the Father of the Constitution, reflected upon the hand of God in the miraculous achievement of such a document: "It is impossible for any man of candour to reflect on this circumstance without partaking of the astonishment. It is impossible for the man of pious reflection not to perceive in it a finger of that Almighty hand which has been so frequently and signally extended to our relief in the critical stages of the revolution."[40] George Washington concurred in this assessment: "[The adoption of the Constitution] will demonstrate as visibly the finger of Providence, as any possible event in the course of human affairs can ever designate it."[41] No wonder that historian Catherine Drinker Bowen, who wrote the best-selling book setting forth the details of the Constitutional Convention, titled it *Miracle at Philadelphia*. The actual word *miracle*, however, was not her invention but was first used by Washington and Madison to describe the convention's historic outcome.

The Constitution was not just a patchwork of ideas from other nation's constitutions. James Madison spoke of the uniqueness of this document in the entirety of history: "Happily for America, happily, we trust, for the whole human race, [the founders of the nation] pursued a new and more noble course. They accomplished a revolution which has no parallel in the annals of human society. *They reared the fabrics of governments which have no model on the face of the globe.*"[42] George Washington added his insight: "[The Constitution] approached nearer to perfection than any government hitherto instituted among men."[43] And John Adams noted that the Constitution was "if not the greatest exertion of human understanding, the greatest single effort of national deliberation that the world has ever seen."[44] In other words, it was inspired. What powerful on-the-scene witnesses of God's hand in the formation of the Constitution!

With the benefit of hindsight, the honest observer must marvel at the novelty and brilliance of the Constitution which was not the creation of mortal genius alone. *New York Times* best-selling author Eric Metaxas said of the American form of government, "Nowhere on the globe was there a nation that had come near to throwing away the very idea of monarchy and declaring, 'We will have no government but the people themselves.' It was a decidedly radical notion, if not a preposterous one… It was a singular moment in the history of the world. We so take self-government for granted in our time that it is almost impossible for us to behold the utter foreignness of it in its day, to see the astonishing and startling nature of its birth in history."[45]

David McCullough likewise noted this distinctive and remarkable accomplishment: "Never, *never anywhere*, had there been a government instituted on the consent of the governed… Sadly, too many today take for granted public schools, freedom of religion, freedom of speech, equality before the law, forgetting that these were ever novel and daring ideas."[46] Historian Catherine Bowen was in accord: "In the year 1787 the Convention's proposals were essentially new, untried."[47] The drafting and ratification of the Constitution was indeed a providential moment in history.[48]

Some have suggested that the Founding Fathers prepared the Constitution primarily to benefit themselves as property owners. In truth, this claim is nothing less than revisionist history absent any compelling historical evidence.[49] To the contrary, Madison wrote, "There was never an assembly of men…who were more pure in their motives."[50] One must ask, "If these men were so self-centered and so profit-motivated, why was God's hand so abundantly manifested in their lives as witnessed by our nation's founding documents?"

There can be no honest question about the Founding Fathers' belief that the Constitution was inspired. But why was this inspiration so essential? Because it was not enough to merely enumerate man's unalienable rights as set forth in the Declaration of Independence. It was also essential to set forth laws of government that would protect those God-given rights, hence the need for heaven-sent men to draft an inspired Constitution.

But the next question becomes, How is the Constitution inspired? Dallin H. Oaks, a former law professor at the University of Chicago and justice of the Utah Supreme Court,[51] tells of a professor who, over time, spoke to a number of religious students. The professor then made this surprising comment: "They all seemed to believe that the Constitution was divinely inspired but none of them could ever tell me what this meant or how it affected their interpretation of the Constitution."[52] Professor Oaks took that as a challenge and then wrote a brilliant article setting forth five ways in which the Constitution is inspired, as summarized below:

1. Separation of powers—as evidenced by the executive, legislative, and judicial branches of government that exert checks and balances on each other. As to this separation of powers, George Washington commented, "The balances arising from the distribution of the legislative, executive, and judicial powers are the best that have [ever] been instituted."[53] In essence, this system of checks and balances promotes the virtues of each governmental branch but simultaneously provides a restraint on human nature's quest for power and its misuse. This is accomplished by requiring laws to pass both chambers of Congress and then requiring the president's approval, or if he vetoes the legislation, the capacity to override his veto by a two-thirds vote in both chambers—an ingenious, even inspired method to prevent the abuse of power in the hands of one or a few.
2. A written bill of rights that includes the protection of individual liberties such as freedom of religion, assembly, and speech, all of which are essential to establish and preserve a nation under God.

3. Division of powers between the nation and the states which Professor Oaks noted "was unprecedented in theory or practice." He further observed, "The particular powers that are reserved to the states are part of the inspiration. For example, the power to make laws on personal relationships is reserved to the states. Thus, laws of marriage and family rights and duties are state laws." (This latter issue will be discussed in subsequent chapters). This separation of powers was intended to give to the federal government only those specific powers necessary to keep the states united and its citizens protected as to the express and implied liberties enumerated in the Bill of Rights. All remaining power was reserved for the states.
4. Popular sovereignty—meaning that the people, not a monarch or dictator, are the ultimate source of government power. In essence, "we the people," not "we the executive" or "we the judiciary" are the highest tribunal of government. This is known as consent of the governed.
5. The rule of law and not of men—meaning that the citizens at large are trusted to have the moral integrity to (1) obey the Constitution and (2) enforce its laws justly.[54] The ultimate goal was to provide the minimum laws necessary to maximize moral agency but at the same time institute sufficient laws to restrain carnal and selfish desires.

In addition to the foregoing, the Constitution had a built-in mechanism for correction—a method to amend it as necessary, as confirmed by the words found in America the Beautiful—"[to] mend thine every flaw."

Fortunately, God raised up the Founding Fathers to produce the divinely inspired Constitution. It is no wonder that William Pitt, former British Prime Minister, should observe, "[The American Constitution] will be the wonder and admiration of all future generations and the model of all future constitutions."[55] William Gladstone, another British Prime Minister, made a similar observation: "The American Constitution is, so far as I can see, the most wonderful work ever struck off at a given time by the brain and purpose of man."[56] And in current times, Supreme Court Justice Neil Gorsuch stated that the Constitution was "the greatest charter of human freedom the world has ever known."[57] What a tragedy if we as a people ever take the Constitution for granted or fail to recognize its inspired nature.

Heroes or Villains?

Were the Founding Fathers heroes or, as some claim, villains? Ted Stewart, a federal judge and author, put this question in its proper light:

> Today, it is common to criticize the founders of America. Judging them by today's standards of equality and justice they do fail. Some owned slaves, none fought to give women equal rights. Most were wealthy white men. Yes, judging the founders by today's standards of equality and justice they fail.
>
> But there is just one problem with judging them by today's standards and it is this: but for those imperfect founders and the sacrifices that they made and the instruments of government which they created, there would *be* no current, enlightened standards of equality and justice by which to judge them.[58]

Judge Stewart is so right. The reason the critics can freely criticize, protest, vote for change, run for office, and exercise freedom of religion or irreligion as they choose is for one reason and one reason only—because the Founding Fathers made it so. We are part of the greatest democracy the world has ever known.

Some might argue that even without our Founding Fathers, our democracy would have eventually evolved, and therefore they did nothing special. But history would not be kind to such a proposition. At the time of our Founders' noble experiment, there was nothing like it in the world.[59] For centuries, even millennia of prior recorded history, there was no comparable democracy that had the breadth of liberties and lasting power of what they created. Theirs was a bold and ingenious initiative, from which many other countries would subsequently pattern their governments. If nothing else, the burden of proof shifted. That the Founders established our democracy is a certainty. That there would have been a similar democracy without them, as claimed by some naysayers, is no more than a speculative possibility without historical precedent.

Historian Catherine Bowen realized that the Founding Fathers seized upon the golden moment for democracy: "Actually, it was the one moment, the one stroke of the continental clock when such an experiment [democracy] had a chance to succeed. Five years earlier and the states would not have been ready. Five years later and the French Revolution, with its violence and blood, would have slowed the states into caution, dividing them [as it indeed divided them] into opposing ideological camps. Tom Paine had recognized the moment. 'The Time hath found us,' he wrote."[60]

If unwilling to acknowledge the Founding Fathers' inspired and timely experiment, one must wonder, "Do the critics believe our liberties came about by chance or that they were spawned by evil men?" If so, how do they reconcile such a position with the unerring logic of the Savior: "Ye shall know them by their fruits" (Matt. 7:16). It seems somewhat hypocritical to partake of and enjoy the fruits of liberty while at the same time criticizing the very tree that produced such fruit. The Savior made it clear: "A good tree cannot bring forth evil fruit, neither can a corrupt tree bring forth good fruit" (Matt. 7:18). Lest there be any question, the Founding Fathers were that good tree that brought forth the good fruits of liberty we enjoy today.

There is no question but that the Founding Fathers appeared on the scene at a pivotal moment in our country's history. We were at a crossroads. Would our nation be content to be a glorified colony, or would it aspire to the stature of a free and independent nation? Would it submit to taxation without representation as required by the Stamp Act of 1765 and the Townshend Acts of 1767 and 1768?

Would it yield to the Intolerable Acts of 1774 that included the quartering of soldiers at the expense of the colonists? Would it passively acquiesce to George III's declaration that the colonies who sought their God-given liberties were in a state of rebellion and that members of the Continental Congress were traitors to the cause? Would the people capitulate to a monarchy—a king who claimed the divine right to rule our nation—or would they rise up and create a government ruled by the consent of the people? And if the latter, who would lead that charge? Would it be the Loyalists? No. Would it be those who chose neutrality in this political conflict? No. It would be the Founding Fathers! They led that incredible charge, reminiscent of these lines from Tennyson's "The Charge of the Light Brigade":

> Cannon to right of them,
> Cannon to left of them,
> Cannon in front of them
> Volley'd and thunder'd;
> Storm'd at with shot and shell,
> Boldly they rode and well,
> Into the jaws of Death,
> Into the mouth of hell.[61]

And so was their charge, boldly and directly into the hell of war against the most formidable nation on earth. They demonstrated an indomitable courage in spite of overwhelming odds against them.

While the Founding Fathers' actions were of historic proportions, there is no claim these men were perfect. As noted, some had slaves, some lived lifestyles not totally compatible with the Christianity they professed, but fortunately they had the vision and unwavering commitment to put their lives and fortunes and reputations at risk to make us a nation free from the tentacles of Great Britain—to become a people who could not only dream of but indeed fully experience their God-given rights of life, liberty, and the pursuit of happiness.

These rights would not come all at once, particularly for Black Americans and women, but the efforts of the Founding Fathers were a giant step forward. It reminds one of Isaiah's observation that the Word of the Lord would come to the people "line upon line…here a little, and there a little" (Isa. 28:13). And so it was with our God-given liberties. The Founding Fathers opened the door so that these liberties could be obtained "here a little, and there a little." At first it was the Declaration of Independence, then the Constitution, then the Northwest Ordinance of 1789 that prohibited slavery within its territory, then the Bill of Rights ratified in 1791, then the Act of 1807 that prohibited the importation of slaves after January 1, 1808, then the Civil War in which over three hundred thousand Union soldiers gave their lives as many sang this line from the Battle Hymn of the Republic: "As He [Christ] died to make men holy, let us die to make men free," then the Thirteenth, Fourteenth, and Fifteenth amendments providing freedom for all Black Americans, then the Nineteenth amendment giving voting rights to women, then the case of Brown v. Board of Education that declared segregation of schools, even if equal, to be unconstitutional, then the Civil Rights Act of 1964 and so on. The Founding Fathers laid the foundation upon which the full liberties of all Americans could be achieved, line upon line. They made it possible to become "a more perfect union" because of the groundwork they laid.

Abraham Lincoln was in total concurrence with the foregoing understanding of the Founders' intent. He reprimanded Chief Justice Taney for his opinion in the *Dred Scott* case that the Founding Fathers did not intend to provide equal rights for blacks. Lincoln noted, "They [the Founding Fathers] defined with tolerable distinctness in what respects they did consider all men created equal—equal with 'certain inalienable rights, among which are life, liberty, and the pursuit of happiness.' This they said, and this meant. They did not mean to assert the obvious untruth, that all were then actually enjoying that equality, nor yet, that they were about to confer it immediately upon them. *They meant simply to declare the right, so that the enforcement of it might follow as fast circumstances should permit*."[62]

History confirms that Lincoln's analysis was correct.

There would be some compromises along the way to achieve equality for all, but that equality would evolve as circumstances permitted. Without such compromises, which proved to be stepping-stones to the ultimate goal of liberty for all, there would have been no Union, no United States of America, and without such Union there would have been no defeat of Great Britain. In essence, we would have been free colonies in the North and slave colonies in the South. Instead, the Founding Fathers forged the Union and in so doing opened the door for the ultimate freedom of all—a remarkable achievement. As Ben Shapiro noted, "They [the Founding Fathers] believed the Union was the best way to protect and expand the rights they valued the most."[63] Surely, the wisdom, vision, and sacrifices of our Founding Fathers constituted a magnificent contribution to the establishment of the greatest democracy the world has ever known.

How easily we tend to forget the incredible sacrifices of our Founding Fathers in providing these liberties. They sent repeated peace proposals to the king of England, only to be countered with repeated rejections. Finally, the day of reckoning came—submit as subjects of the Crown or risk their lives in order to be free men and women under God. Perhaps Patrick Henry best expressed their innermost passions and dilemma with his never-to-be-forgotten battle cry: "Give me liberty, or give me death!"[64] These were more than the stirring words of gifted oratory; they were a stark disclosure of the choice that confronted them.

All the odds were stacked against these revolutionaries. They had no trained militia, no navy, no national treasury from which to pay salaries to their soldiers or provide needed ammunition and supplies. As if that were not enough, they faced opposition from loyalists within their own ranks.

By contrast, England had a mighty and well-trained army, a seemingly invincible navy, a government with the power to tax and provide almost unlimited ammunition and supplies, and finally, a kingdom united in its goal to keep America "a glorified serfdom."

From a worldly perspective, a revolutionary war on the part of the colonists was nothing less than a suicide mission. It was the modern-day version of David with his slingshot against the mighty Goliath with his colossal sword and shield.

But something within drove the Founding Fathers onward—an inner vision, nay, even more, a divine assurance that in spite of overwhelming odds, in spite of seemingly certain destruction, Providence would be with them in this quest for their God-given rights of life, liberty, and the pursuit of happiness.

The Founding Fathers could have quietly retreated to the comfort and wealth of their plantations, law offices, and businesses, but they put that all at risk for their children, fellow Americans, and future generations. To not be grateful for their sacrifices, for their willingness to literally put their lives, fortunes, and reputations on the altar of sacrifice would be ingratitude of the highest order. They were nothing less than heaven-sent messengers who gave us the greatest liberties ever enjoyed by any people or nation on earth. They were the advance guard that opened the door to the liberties we now enjoy. As such, we should honor and respect them and their incredibly supporting and sacrificing spouses as the heroes they indeed are.

---

1 Library of Congress, "America as a Religious Refuge: The Seventeenth Century, Part 1," loc.gov.

2 In Cousins, *In God We Trust*, 121. Samuel Adams observed, "I confess I am surprised to find, that so little attention is given to the danger we are in, of the utter loss of those *religious Rights*, the enjoyment of which our good forefathers had more especially in their intention, when they explored and settled this new world" (*Writings of Samuel Adams*, 1:201; spelling modernized; emphasis in original).

3 Schlesinger, *The Birth of the Nation*, 80.

4 Fiske, *The Beginnings of New England*, 242–43.

5 In Bennett, *Our Sacred Honor*, 365–66; emphasis added. Robert R. Mathisen, a professor of history and political science at Corban University, made a similar observation about God's hand in the settling of America: "Particularly noteworthy was the ever present religiously oriented sense of mission which guided people of all ranks to the New World early during the period between 1607 and 1820. A favoring Providence was seen as directing the destiny of His 'chosen people' in the abundant wilderness called America" (*The Role of Religion in American Life*, 1).

6 Boreham, *Mountains in the Mist*, 166–69, emphasis added.

7 Cousins, *In God We Trust*, 2.

8 Krauthammer, *The Point of It All*, 260. Historian Benson Bobrick concurred in this observation: "Although outstanding figures may occasionally emerge in response to a historical crisis, those who arose to lead the Revolution surpassed all that might have been hoped for or have since been seen" (Bobrick, *Angel in the Whirlwind*, 95).

9 In Stanly, "Funeral Oration," founders.archives.gov.

10 Schlesinger, *The Birth of a Nation*, 245.

[11] Commager, *Freedom and Order*, 150.

[12] Tuchman, *The March of Folly*, 18. While Thomas Jefferson was serving in Paris as an ambassador for the United States, he read the list of those attending the Constitutional Convention and commented that they were "an assembly of demi-gods" (in Bowen, *Miracle at Philadelphia*, 4). Franklin noted that the members of the Constitutional Convention were "the most august and respectable assembly he ever was in in his life" (in *Miracle at Philadelphia*, 89).

[13] Schlesinger, *The Birth of a Nation*, 246.

[14] Carson, *America the Beautiful*, 61.

[15] Franklin, "Information for Those Who Would Remove in America," 444.

[16] In McCullough, "The Glorious Cause of America," speeches.byu.edu.

[17] McCullough, "The Glorious Cause of America," speeches.byu.edu.

[18] In McCullough, "The Glorious Cause of America," speeches.byu.edu.

[19] Shakespeare, *Henry V*, act 4, scene 2, lines 276–79.

[20] Shakespeare, *Henry V*, act 4, scene 3, lines 3–5.

[21] Washington, "George Washington to Continental Army" loc.gov; emphasis added; spelling modernized.

[22] Ferling, *Almost a Miracle*, 569.

[23] Washington, "George Washington to Samuel Langdon," loc.gov.

[24] In Skousen, *The 5000 Year Leap*, 99.

[25] McCullough, *1776*, 191.

[26] Jefferson, "Thomas Jefferson to Walter Jones," loc.gov; emphasis added. Historian Catherine Drinker Bowen noted, "Abigail Adams could be sharp-tongued, nor was she given to flattering personal descriptions. Yet on meeting the General [Washington] she made no apology for quoting Dryden's high-flown lines, which she said 'instantly occurred' to her: Mark his majestic fabric; he's a temple Sacred by birth, and built by hands divine; His soul's the deity that lodges there; Nor is the pile unworthy of the God" (*Miracle at Philadelphia*, 194).

[27] In 1974, Flexner wrote an influential biography of Washington, subtitled *The Indispensable Man*.

[28] In Cousins, *In God We Trust*, 57.

[29] In Sparks, *The Life of Benjamin Franklin*, 1:408. It is reported that "Jefferson loved the story of how Benjamin Harrison, an enormously fat Virginian, once told the wispy Elbridge Gerry of Massachusetts, 'Gerry, when the hanging comes, I shall have the advantage; you'll kick in the air half an hour after it is all over with me'" (in Mecham, *American Gospel*, 76).

[30] Rush, "To John Adams from Benjamin Rush," founders.archives.gov.

[31] Quoting Shakespeare, *Hamlet*, act 5, scene 2, line 10; in *The Works of Daniel Webster*, 1:133.

[32] Frédéric Bastiat, the well-known French economist and journalist, wrote his masterful book *The Law* in 1850. In it he noted that before man's laws existed, "God…bestowed upon every one of us the right to defend his person, his liberty, and his property" (page 2).

[33] Kennedy, "Inaugural Address of John F. Kennedy," avalon.law.yale.edu.

[34] Panel 3 of Jefferson Memorial, Washington, DC.

[35] Hamilton, *The Farmer Refuted*, 38.

[36] Washington, "Washington's Inaugural Address of 1789," archives.gov; emphasis added.

[37] In Bennett, *Our Sacred Honor*, 384–85; emphasis added.

[38] Ezra Taft Benson, former US Secretary of Agriculture, wrote, "Some historians have ignored this dimension [Franklin's motion requesting daily prayer] because Madison who reported the Constitutional Convention, said nothing about it. Others report that the motion was not acted upon. Another member of the convention, Jonathan Dayton of New Jersey, who also reported it, said the motion was acted on favorably by the convention" (God's Hand in Our Nation's History, speeches.buy.edu). Some have noted that the motion by Franklin to hire a minister to offer daily prayer did not pass because the Convention had no money available for a paid minister. On the other hand, President John F. Kennedy noted, "During the deliberations in the Constitutional Convention they [the Founding Fathers] were called to daily prayers" ("Proclamation 3436: National Day of Prayer, 1961," 146).

[39] Franklin, "A Comparison," 162.

[40] Madison, "The Difficulties of the Constitutional Convention in Devising a Proper Form of Government," 74. Madison also said, "It is impossible to consider the degree of concord [in drafting the Constitution] which ultimately prevailed as less than a miracle" ("From James Madison to Thomas Jefferson," founders.archives.gov).

[41] Washington, "From George Washington to Lafayette," founders.archives.gov. Charles Pinckney, a delegate to the Constitutional Convention, added his witness of God's intervention in this remarkable document: "When the great work [the Constitution] was done and published, I was…struck with amazement. Nothing less than the superintending hand of Providence, that so miraculously carried us through the war…could have brought it about" (Pinckney, "A Republican," 412).

[42] Madison, *The Federalist Papers*, no. 14, page 44; emphasis added. John Adams called the Constitution "the greatest single effort of national deliberation that the world has ever seen" ("From John Adams to William Stephens Smith," founders.archives.gov).

[43] Washington, "From George Washington to Sir Edward Newenham," founders.archives.gov.

[44] Adams, "From John Adams to William Stephens Smith," founders.archives.gov.

[45] Metaxas, *If You Can Keep It*, 26, 30–31.

[46] McCullough, *The American Spirit*, 28–29; emphasis in original.

[47] Bowen, *Miracle at Philadelphia*, 123.

[48] Benjamin Rush had a somewhat different perspective: "I do not believe that the Constitution was the offspring of inspiration, but I am as perfectly satisfied that

the union of the states, in its form and adoption, is as much the work of divine providence as any of the miracles recorded in the old and new testament were the effects of a divine power" (In Meacham, *American Gospel*, 99).

49 Catherine Drinker Bowen quoted several of the Founding Fathers who had a vision for a Constitution that would serve future generations, not just be for the current moment, noting with irony that those are "strange words for propertied gentlemen, intent, as some historians have hinted, only on commerce and their own financial security" (*Miracle at Philadelphia*, 89).

50 In Newton, *Angry Mobs and Founding Fathers*, 93; see also Ezra Taft Benson, God's Hand in Our Nation's History, speeches.byu.edu.

51 He now serves as a member of the First Presidency of the Church of Jesus Christ of Latter-day Saints.

52 Oaks, "The Divinely Inspired Constitution," 68.

53 In Skousen, *The 5000 Year Leap*, iv. J. Reuben Clark, former Undersecretary of State, wrote, "It is this union of independence and dependence of these branches—legislative, executive, and judicial—and of the governmental functions possessed by each of them, that constitutes the marvelous genius of this unrivalled document. The Framers had no direct guide in this work, no historical governmental precedent upon which to rely. As I see, it, it was…truly a miracle" (*Stand Fast by Our Constitution*, 147–48).

54 Oaks, "The Divinely Inspired Constitution," 68–74.

55 In Thompson, "Some Dangerous Tendencies in Government," 169.

56 Gladstone, "Kin beyond Sea," 185.

57 Gorsuch, *A Republic, If You Can Keep It*, 34.

58 Stewart, Utah State University commencement address, May 6, 2017; emphasis in original.

59 Chris Stewart (a US congressman) and Ted Stewart (a federal district court judge) wrote that as late as 1860, "the world was full of dictatorships, noble monarchies, fledgling parliamentary governments, and military tyrannies, but there wasn't another functioning example of a democracy outside of the United States" (*Seven Miracles That Saved America*, 154).

60 Bowen, *Miracle at Philadelphia*, 135.

61 Tennyson, "The Charge of the Light Brigade," in *Harvard Classics*, 42:1006.

62 In Barrett, *Life of Abraham Lincoln*, 140; emphasis added.

63 Shapiro, *How to Destroy America in Three Easy Steps*, 127.

64 Henry, Second Virginia Convention, March 23, 1775

CHAPTER 4

The Preservation and Future of America

God's Hand Continues to Bless America

God did not help establish this country as a stronghold of democracy and a light to the world, only to withdraw to some distant corner of the universe and leave America on its own. The Founding Fathers knew this and thus wrote of our nation's destiny, as found in the Declaration of Independence: "with firm reliance on the protection of divine Providence." That Providence was manifest in the War of 1812—a war between the United States and England—and in key subsequent events of America's history, a few of which are shared below.

The War of 1812 and the National Anthem

President James Madison proclaimed two days of national prayer and fasting during the War of 1812. He had recognized God's help in the past and now sought it once again.

Sarah Zielinski, a contributing writer for the *Smithsonian* magazine, wrote of a key moment during the war—the British invasion of Washington, DC, on August 24–25, 1814. As British soldiers moved throughout Washington, setting fire to most of the city, residents could see from the darkening sky:

> A bad storm was on its way and they quickly took shelter. The British, though, had no idea how bad a D.C. storm could get.
>
> The clouds began to swirl and the winds kicked up. A tornado formed in the center of the city and headed straight for the British on Capitol Hill. The twister ripped buildings from their foundations and trees up by the roots. British cannons were tossed around by the winds. Several British troops were killed by falling structures and flying debris.
>
> The rain continued for two hours, dousing the flames. The British decided it was time to leave.[1]

Concerning this event, meteorologists later wrote, "As the British troops were preparing to leave, a conversation was noted between the British Admiral and a Washington lady regarding the storm: The admiral exclaimed, 'Great God, Madam! Is this the kind of storm to which you are accustomed in this infernal country?' The lady answered, 'No, Sir, this is a special interposition of Providence to drive our enemies from our city.' The admiral replied, 'Not so Madam. It is rather to aid your enemies in the destruction of your city.'"[2]

Who was right? Zielinski noted that the city was rebuilt, and since that day in August 1814, there have been only seven other reported tornadoes in the city's history,[3] and none at such a critical point in time. Coincidence or providence? As the seeming coincidences multiply, shown from the examples below, the evidence of God's hand becomes more difficult to dismiss.

Francis Scott Key was a lawyer and deeply religious man who had an intense love for his country. He was also a poet. During the War of 1812, one of Key's good friends, Dr. William Beanes, was taken prisoner by the British. He was being held aboard a ship known as the

Tonnant. Key found this ship near the mouth of the Potomac River. With a white flag in his hand, he was allowed to board. He pleaded for the release of his friend, who had rendered medical services to both English and Americans alike, even saving some lives of British soldiers.

The British general was convinced Dr. Beanes should be freed, but not now. The British were about to attack Baltimore, and Key was told he must stay on board until the attack was over to preserve the element of surprise. The entrance to Baltimore was protected by Fort McHenry. There behind the guns hung a huge American flag. It was thirty-two by forty-two feet and was made of four hundred yards of material. It could be seen for miles.

On Monday, September 12, 1814, British forces started to land. In order to give protection, the British ships started to fire on Fort McHenry on September 13. All day long, Key watched the battle. He could see the red and white stripes of the flag flying above the fort. One of the British guards reportedly told him to take a good look, because by tomorrow it would no longer be there.

Night came, and the battle continued. The British ships were bombarding Fort McHenry unmercifully for more than twenty-five straight hours. The sky was bright with blazing red lights of rockets and bursting bombs. It was hard to see the flag through the smoke of the cannons. Finally, the dark of the night changed into the gray of dawn. Francis Scott Key strained to see. "There it is!" he cried. "The flag is safe."[4] The British were returning to their boats. They had been defeated. Key recognized the hand of God in this unlikely victory. He pulled an old letter from his coat pocket—the only paper he had—and began to compose the lyrics to what has become our national anthem, "The Star-Spangled Banner":

> Blessed with victory and peace, may the heav'n rescued land
> Praise the Pow'r that hath made and preserved us a nation!
> Then conquer we must, when our cause it is just.
> And this be our motto: "In God is our trust!"

> And the star-spangled banner in triumph shall wave
> O'er the land of the free and the home of the brave!

Francis Scott Key recognized the protecting hand of God, who, through this battle, had "preserved us a nation!"

Abraham Lincoln Seeks Divine Aid

Time marched on, and once again the hand of God was unmistakable in the preservation of this country. As Abraham Lincoln was about to accept the presidential chair, and with that wisdom that so often surpassed the ages, he offered this formula for unequivocal success of our nation: "Washington...never would have succeeded except for the aid of Divine Providence, upon which he at all times relied. I feel that I cannot succeed without the same Divine Aid which sustained him, and on the same almighty Being I place my reliance for support, and *I hope you my friends, will all pray that I may receive that Divine assistance without which I cannot succeed, but with which success is certain*."[5]

Sensing the nation was forgetting the very God who had begotten it and preserved it, Lincoln issued a proclamation calling for a national day of fasting and prayer:

> "We have grown in numbers, wealth and power, as no other nation has ever grown. But we have forgotten God... Intoxicated with unbroken success, we have become too self-sufficient to feel the necessity of redeeming and preserving grace, too proud to pray to the God that made us!
> "It behooves us then, to humble ourselves before the offended Power, to confess our national sins, and to pray for clemency and forgiveness."[6]

Lincoln repeatedly acknowledged the divine hand in the shaping of America. Before issuing the Emancipation Proclamation, he declared, "It is my earnest desire to know the will of Providence. And if I can learn what it is I will do it!"[7] As noted by one set of biographers, Lincoln "saw himself more and more as an especially appointed agent of the Almighty."[8]

On one occasion, Major General Daniel E. Sickles, who lost a leg at Gettysburg, asked Lincoln why he was so sure of success in that fateful battle. Lincoln paused and then responded, "I felt that the great crisis had come. I went to my room and got down on my knees in prayer. Never before had I prayed with so much earnestness. I felt I must put all my trust in Almighty God. He gave our people the best country ever given to man. He alone could save it from destruction. I had tried my best to do my duty and found myself unequal to the task. The burden was more than I could bear. I asked him to help us and give us victory now. I was sure my prayer was answered. I had no misgivings about the result at Gettysburg."[9] Lincoln knew with certainty that God's hand was with the Union in this decisive battle at Gettysburg—the turning point of the Civil War.

When Vicksburg fell to the Union Army, Lincoln issued a Proclamation of Thanksgiving with these words: "It is meet and right to recognize and confess the presence of the Almighty Father and the power of His hand equally in these triumphs and in these sorrows."[10]

Perhaps Lincoln best summarized God's influence in the destiny of this nation in these words: "That the Almighty does make use of human agencies, and directly intervenes in human affairs, is one of the plainest statements in the Bible. I have had so many evidences of His direction, so many instances when I have been controlled by some other power than my own will, that I cannot doubt that this power comes from above."[11]

I have a tender place in my heart for Abraham Lincoln. A portrait of him hangs in my office. My father loved him and spoke of him often in our home. In fact, he named me after Lincoln's son, Tad.[12] My father revered Lincoln as a man of keen wit, of profound wisdom, of sound practical judgment, and of moral integrity, but most of all as a man of God. Lincoln embodied and exemplified that which is good and moral in America. He loved this country, he was not afraid to acknowledge God's hand in its development and preservation, and he recognized the absolute need for us individually and as a nation to seek God's hand in all our affairs.

It is no coincidence that the two greatest presidents of our country—George Washington and Abraham Lincoln—were devout men of God. They sought God's aid and wisdom, not only in the intimacy of their private prayers but also in the openness of their public dealings. In their minds, the greatness of this nation and the need for God's influence were inseparably connected. They knew that God's hand was needed not only in the founding of America but in its ongoing preservation.

World War II

God's influence did not end with Lincoln's presidency and the Civil War. It continued to be present, especially during America's greatest times of need, when its survival and that of its allies were at stake, such as World War II. Following are some examples of pleas for God's help during this devastating war and the divine responses:

- Dunkirk was one such miracle. Hitler was rampaging through Western Europe at lightning speed. His army seemed unstoppable. He had driven the British troops and their allies to the west coast of France—to Dunkirk. There was nowhere else to retreat. They were hemmed in by the enemy with their backs to the sea. The German High Command was confident that they were about to annihilate the Allied Army. After all, they had approximately one million German troops, with superior armory, surrounding a little over three hundred thousand allied forces. Then God, who has both the power to turn the hearts of rulers (see Proverbs 21:1) and control the weather (see Matthew 8:27), stepped in. For reasons that are unclear and still debated by historians, on May 24, 1940, Hitler halted the advance of his Panzer troops for three days.

Following the war, Field Marshall Karl Von Rundstedt (often referred to as Gerd von Rundstedt) who commanded the armored units, called Hitler's stop order "an incredible blunder."[13] What seems undisputed by historians is that if Hitler had not hesitated, he could have delivered a devastating, perhaps knockout blow to the Allied forces. However, evangelical minister J. John noted God's hand in these events:

> On 23rd May, King George VI requested that the following Sunday should be observed as a National Day of Prayer. Late on the Saturday evening the military decision was taken to evacuate as many as possible of the Allied forces. On the Sunday, the nation devoted itself to prayer in an unprecedented way.
>
> Eyewitnesses and photographs confirm overflowing congregations in places of worship across the land. Long queues formed outside cathedrals. The same day an urgent request went out for boats of all sizes and shapes to cross the English Channel to rescue the besieged army, a call ultimately answered by around 800 vessels.
>
> Bad weather on the Tuesday grounded the Luftwaffe, allowing Allied soldiers to march unhindered to the beaches. In contrast, on Wednesday the sea was extraordinarily calm, making the perilous evacuation less hazardous. By the time the German Army was finally ordered to renew its attack, over 338,000 troops had been snatched from the beaches… Many of them were to return four years later to liberate Europe.[14]

In retrospect, one might ask, "Why did Hitler delay the attack on the besieged troops when he had them on the ropes, why the bad weather for the German air force but the unexpected good weather for hundreds of vessels to make repeated journeys across the English Channel to rescue the stranded soldiers? And why all this occurring concurrently with Britain's day of national prayer?" Some might call this a coincidence, but for those who lived through it, it is widely known as the miracle of Dunkirk. When one connects the dots, it is compelling evidence of divine intervention that greatly blessed America by preserving its allies to fight another day.

- D-Day was another example of divine intervention. June 5, 1944, was the planned day for the invasion of Normandy, but the weather forecast was bleak for a predicted week—rain, clouds, and rough seas. Then came a surprise announcement, that there would be a break in the bad weather for the midafternoon on June 6. General Dwight D. Eisenhower, the Allied Supreme Commander in Europe, made the decision to launch the attack. Victor Penrosa, an author and veteran of a later war, noted, "Because of the bad weather, many of the top German generals were away participating in war games. Many thought it would be a good time to take an extra day for a holiday and left a day early on June 5, since the weather was not supposed to get better for another week. This left only lower-ranking officers in charge who had little power to move troops." Penrosa also noted that Field Marshal Erwin Rommel, one of Hitler's key generals, had returned from the Western Front to Germany in order to be present for his wife's birthday on June 6.

Noticing the absence of key generals and the favorable turn of the weather for a brief period, Penrosa observed, "There were too many things happening all at the same time for it to be just a coincidence… I believe God was very much involved and helped the Allies on D-Day."[15]

On the eve of the D-Day invasion, General Eisenhower sent a message to his troops. With incredible military might at his command, he still understood the need for divine help: "The hopes and prayers of liberty-loving people everywhere march with you. Let us all beseech the blessing of Almighty God upon this great and noble undertaking."[16] One wonders how many thousands of prayers were offered in response to that plea for divine aid. And it came. The invasion was successful. And the liberty of the US and its allied nations, for a time teetering in the balance, was preserved.

President Ronald Reagan, recounting the events of that day on its fortieth anniversary, noted the courage of the Allied Forces and the faith of the American people: "Something else helped the men of D-day: their rockhard belief that Providence would have a great hand in the events that would unfold here; that God was an ally in this great cause. And so, the night before the invasion, when Colonel Wolverton asked his parachute troops to kneel with him in prayer he told them: Do not bow your heads, but look up so you can see God and ask His blessing in what we're about to do. Also on that night, General Matthew Ridgway [lay] on his cot, listening in the darkness for the promise God made to Joshua: 'I will not fail thee nor forsake thee.'"[17] And fail them God did not.

- The Battle of the Bulge was one more example of divine intervention. The German Army was in retreat, but on December 16, 1944, it made one last offensive attack through the Ardennes in Belgium. The American 101st Airborne Division fought valiantly but was eventually surrounded in the city of Bastogne by the German Army. General George W. Patton was sent to rescue them, but the weather was a major problem that prevented the necessary air support. Patton, known as a rough and tough general, sought a prayer from his chaplain that would clear the weather. The chaplain was somewhat reluctant about providing a prayer so that German soldiers could be killed. Penrosa then records Patton's response to the chaplain: "I want that prayer now. We need God on our side, or those soldiers in Bastogne will all die."

The chaplain then provided the following prayer: "Almighty and most merciful Father…grant us fair weather for battle. Graciously hearken to us as soldiers who call upon Thee that, armed with Thy power, we may advance from victory to victory, and crush the oppression and wickedness of our enemies and establish Thy justice among men and nations."

Penrosa then commented, "The next day, December 23, the weather cleared. In fact, it was perfect weather for six days. General

Patton was so pleased with his chaplain that he gave him a medal, and said, 'This man stands in good with the Lord.'"[18] Patton, a military genius and not shy about taking credit, was nonetheless quick to recognize the hand of God in this most decisive battle.

If the enemy had prevailed in World War II, democracy would have been replaced by dictatorship, and personal liberty, including religious liberty, might well have been extinguished. The divine promise as recorded in 2 Kings 17:39 seems so apropos: "But the Lord your God ye shall fear; and he shall deliver you out of the hand of all your enemies." Once again, God came to America's rescue and preserved this great land and the liberties for which it stands. Suffice it to say, the fingerprints of God are everywhere to be found in the discovery, establishment, and preservation of America. His influence has been both persistent and profound.

What Difference Can God Make in the Destiny of a Nation?

Every nation needs God. Why? Because God and God alone has the capacity to make a nation great. He said to the prophet Abraham, "I will make of thee a great nation" (Gen. 12:2). The Psalmist wrote, "Blessed is the nation whose God is the Lord" (Ps. 33:12). But there is a condition to that greatness: "All nations whom thou hast made shall come and worship before thee, O Lord; and shall glorify thy name" (Ps. 86:9). And in Proverbs 14:34, we read, "Righteousness exalteth a nation." Isaiah issued this warning to those nations that believe they can achieve greatness without God: "The nation and kingdom that will not serve thee [God] shall perish; yea, those nations shall be utterly wasted" (Isa. 60:12).

These biblical passages teach three fundamental truths. One, we have a duty to serve and obey God. Two, if we do, He will bless our nation and make it great. And three, if we do not, our nation will perish. Today we are engaged in a real war between secularism and spirituality—between the ways of the world and the ways of God. Will we choose a nation under God or without God? God has made clear the consequences of that choice. Lincoln was not shy in expressing the choice that should be made: "It is the duty of nations, as well as of men…to recognize the sublime truth, announced in the Holy Scriptures and proven by all history, that those nations only are blessed whose God is the Lord."[19]

Fortunately, presidents such as John F. Kennedy have encouraged us as a nation to seek the blessings of God. In connection with his proclamation of a national Thanksgiving Day, October 28, 1961, he said, "I ask the head of each family to recount to his children the story of the first New England Thanksgiving, thus to impress upon future generations the heritage of this nation born in toil, in danger, in purpose, and in the conviction that right and justice and freedom can through man's efforts persevere and come to fruition with the blessing of God."[20]

Why Is God So Concerned about the Destiny of America?

But why is God so passionate about this country, so intimately involved in its discovery, establishment, and preservation? Was it so He could create a political juggernaut to rule the world? Or was it so He could create an environment of religious freedom where faith in God could flourish and God could be worshipped without fear, without restraint, without embarrassment—even honored and recognized as the God of the land? When the latter happens, then such a society is eligible for its maximum spiritual growth and happiness—God's ultimate goal for His children.

The Founding Fathers knew that God's hand in America would have implications far beyond the boundaries of one single nation. Patrick Henry declared that "America lighted the candle to all the world."[21] Benjamin Rush noted, "I was constantly animated by a belief that I was acting for the benefit of the whole world, and of future ages."[22] Jefferson envisioned that the Constitution "will prove in the end a blessing to all the nations of the earth."[23] He also predicted that the government established by the Founding Fathers "will be a standing monument and example for the aim and imitation of the people of other countries."[24] And Lincoln, knowing all this, called America "the best great hope of Earth."[25] One of Lincoln's biographers, William J. Wolf, observed that Lincoln believed "that America was a chosen nation destined to further God's plan for mankind."[26] Therefore, it should not be surprising that Marquis de La

Fayette, a revered defender of the American Revolution, prophetically declared, "The happiness of America is intimately connected with the happiness of all mankind."[27]

No wonder that God, who created the world and all mankind, has such a vested interest in America. It is His beacon on the hill for all the world to see, where religious and other liberties flourish, and where His name can and should be revered both privately and publicly as the God of the land. God loves America, has preserved it, and desires to hold it up as a standard for all the world to emulate.

Accordingly, we should likewise love America and the ideals for which it stands.

---

1 Zielinski, "The Tornado That Saved Washington," smithsonianmag.com.

2 In Zielinski, "The Tornado That Saved Washington," smithsonianmag.com.

3 Zielinski, "The Tornado That Saved Washington," smithsonianmag.com.

4 The battered storm flag that survived the night of battle was lowered and replaced in the morning by the forty-two-foot flag that Key saw in the early morning hours.

5 Lincoln, "President Lincoln's Farewell Address," loc.gov; emphasis added. This address was given "to his old neighbors" in Springfield, Illinois, as Lincoln began his service in Washington, DC.

6 Lincoln, "A Proclamation," loc.gov.

7 In Kunhardt, *Lincoln*, 336.

8 Kunhardt, *Lincoln*, 336.

9 In Kunhardt, *Lincoln*, 336.

10 Lincoln, "Proclamation 103," presidency.ucsb.edu.

11 In Wolf, *The Almost Chosen People*, 156.

12 His real name was Thomas, but Lincoln nicknamed him Tad.

13 In Penrosa, *God's Hand in History During World War II*, 12–13. Winston Churchill gives Hitler a little more credit: "Hitler's belief that the German Air Force would render escape impossible, and that therefore he should keep his armoured formations for the final stroke of the campaign, was a mistaken but not unreasonable view" (*The Second World War*, 2:91). Whatever the reason, the consequences of the delayed attack were the same—the rescue of the Allied army.

14 John, "How a Day of Prayer Saved Britain at Dunkirk," premierchristianity.com.

15 Penrosa, *God's Hand in History During World War II*, 97–98.

16 Eisenhower, statement to soldiers, sailors, and airmen of the Allied Expeditionary Force, June 6, 1944.

[17] Reagan, "Remarks at a Ceremony Commemorating the 49th Anniversary of the Normandy Invasion, D-day," reaganfoundation.org; quoting Joshua 1:5.

[18] Penrosa, *God's Hand in History During World War II*, 102–3.

[19] Lincoln, "A Proclamation for a Day of Humiliation, Fasting and Prayer," loc.gov; emphasis added.

[20] Kennedy, "Proclamation 3438: Thanksgiving Day, 1961," 63.

[21] In Hiedler and Hiedler, *Washington's Circle*, 140.

[22] In Schlesinger, *The Birth of the Nation*, 238.

[23] Jefferson, "From Thomas Jefferson to Joseph Cabell Breckinridge," founders.archives.org.

[24] Jefferson, "From Thomas Jefferson to John Dickson," founders.archives.org.

[25] In Maltby, *The Life and Public Services of Abraham Lincoln*, 191. Lincoln also said, "I must trust in that Supreme Being who has never forsaken this favored land" (in Wolf, *The Almost Chosen People*, 151).

[26] Wolf, *The Almost Chosen People*, 149.

[27] In Tower, *The Marquis de la Fayette*, 1:58.

CHAPTER 5

America's Survival Depends upon a Moral People

The Founding Fathers Viewed Morality as Essential to Liberty and Happiness

John Jay, one of the authors of *The Federalist Papers* and the first chief justice of the US Supreme Court, wrote a letter to a friend about a conversation he had with an atheist physician: "I very concisely remarked, that if there was no God, there could be no moral obligations, and I did not see how society could subsist without them. He [the atheist] did not hesitate to admit, that if there was no God, there could be no moral obligations, but insisted that they were not necessary, for that society would find a substitute for them in enlightened self-interest."[1] The proposal of the atheist seems somewhat naïve and impractical. If enlightened self-interest is to replace morality, whose self-interest do we adopt? That of the atheist or believer? Those who advocate pro-life or pro-choice? That of the capitalist or socialist?

Without moral guidelines from God, there are no fixed boundaries to address the burning social issues of our day, no rock foundation on which to build an enduring nation. In essence, we would end up with a nation of moral relativism, built upon a foundation of sand that would shift or collapse with the constantly changing tides of public opinion. Fortunately, the Founding Fathers understood the need for God's moral law as a counter to personal prejudices and as the cornerstone of a stable and righteous nation.[2]

The Declaration of Independence sets out our unalienable, meaning divine, rights. But with those rights come moral duties. Just as choices and consequences are inseparable, likewise divine rights and divine duties are inseparable. You cannot have one without the other.

James Madison wrote, "Is there no virtue among us? If there be not, we are in a wretched situation. No theoretical checks—no form of government can render us secure. To suppose that any form of government will secure liberty or happiness without any virtue in the people, is a chimerical idea."[3] John Adams also supported this line of reasoning: "We have no Government armed with Power capable of contending with human Passions unbridled by morality and religion. Avarice, Ambition, Revenge or Gallantry would break the strongest Cords of our Constitution as a Whale goes through a net. *Our Constitution was made only for a moral and religious People. It is wholly inadequate to the government of any other.*"[4]

Samuel Adams, a Founding Father, warned of the consequences of a society devoid of divine morals: "I have long been convinced that our enemies have made it an object, to eradicate from the minds of the people in general a sense of true religion and virtue, in hopes thereby the more easily to carry their point of enslaving them. The diminution of public virtue is usually attended with that of public happiness, and the public liberty will not long survive the total extinction of morals."[5] His observation is prophetic. Today there is an onslaught by some to eliminate divinely determined moral values from the public sector—to replace absolute morals with relativism, and God with atheism. And thus, the destructive march toward secularism.

Montesquieu was a French attorney and philosopher who was frequently quoted by the Founding Fathers. He spoke of the nexus between love of country and morals: "The love of our country is conducive to a purity of morals, and the latter is again conducive to the former."[6] In other words, the greater our love for morals, the greater our love for country. And the less our love for morals, the less our love for country. Love of morals and country seem to be inextricably bound.

There can be no doubt that the Founding Fathers understood the need for the new nation and government to be built on a foundation of universal morals, not individual self-enlightenment. They knew that morals were essential to liberty, happiness, and love of country. They knew that history has repeatedly taught that if there is no morality, then man will be selfish and carnal regardless of any governmental laws to the contrary. In other words, we can choose to be governed by morals internally imposed or laws externally mandated.

What Is Moral Law, and Who Determines It?

Realizing that a moral people are essential to maintaining our God-given liberties, then one might ask, "What is moral law and who determines it?" The morals of which the Founding Fathers spoke were not man-made guidelines or arbitrary rules that fluctuated with every transient philosophy of life. They were not some vague form of self-enlightenment or determined by opinion polls or social norms. Rather, the Founding Fathers sought a manifestation of God's will as the moral code for this nation. Their understanding of this truth came from both conscience and such political authorities as Sir William Blackstone (an English judge and law professor) and John Locke (a British philosopher), both of whom were assiduously studied by the Founding Fathers. Blackstone wrote, "As man depends absolutely upon his maker for every thing, it is necessary that he should in all points conform to his maker's will. This will of his maker is called the law of nature... No human laws are of any validity, if contrary to this [God's will]."[7] Locke was in concurrence: "The rules that they [legislators] make for other men's actions must...be conformable to the law of Nature, i.e., to the will of God."[8]

Jefferson was of a like mind: "Whatever is to be our destiny, wisdom, as well as duty, dictates that we should acquiesce in the will of Him whose it is to give and take away."[9] He added that Jesus's moral laws are "the most sublime and benevolent code of morals which has ever been offered to man."[10]

John Jay felt similarly: "The moral or national law was given by the Sovereign of the universe to all mankind."[11] Washington concurred, "It is the duty of all Nations to acknowledge the providence of Almighty God, to obey his will [the moral law], to be grateful for his benefits, and humbly to implore his protection and favor."[12]

James Wilson, who signed both the Declaration of Independence and the Constitution and later became one of the original justices on the US Supreme Court, wrote of God's will as the supreme law by which we should be governed:

"Having thus stated the question—what is the efficient cause of moral obligation?—I give this answer—the will of God. This is the supreme law. His just and full right of imposing laws, and our duty in obeying them, are the sources of our moral obligations.

"How shall we, in particular cases, discover the will of God? We discover it by our conscience, by our reason, and by the Holy Scriptures."[13]

Our conscience, to which Wilson referred, is much more than a network of cerebral circuitry parroting our personal prejudices on moral issues. It is much more than man's reasoning and experience fused in such a fashion to determine moral truth. Rather, it is the light of Christ, which, according to the gospel of John, "lighteth every man that cometh into the world" (John 1:9). No wonder Isaiah said, "Let us walk in the light of the Lord" (Isa. 2:5). Our conscience is a reflection of God's will and should be our moral compass, our divine navigational system. When all is said and done, conscience is more powerful, more persuasive than secular law. It governs conduct even when no mortal reward or punishment is given. It is this compass of conscience that the Founding Fathers sought to follow in laying the foundation of our nation and which they enjoined us to pursue. They knew it was the only foolproof restraint against one's carnal desires. Lincoln, in the same spirit manifested by the Founding Fathers, declared, "I have desired that all my works and acts may be according to His [God's] will, and that it might be so, I have sought His aid."[14]

But why is it so important to learn and follow God's will? Because God is not only the most intelligent and powerful being in the universe but also the happiest person in the universe. Accordingly, when we follow His will, we taste in part of that joy. The Savior acknowledged this truth: "These things I speak in the world [My will], that they might have my joy fulfilled in themselves" (John 17:13). And on another occasion, He said, "These things have I spoken unto you, that my joy might remain in you, and that your joy might be full" (John 15:11).

Contrary to the opinion of some, there is nothing negative about God's moral standards. Rather, they are positive and uplifting and liberating. They build relationships of trust, they enhance self-esteem, they foster a clear conscience, they promote happiness, and they invite the Spirit of the Lord to bless our individual, family, and community lives. Is it any wonder that our Founding Fathers, wise and devoted as they were, sought these moral standards as their guide? They knew that liberty was not the right to do anything, anytime, anywhere. They understood the need for divine restraints and direction, meaning moral standards, so that our actions would not adversely affect society and the rights of others. President Lyndon Johnson made this significant observation: "God will not favor everything that we do. It is rather our duty to divine His will."[15] The holy scriptures speak directly to those who fail to seek God's will: "Be ye not unwise, but understanding what the will of the Lord is" (Eph. 5:17).

America will never be destroyed by external forces but rather only by its internal choices—choices to follow man's will (secularism) rather than God's.

Lincoln so prophesied, "As a nation of freemen, we must live through all time, or die by suicide."[16] Secularism is the poison pill that brings about that demise.

Morality Requires Religion, and Religion Requires God

Is it possible, however, to have moral standards—to know and live God's will without religion? George Washington believed the two to be inseparable, that they went hand in hand: "Of all the dispositions and habits which lead to political prosperity religion and morality are indispensable supports." Washington further declared,

"Let us with caution indulge the supposition that morality can be maintained without religion. Whatever may be conceded to the influence of refined education or minds of peculiar structure, *reason and experience both forbid us to expect national morality can prevail in exclusion of religious principle.*"[17] While there certainly exist some nonbelievers who are moral people (who follow God's will but question belief in Him), it is a pretense to believe that morality can be achieved, at least in a collective and ongoing setting, independent of religious influence. Robert Bork concurred in this observation: "Religion is regarded by most Americans as the sole or primary source of moral belief."[18]

De Tocqueville likewise understood this, for he declared, "Liberty cannot be established without morality, nor morality without faith."[19] Eric Metaxas added, "If you take God and faith and morality out of the equation [of how to govern society], everything inevitably falls apart. It cannot be otherwise."[20] Perhaps Reverend Billy Graham said it about as well as it can be said, "Only the living God can fill the moral vacuum that exists in our world."[21]

The nexus between morality and religion was a constant recurring theme in the hearts and minds of the Founding Fathers. In a letter to Benjamin Rush, John Adams wrote, "Religion I hold to be essential to Morals."[22] Alexander Hamilton opined, "Morality must fall without religion."[23] And James Madison added, "Belief in a God All Powerful, wise, and good is so essential to the moral order of the world and to the happiness of man that arguments which enforce it cannot be drawn from too many sources."[24]

Thomas Paine, sometimes mistakenly referred to as an atheist, wrote that "the God in whom we believe is a God of moral truth."[25] He also believed that "morality and religion, which is the most solid support thereof, are necessary to the maintenance of society, as well as to the happiness of the individual."[26] Patrick Henry spoke of "the great pillars of all government and of social life; I mean virtue, morality, and religion. This is the armor, my friend, and this alone, that renders us invincible."[27] Statements to this effect by the Founding Fathers are almost legion in number. There is no doubt where they stood on this issue.

Following is an observation attributed by many to de Tocqueville, though the true author is unknown. Regardless of its origin, its message is consistent with our history and the Founding Fathers' beliefs that morals and religion must be the bedrock of a great nation:

> I sought for the greatness and genius of America in her commodious harbors and her ample rivers—and it was not there…in her fertile fields and boundless forests—and it was not there…in her rich mines and her vast world commerce—and it was not there…in her democratic Congress and her matchless Constitution—and it was not there. Not until I went to the churches of America and heard her pulpits aflame with righteousness did I understand the secret of her genius and power. America is great because she is good, and if America ever ceases to be good, America will cease to be great.[28]

In other words, America's greatness is not to be found in her economic prowess, political correctness, diversity, or in her governmental programs, but in her goodness. And goodness comes by learning the will of God and doing it. That is one reason religion is so critical to the welfare of America, because it reveals and reinforces the will of God, the moral principles by which we should live. It is our nation's best catalyst for goodness. It is a counterbalance to man's natural selfish interests and desire for power. No wonder the Savior instructed us to pray: "Thy kingdom come. *Thy will be done in earth*, as it is in heaven (Matt. 6:10; emphasis added). And no wonder He said in the same sermon, "Not every one that saith unto me, Lord, Lord, shall enter into the kingdom of heaven; but he that doeth the will of my Father which is in heaven" (Matt. 7:21).

The political kingdom in which we now live is but a temporary kingdom, a probationary period of sorts to see if we will obey God's will. That is why it is so important to learn and do His will now, for it determines our eternal destiny.

The Founding Fathers saw belief in God as not only integral to our eternal salvation but as the essential element of our nation's fabric, because to them, the nation's success was dependent on morality, morality was dependent on religion, and religion was dependent on learning and living God's will. Morality, religion, and God are inseparable partners in maintaining the integrity and effectiveness of the Constitution, and thus the success of this nation. If God's moral law is not the foundation for our society, then secularism will rapidly and radically replace God's divine law as our governing standard.

Justice Antonin Scalia summarized it well: "The Founders believed morality was essential to the well-being of the republic, *and that religion was the best way to foster morality*."[29] De Tocqueville also recognized this necessary link: "Despotism may govern without faith, but liberty cannot. Religion is…more needed in democratic republics than in any others."[30] And Jon Meacham, well-known author and Pulitzer Prize winner, made this significant observation: "Is religion in America a necessary evil, or can it be a positive force for good? Taken all in all, I think history teaches that the benefits of faith in God have outweighed the costs. To argue against a role for faith in politics is essentially futile."[31] Abigail Adams spoke directly to this point: "A true patriot must be a religious man."[32]

Does Religion Foster Morality?

But one might ask, "What concrete proof do we have that religion fosters morality?" Arthur Brooks, a professor of business and government policy and frequent contributor to the *Wall Street Journal*, wrote a book entitled *Who Really Cares*. It is a candid fact-filled book on who gives for charitable purposes, who renders community service, and who does not. His conclusions are not mere anecdotal statements but supported by substantial national and international datasets. After providing a plethora of facts, he shares these conclusions: "Religious people are far more charitable with their time and money than secularists. Religious people are more generous in informal ways as well, such as giving blood, giving money to family members, and behaving honestly." He then goes on to note that "charitable giving is learned, reinforced, and practiced with intact families—especially religious families."[33] Brooks makes this candid confession, which adds substantial weight to his conclusions: "I confess the prejudices of my past here to emphasize that the findings in this book—many of which may appear conservative and support a religious, hardworking, family-oriented lifestyle—are faithful to the best available evidence, and *contrary* to my political and cultural roots. Indeed, the irresistible pull of empirical evidence in this book is what changed the way I see the world."[34]

Brooks was only one of many in his positive assessment of religion. Timothy P. Carney, author and commentary editor at the *Washington Examiner*, wrote, "From time to time, the media will trumpet some study finding some malady among the religious—they're angrier, or stupider, or greedier. But ask almost any social scientist, Left or Right, religious or secular, and he or she will tell you with high confidence that religious people are better off socially and economically and fall into fewer negative behaviours [crime, teenage pregnancy, drug abuse, suicide] than nonreligious people. Popular culture likes to paint the dark picture of religion in America, but the actual data point the other way." He then went on to say, "Gallup, the pollster, has a 'Well-Being Index,' which measures emotional health, physical health, healthy behaviors, and more. [It] found that very religious people have better lives than similarly situated nonreligious people. So America's growing irreligiosity is a problem. Only the most stubborn enemies of religion deny that."

Carney continued, "Nonchurchgoers are more depressed, more likely to be in poverty, more likely to die of despair. Nonchurchgoers are less likely to be connected to their community, and frankly less likely to see the value of the community."[35]

The Pew Research Center is in accord with these findings. It discovered that actively religious people (those who attend religious services at least once a month) are more likely than less religious people to describe themselves as "very happy," to join nonreligious organizations such as charities and clubs, and to vote.[36]

Studies have also shown that religion has a profound effect for good upon children, including teenagers. Researchers from Harvard's

School of Public Health conducted a study in 2018 which revealed that children who attend church at least once a month have greater satisfaction in life, volunteer more, and have a "greater sense of mission, more forgiveness, and lower probabilities of drug use and early sexual initiation" than those with no or less religious activity in their lives. The study also confirmed similar results in prior studies with these comments: "Consistent with prior literature, our results suggest associations of frequent religious participation in adolescence with greater subsequent psychological well-being, character strengths, and lower risks of mental illness and several health behaviors."[37] Who would not want their children to have those substantial benefits in life?

David Horowitz, a Jewish agnostic and *New York Times* best-selling author, noted the difference between the consequences of a religion-inspired society versus an atheistic one. The leaders of the New Atheism movement, he observed, "are blind to all the positive influences religion has had on human behavior, and they ignore all the atheist-inspired genocides of the last 250 years. In the twentieth century alone, Communist atheists slaughtered more than 100 million people in Russia, China, and Indochina."[38]

Is it any wonder the Founding Fathers saw religion as a necessity to foster morals and maximize happiness, and thus serve as the backbone of an enlightened and righteous society?

William P. Barr, former US attorney general, spoke of the absolute need for religion in order to maintain a moral and free people: "In the Framers' view, free government was only suitable and sustainable for a religious people—a people who recognized that there was a transcendent moral order antecedent to both the state and man-made law and who had the discipline to control themselves according to those enduring principles." He then made this tragic but truthful commentary: "We see the growing ascendancy of secularism and the doctrine of moral relativism. Suffice it to say that the campaign to destroy the traditional moral order has brought with it immense suffering, wreckage, and misery. And yet, the forces of secularism, ignoring these tragic results, press on with even greater militancy." He then noted that this militant secularism "has itself become a religion, pursued with religious fervor. Those who defy the creed risk a figurative burning at the stake—social, educational, and professional ostracism and exclusion waged through lawsuits and savage social media campaigns."[39]

What then should be the foundation of our society—religion or secularism?

As previously noted, the Savior gave a very practical test to determine truth, "by their fruits ye shall know them" (Matt. 7:20). In general, the fruits of religion are represented by a people who are happy, who are compassionate as evidenced by their charitable giving, who participate in charitable and civic organizations, who are honest, and who are of strong family orientation. Judeo-Christianity and many other religions actively teach their people to be law-abiding citizens, to be faithful spouses, to promote self-reliance, and to respect and honor God—all morals valued by the Founding Fathers. Of course there are exceptions, but in the main, religion is a powerful tool to teach and promote moral values—an essential element of a free society. On the other hand, secularism is the polar opposite of morality. It is immorality couched in politically correct terms. That being the case, why would we not want to promote religion in general (not a specific religion) at every reasonable opportunity in both the private and public sectors?

Daniel Webster, a highly respected American statesman who lived between 1782 and 1852, spoke of the consequences when a nation either accepts or rejects religion: "If we and they [our posterity] shall live always in the fear of God, and shall respect His commandments…we may have the highest hopes of the future fortunes of our country. It will go on prospering… But if we and our posterity reject religious instruction and authority, violate the rules of eternal justice, trifle with the injunctions of morality, and recklessly destroy the political constitution which holds us together, no man can tell how suddenly a catastrophe may overwhelm us, that shall bury all our glory in profound obscurity."[40]

When Justice Antonin Scalia passed away, his son Paul made this significant observation: "Dad understood that the deeper he went in his Catholic faith, the better a citizen and public servant he became. God blessed him with a desire to be the country's good servant, *because* he was God's first."[41] This seems to be an eternal truth. If we will put God first in our life, then He will make of us better patriots, better citizens, and better public servants than we might otherwise be.

That is why religion is so critical to the well-being of our society.

The Role of Judeo-Christianity and the Bible in Shaping America's Moral Code

The primary source for the ideals of the Founding Fathers was not just religion in general but more specifically Christianity. As John Adams observed, "The general principles on which the fathers achieved independence were the only principles in which that beautiful assembly of young gentlemen could unite. And what were these general principles? I answer, the general principles of Christianity."[42] Christianity was so engrained in the Founders' way of life—such a manifest part of their culture—that references to it surfaced repeatedly in their public as well as private lives. Consistent with this, Washington directed his troops as follows: "The general hopes and trusts that every officer and man will endeavor so to live and act as becomes a Christian soldier."[43] President John F. Kennedy wrote to Brazil's president, Jânio da Silva Quadros, "To each of us is entrusted the heavy responsibility of guiding the affairs of a democratic nation founded on Christian ideals."[44] And one of those Christian ideals is to promote religious freedom for all religions, whether or not Christian in nature.

In fact, so universal was the understanding that this was a Christian nation that the US Supreme Court unanimously declared the same in *Church of the Holy Trinity v. United States* (1892): "From the discovery of this continent to the present hour, there is a single voice making this affirmation… We find everywhere a clear recognition of the same truth… This is a Christian nation."[45]

Mark David Hall, Herbert Hoover distinguished professor of political science at George Fox University, acknowledged this underlying Christian culture: "While America did not have a Christian Founding in the sense of creating a theocracy, its Founding was deeply shaped by Christian moral truths," or perhaps more precisely stated, the principles of Judeo-Christianity. Hall went on to cite a study by Donald Lutz, "who examined 15,000 pamphlets, articles, and books on political subjects published in the late 18th century. His study found that the Bible was cited far more often than any other book, article, or pamphlet. In fact, the Founders referenced the Bible more than all enlightenment authors combined."[46] In essence, the Bible and Judeo-Christian beliefs became the foundation of our nation's moral code.[47]

President Andrew Jackson concurred, "[The Bible] is the rock on which our Republic rests."[48] Lincoln was in total agreement that our moral structure emanates from the Bible: "[The Bible] is the best gift God has given to men. All the good the Saviour gave to the world was communicated through this book. But for it we could not know right from wrong."[49]

Presidents of more recent vintage felt similarly. President Calvin Coolidge observed, "The foundations of our society and our government rest so much on the teachings of the Bible that it would be difficult to support them if faith in these teachings would cease to be practically universal in our country."[50] And Franklin D. Roosevelt noted, "In the formative days of the Republic the directing influence the Bible exercised upon the fathers of the Nation is conspicuously evident… We cannot read the history of our rise and development as a Nation, without reckoning with the place the Bible has occupied in shaping the advances of the Republic."[51]

Ben Carson made this significant observation as to the role of the Bible in our nation's development: "When our nation was rising rapidly to the pinnacle of the world, we were not ashamed of our relationship with God. In fact, reading from the Bible was not only common, it was expected in early public schools. The founders wanted generally accepted religious values to be taught in our schools without favoring any particular denomination, *but they never intended to exclude God from the classroom, because they knew that you had to have something upon which to base your system of values.* If we only believe in evolution and survival of the fittest, whose values do we use to govern society?"[52]

In spite of these deserved tributes to the Bible and the key role it played in shaping our nation's moral code, there are some who would like to ban it from the public square and abandon its teachings in favor of more secular dogma. To do so, however, would be an affront to God, to the Founding Fathers, and to many of our national heroes. It would be nothing less than a tragic step backward that would diminish our moral values and take us further down the path of secularism.

Some might ask, "What specific principles of religion are we to enforce in order to enhance our nation's moral values without establishing a national religion?" The answer, the basic moral principles of Judeo-Christianity upon which this nation was founded, principles which foster freedom of speech, freedom of assembly, and freedom of religion even for non-Jewish and non-Christian sects.

How Can We Best Interpret the Bible to Discover Moral Truth?

It is one thing to acknowledge that moral truths are essential to the well-being of our country as repeatedly taught by the Founding Fathers. But that raises a difficult question: what should be the guiding principles to discover those moral truths, particularly in a nation that is so diverse? As important as the Bible is for this purpose, how do we reconcile Biblical conflicts such as the one encountered during the Civil War when both sides—North and South—referred to the Bible as support for their cause? As Lincoln noted, "Both [North and South] read the same Bible, and pray to the same God; and each invokes His aid against the other."[53] Either the Bible gave conflicting messages or one side misinterpreted those messages. Lincoln believed the latter. Following are some principles taught in the Bible that can help us interpret its passages correctly and thus be unified in the moral principles it teaches.

The Need for Multiple Witnesses

Most are familiar with the proverb, "One swallow does not a summer make." In that same spirit, one scripture does not necessarily a truth make. The apostle Paul taught, "In the mouth of two or three witnesses shall every word be established" (2 Cor. 13:1). In other words, is there more than one scripture to justify one's position? For example, on the question of slavery, the scriptures teach us (1) that we are all the "children of God" (Rom. 8:16–17), (2) that "God is no respecter of persons" (Acts 10:34), and (3) that we should "love one another; as I [God] have loved you" (John 3:34), all of which are in direct opposition to slavery. These are but a few of the many scriptures that echo this sentiment and establish a pattern for us to determine the truth. The frequent repetition of this theme in the scriptures should be convincing evidence of God's true will on the subject.

The Power of Reason

The Bible has also given us other principles that can help us understand its various passages. The Lord declared to Isaiah, "Come now, and let us reason together" (Isa. 1:18). The need to reason through an issue is a common theme in the Bible (see 1 Samuel 12:7; Acts 17:2; Acts 18:4; 1 Peter 3:15). The Lord expects us to use our God-given powers of reason, but if exercised alone, without the aid of the scriptures and the Holy Spirit, they can lead to secularism. When reason, however, is combined with the scriptures, it leads to moral truth as God would have us know and live it. Lincoln was a master at combining the two. In obvious reference to the scriptures and the evils of slavery, Lincoln reasoned as follows: "It may seem strange that any men should dare to ask a just God's assistance in wringing their bread from the sweat of other men's faces; but let us judge not, that we be not judged."[54] If someone had a general belief in God and the Bible, then it became very difficult to honestly refute this logic of Lincoln founded in his moral inferences from the Bible.

Learning from Our Past Experiences

When Jacob (Isaac's son) wanted to leave Laban's homeland and establish his own home, Laban responded, "I have learned by experience that the Lord hath blessed me for thy sake" (Gen. 30:27). Experience can be a powerful teacher. Hank Smith, a religious leader and teacher, noted, "A man with an experience is never at the mercy of a man with an opinion."[55] For example, experience should demonstrate to us that the principles underlying socialism, as evidenced in history (discussed in chapter 15), are contrary to the moral laws of God.

Seeking the Influence of the Holy Spirit

Will there still be difficult issues to resolve even after making references to the Bible, exercising our powers of reason, and benefiting from our experiences? Yes. That is why it is so important to follow our conscience, which is a manifestation of the light of Christ and the Holy Spirit. The Bible tells us that the Holy Spirit gives us knowledge (see 1 Corinthians 12:8), good judgment (see Matthew 12:18), is a guide to all truth (see John 16:13), and helps us distinguish between man's wisdom and God's (see 1 Corinthians 2:11). Who would not want each of those divine powers to help them determine moral truth? That is one reason it is so important to elect men and women of God who seek the Holy Spirit in their lives and thus can discern between the wisdom of the world and the wisdom of God.

The truths of the Bible, as evidenced by multiple supporting scriptures, and combined with the powers of reason, experience, and the Holy Spirit, are the resources God has given us and directed us to use in order to determine His moral law. When these resources are collectively used, moral truth is most likely to be discovered.

Why Is It Important to Know God's Moral Law and Live It?

The following facts and principles are designed to help us understand why it is important to both know God's moral law and to live it.

First: We are the spirit children of God. The Bible refers to us as "the children of God" (Rom. 8:16), "his offspring" (Acts 17:28), and to God as "the Father of [our] spirits" (Heb. 12:9).

Second: Because we are God's children, he loves us immensely. The apostle John confirmed this truth: "For God so loved the world, that he gave his only begotten Son" (John 3:16).

Third: Because God loves us immensely, he blessed us with certain unalienable rights, among them life, liberty, and the pursuit of happiness, which individually and collectively maximize our quest for true happiness. He also gave us moral laws or commandments that best protect those rights so that we can return to Him, become more like Him, and experience a fulness of joy (see Psalm 16:11; Matthew 5:48; John 15:11; Hebrews 5:9).[56]

Fourth: Because the Founding Fathers were inspired, they were able to clearly enunciate those unalienable rights and moral laws in the creation of the Declaration of Independence and Constitution. In those charter documents, they also defined the basic governmental rights and moral obligations that would best protect those divine entitlements.

Fifth: In order for the Declaration of Independence and Constitution to be effective, however, the Founding Fathers declared the necessity of a moral people. They further understood that we could not have a moral people at large without religion—the most powerful societal force available to teach and implement these moral laws.

Sixth: Since religion is the best source we have to encourage the living of God's moral laws, the Founding Fathers demonstrated by their actions that religion in general should be encouraged in the public as well as private sector (see chapter 8) without ever fostering a national religion.

Seventh: If we as a people obey God's moral laws, He makes the following promises to us and to our nation: "Righteousness exalteth a nation" (Prov. 14:34) and "If my people, which are called by my name, will humble themselves, and pray, and seek my face, and turn from their wicked ways; then will I hear from heaven, and will forgive their sin, and will heal their land" (2 Chron. 7:14). And oh, what a healing we could use—healing from contention and bigotry and political divisiveness! On the other hand, Isaiah taught, "The nation and kingdom that will not serve thee [God] shall perish; yea, those nations shall be utterly wasted" (Isa. 60:12). George Washington was in concurrence: "The propitious smiles of Heaven, can never be expected on a nation that disregards the eternal rules of order and right, which Heaven itself has ordained."[57]

What If I Don't Believe in God?

If one does not believe in God, then one is left to his or her own devices to determine what is moral and what is not. As a result, one's moral code becomes a function of how one views society, his or her reasoning powers, passions, interpretation of facts, personal perspective, and personal integrity. This becomes a subjective test that can differ in each person's mind and therefore result in a lack of uniformity and stability. In this scenario, one person's sincere beliefs may be no better than another's. What happens when these viewpoints are in opposition? Who is to be believed? And what viewpoint should govern?

In response to the question why some are "so determined to remove God from our lives," Ben Carson offered this assessment: "They recognize that if we have no higher authority to answer to than man, we become gods unto ourselves and get to determine our own behavior. In their world, 'If it feels good, do it.' They can justify anything based on their ideology because in their opinion, there is no higher authority other than themselves to overrule them. They have a visceral reaction to the mention of God's word, because it tears at the fabric of their justification system."[58] The result, as Ben Shapiro observed, is a society in which "where children had once learned from *Pinocchio* to 'always let your conscience be your guide,' now they were taught by *Frozen*, 'no right, no wrong, no rules for me / I'm free! / Let it go!'"[59]

Alexis de Tocqueville commented on the difference between those nations who believed in God verses those who did not: "There are certain populations in Europe whose unbelief is only equalled by their ignorance and their debasement, whilst in America one of the first and most enlightened nations in the world, the people fulfill all the outward duties of religion with fervor."[60]

Removal of God from society is an ill-advised attempt by some to sanction immoral acts without suffering guilt or other adverse consequences. But it is a futile effort, because ultimately there is no escape for individuals and societies from the consequences of breaking God's moral laws. Such action always results in a loss of God's guiding hand and protecting power. There are no exceptions, or as one Christian leader said, "There are no successful sinners."[61] When a nation fails to learn the lessons surrounding godlessness and moral depravity, it becomes one more tragedy in the annals of history.

God's Knows What Is Best for Us as Individuals and as a Nation

In a real sense, each of us faces this crossroad in life: will we choose man's wisdom or God's will? The latter provides the direction and perspective of someone who is all-knowing, all-loving, and all-powerful, and therefore His will constitutes perfect moral judgment. If given the choice, whose moral code would you adopt—man's or God's? Gallup polls report that approximately 90 percent of Americans believe in God.[62] They don't all have a designated religion, they don't all attend church, but they believe in a supreme being who governs the universe. Accordingly, it is His will we should seek and follow. This makes sense, because He knows better than any individual man or woman or society as to what will bring stability and happiness to us as individuals and as a nation.

One Christian leader told of "two frivolous girls clattering through a great museum and then flippantly remarking as they left the building that it hadn't impressed them much. One of the door-keepers standing by commented to them, 'Young ladies, this museum is not on trial here today. Its quality cannot be contested. You are the ones who are on trial.'"[63] Likewise, God's moral laws are not on trial.

They have been tested and proven over the ages and confirmed by the Holy Spirit. Rather, it is we who are on trial to see if we will embrace them, endorse them, and live by them. And when we do so as a nation, we will be entitled to fulfillment of that divine petition "God bless America."

---

1 Letter from John Jay to John Bristed, Apr. 23, 1811, in *The Life of John Jay*, 347.

2 For the purpose of this book, the term *morals* and related terms are used in a broad sense to include those virtues that help refine and perfect: integrity, unselfishness, chastity, self-restraint, civility, and the like—in essence, every virtue that makes us more godlike (see Matthew 5:48).

3 Madison, *The Writings of James Madison*, 223. Washington concurred: "There is no truth more thoroughly established, than that there exists in the economy and course of nature, an indissoluble union between virtue and happiness" ("Washington's Inaugural Address of 1789," archives.gov).

4 Adams, "From John Adams to Massachusetts Militia," founders.archives.gov; emphasis added. Adams also noted that "without Virtue, there can be no political Liberty" ("From John Adams to Thomas Jefferson," Dec. 21, 1819, founders.archives.gov).

5 In Cousins, *In God We Trust*, 351.

6 Montesquieu, *The Spirit of Laws*, 1:46.

7 Blackstone, *Commentaries on the Laws of England*, 1:39–40.

8 Locke, *Two Treatises of Civil Government*, 262.

9 Jefferson, *The Writings of Thomas Jefferson*, 4:547.

10 Jefferson, "Thomas Jefferson to John Adams," founders.archives.gov.

11 Letter from John Jay to John Murray Jr., Apr. 15, 1818, in *The Life of John Jay*, 385.

12 Washington, "Thanksgiving Proclamation," founders.archives.gov. In more recent times, President Franklin Roosevelt offered a prayer during a nationwide radio address on the occasion of the D-Day invasion. His prayer included these words: "O Lord, give us faith. Give us faith in thee. Thy will be done, Almighty God. Amen" ("Text of Radio Address," fdrlibrary.org).

[13] Wilson, *The Works of James Wilson*, 1:105–6.

[14] In Wolf, *The Almost Chosen People*, 154.

[15] In Meacham, *American Gospel*, 197.

[16] Lincoln, "Address Before the Young Men's Lyceum of Springfield, Illinois," Collected works, 109.

[17] Washington, "Washington's Farewell Address," avalon.law.yale.edu; emphasis added. I have a friend who is an agnostic but who lives what most Christians would deem a moral life. I do not think that George Washington was saying that an individual agnostic or atheist cannot live a moral life, but that both reason and history experience have demonstrated that a collective society of such will not produce a moral nation.

[18] Bork, *The Tempting of America*, 248.

[19] De Tocqueville, *Democracy in America*, Vol. 1:xviii–xix.

[20] Metaxas, *If You Can Keep It*, 48.

[21] In Meacham, *American Gospel*, 215.

[22] Adams, "From John Adams to Benjamin Rush," founders.archives.gov.

[23] Hamilton, "The Stand No. III," founders.archives.gov; emphasis in original.

[24] Madison, "From James Madison to Frederick Beasley;" typography modernized. Alexander Hamilton said, "Can we in prudence suppose that national morality can be maintained in exclusion of religious principles? Does it not require the aid of a generally received and divinely authoritative religion?" (in Meacham, *American Gospel*, 28).

[25] Paine, The *Age of Reason*, 44. Norman Cousins wrote about Paine, "A man who was willing to travel anywhere in the world to combat atheism and to establish the proof of the existence of God can hardly be denounced as an atheist himself, but this is what happened to Thomas Paine. His crusade was based on the love of God and man, yet he was flayed as an infidel and enemy of religion… Paine was particularly disturbed about the widespread atheism in France and set out to combat it." As part of this effort, Paine established the Theophilanthropy movement in France, which he said was based on the "existence of God and the immortality of the soul" (Cousins, *In God We Trust*, 389–90).

[26] Paine, *The Theological Works of Thomas Paine*, 191. Benjamin Franklin was yet another advocate for the need of religion: "History will also afford frequent opportunities of showing the necessity of a public religion, from its usefulness to the public; the advantages of a religious character among private persons… and the excellency of the Christian religion above all others ancient or modern" (in Meacham, *American Gospel*, 21).

[27] In Arnold, *The Life of Patrick Henry*, 254.

[28] In Billington, *Respectfully Quoted*, 160.

[29] Scalia, *Scalia Speaks*, 73; emphasis added. Jon Meacham concurred with this observation: "The Founders came to believe that religion, for all its faults, was an essential foundation for a people's moral conduct and for American ideas about justice, decency, duty, and responsibility" (*American Gospel*, 27).

[30] De Tocqueville, *Democracy in America*, 1:288.

[31] Meacham, *American Gospel*, 31–32.

[32] Adams, "Abigail Adams to John Adams," founders.archive.gov; capitalization standardized.

[33] Brooks, *Who Really Cares*, 177–78.

[34] Brooks, *Who Really Cares*, 12–13 emphasis in original. The Philanthropy Roundtable came to the same conclusion: "Religion motivates giving more than any other factor. The biggest givers are found to be concentrated in 'Bible Belt' states in the South or where Mormons make up a large portion of the population" ("Who Gives Most to Charity?" philanthropyroundtable.org).

[35] Carney, *Alienated America*, 126, 130, 139. Carney also noted, "According to our analysis of the American Time Use Survey, spending two or more hours devoted to religious activity on a given Sunday had a stronger effect on life satisfaction than did making more than $75,000 per year. So, for someone at the national median income level of $56,500…spending two hours a week at church is associated with more happiness in the long run than getting a $20,000 raise" (*Alienated America*, 267).

[36] Marshall, "Are Religious People Happier, Healthier? Our New Global Study Explores This Question," pewresearch.org.

[37] Chen and VanderWeele, "Associations of Religious Upbringing With Subsequent Health and Well-Being," 2357, 2361.

[38] Horowitz, *Dark Agenda*, 5–6.

[39] Barr, "Remarks to the Law School," justice.gov.

[40] Webster, "Extract from the Address before the Historical Society of New York, February, 1852," 125.

[41] In Scalia, *On Faith*, 217; emphasis in original.

[42] Adams, "From John Adams to Thomas Jefferson," June 28, 1813, founders.archives.gov; typography modernized. On another occasion, Adams wrote in his usual direct manner, "Without religion this world would be something not fit to be mentioned in polite company, I mean hell" ("From John Adams to Thomas Jefferson," Apr. 19, 1817; typography modernized).

[43] In Meacham, *American Gospel*, 77.

[44] Kennedy, "Message Greeting President Quadros," 28.

[45] Justice Josiah David Brewer wrote the opinion, *Church of the Holy Trinity v. United States*, 143 U.S. 457, 465, 471 (1892); emphasis added. In 1797, the United States entered a treaty with Tripoli, which contained language that "America is not in any sense founded on the Christian religion" and then went on to explain what that language meant (i.e. America has no hatred "against the laws, religion or tranquility of [Muslims])." In other words, America's government is not a theocracy, nor does it adopt any so-called "Christian" principles or otherwise that oppose the worship of Allah. Rather, as stated by the Founding Fathers on scores of occasions, America's government is based on

righteous Judeo-Christian morals, which include freedom of worship by and for all religions (Barton, *Original Intent,* 133).

[46] Hall, "Did America Have a Christian Founding?" Eric Metaxas made a similar observation: "When the founders were advocating for liberty, their single-most-quoted source was the Bible" (*Metaxas, If You Can Keep It,* 155).

[47] Alexis de Tocqueville also noticed the observable effect of Christianity upon the morals adopted in America: "The [Christian] sects which exist in the United States are innumerable. They all differ in respect to the worship which is due from man to his Creator; but they all agree in respect to the duties which are due from man to man. Each sect adores the Deity in its own peculiar manner; but all the sects preach the same moral law in the name of God. There is no country in the whole world in which the Christian religion retains a greater influence over the souls of men than in America" (*Democracy in America,* 1:284–85).

[48] In Reagan, "Proclamation 5018—Year of the Bible, 1983," presidency.ucsb.edu.

[49] Lincoln, *Complete Works,* 10:218.

[50] In Federer, *America's God and Country,* 181.

[51] Roosevelt, "Statement on the Four Hundredth Anniversary of the Printing of the English Bible," presidency.ucsb.edu.

[52] Carson, *America the Beautiful,* 124; emphasis added.

[53] Lincoln, "Second Inaugural Address," loc.gov.

[54] Lincoln, "Second Inaugural Address," loc.gov.

[55] This same quotation has been used by Hank Smith in various talks he has given and confirmed to the author in an e-mail dated Sept. 1, 2017.

[56] God decreed, "If ye love me, keep my commandments" (John 14:15). Obedience to God's commandments or moral laws is a measure of our discipleship, our devotion, and our appreciation and love for God.

[57] Washington, "Washington's Inaugural Address of 1789," archives.gov.

[58] Carson, *One Nation,* 41.

[59] Shapiro, *The Right Side of History,* 196.

[60] De Tocqueville, *Democracy in America,* 1:289.

[61] Lee, "'Successful' Sinners," 3.

[62] See Newport, "Most Americans Still Believe in God," June 29, 2016, news.gallup.com.

[63] Packer, *Teach Ye Diligently,* 177.

CHAPTER 6

How Should We Interpret the Constitution—the Living Document Method?

Two Prime Methods to Interpret

Is there a way to interpret the Constitution that best reflects the will of God and thus is consistent with His moral law? While there are multiple ways to interpret the Constitution, there are two prime methods used by lawyers and judges today, one of which seems better designed to learn and implement the will of God as it was understood and embraced by the Founding Fathers.

One method of interpretation is known as the living document or living Constitution theory. This proposes that the text should be interpreted in accordance with the standard set forth in 1958 by the US Supreme Court in the case of *Trop v. Dulles*, namely, "the evolving standards of decency that mark the progress of a maturing society."[1] Justice Ruth Bader Ginsburg explained this methodology as follows: "This is a constitution, not a law meant to last a certain period of time; it was meant to govern through the ages. And of course, to govern through the ages it has to be kept in tune with the people that are governed. It can do that because it has broad themes that were meant to grow with an evolving society."[2] This method is intended to provide flexibility in a world of changing morals and ideals.

The other method of interpretation is known as originalism or strict constructionism. If we believe that the Founding Fathers were inspired and sought the will of God to construct the Constitution, then we would want to make every effort to interpret the Constitution in accordance with the Founders' original intent, hence the term *originalism*. As a consequence, originalists strive to interpret the Constitution in accordance with the exact meaning of the words in the text as understood by the Founders. If the meaning is not self-explanatory, they try to determine the meaning of the words in accordance with the intent of the Framers as preserved in historical documents. This, they believe, will foster the moral values advanced by the Founding Fathers, give stability and predictability to the meaning of the Constitution, and immunize it from the constantly shifting sands of public opinion.

Justice Clarence Thomas explained originalism as follows: "The Constitution means not what the Court says it does but what the delegates at Philadelphia and at the state ratifying conventions understood it to mean. We as a nation adopted a written Constitution precisely because it has a fixed meaning that does not change. Otherwise we would have adopted the British approach of an unwritten, evolving constitution."[3] In other words, the principles enunciated in the Constitution mean the same thing today as they did when it was written in 1787. But what if the Constitution is not clear on a certain matter or fails to address an issue before the court? What is the responsibility of the judges faced with such a dilemma? In this and the following chapter are two different perspectives on how to resolve the answers to those questions.

The Living Document Method—Judicial Interpretation or Legislation?

An evolving standard of interpretation might have some merit if we were assured our society would always be evolving or progressing in its "standards of decency." But history has shown that this is often not the case, and thus it may be a slippery slope on which to build one's judicial philosophy. For example, were there evolving standards of decency in Sodom and Gomorrah as compared to prior ages? Did Mao Zedong and Joseph Stalin bring heightened standards of morality to their societies versus those of previous generations? Have we had progressing standards of decency during the last fifty to seventy years of US history? Are the movies coming out of Hollywood more decent and moral and uplifting than fifty to seventy years ago? Or how do we explain the pornography explosion in recent years? Or what about the increased use of drugs and harmful substances? Or the increase in fornication, adultery, and cohabitation before marriage? Are these evidences of a more refined, sensitive, and moral nation? If not, are our Supreme Court justices, nonetheless, obligated to interpret the Constitution in accordance with these evolving but deteriorating standards in order to be consistent with the philosophy underlying the living document method of interpretation?

The living document methodology gives judges the license to supplant and override the exact textual meaning of the Constitution—the original intent of the Framers as predicated upon God's moral law and to replace it with current popular values (or at least what the judges believe should be current social values). This seems to be in line with the observation of Chief Justice Charles Evans Hughes, "the Constitution is what the judges say it is."[4] In other words, this method converts jurists into super-legislators and self-proclaimed moral arbiters. At the same time, these jurists possess life tenure on the bench and salary guarantees.[5] In other words, they become unelected "legislators" who cannot be removed from office or have their salaries adjusted by the electorate—hardly a check and balance system consistent with the letter and spirit of the Constitution.

Robert Bork tells the story of "two of the greatest figures in our law, Justice Holmes and Judge Learned Hand, [who] had lunch together and afterward, as Holmes began to drive off in his carriage, Hand, in a sudden onset of enthusiasm, ran after him, crying, 'Do justice, sir, do justice.' Holmes stopped the carriage and reproved Hand: 'That is not my job. It is my job to apply the law.'"[6]

James Madison, known as the father of the Constitution, addressed this same concern: "I entirely concur in the propriety of resorting to the sense in which the Constitution was accepted and ratified by the nation. In that sense alone it is the legitimate Constitution. And if that be not the guide in expounding it, there can be no security for a consistent and stable...exercise of its powers. What a metamorphosis would be produced in the code of law if all its ancient phraseology were to be taken in its modern sense." He then observed, "*the language of our Constitution is already undergoing interpretations unknown to its founders*."[7] His warning was clear—don't tamper with the original meaning of the Constitution as understood by the Founding Fathers.

If a change to the original intent of the Constitution is desired, we have an amendment process provided by the Founding Fathers which defers to the will of the people. This is a key constitutional principle which seems to be overlooked or minimized by those of the living document mentality. We all acknowledge that the amendment process is, by design, not an easy one, but it is certainly better than the alternative: a few unelected judges imposing their will on the majority of society.

George Washington addressed this latter possible evil: "If, in the opinion of the people, the distribution or modification of the constitutional powers be in any particular wrong, let it be corrected by an amendment in the way which the Constitution designates. *But let there be no change by usurpation; for though this, in one instance, may be in the instrument of good, it is the customary weapon by which free governments are destroyed*."[8] What wise counsel! And what a usurpation of power we have when unelected judges, deliberately or innocently, circumvent the amendment process to impose their own will upon the people, however beneficial they feel it may be.[9]

Dangerously, we have generated a new mentality—that social issues should be tried and decided in the courts by unelected judges rather than at the ballot box by popular vote. No wonder that some speak of packing the Supreme Court or putting limits on terms of Supreme Court justices or allowing opposing parties to each pick ten judges and then they collectively pick five more. Such propositions are motivated and rooted in the assumption that political philosophies, not the original meaning of the text, should govern the interpretation of the Constitution.

Sadly, as Supreme Court nominees are interrogated by US senators, many of the questions asked have nothing to do with integrity or judicial competence but whether or not such nominee would decide a particular case in conformance with a senator's political bias. Such an approach is intended to make the judiciary nothing more than puppets of the majority party in power—in direct contravention of the separation of powers clause set forth in the Constitution. Justice Scalia noted, "Once the secret is out that the judges are evolving a new constitution rather than applying the old one, the people will see to it that judges are selected who will evolve it the way *they* want to evolve it."[10] Unfortunately, the genie is already out of the bottle.

Scalia further observed, "That, of course, is the very *appeal* of non-originalism for the judges: once they are liberated from the original meaning, they are liberated from any other governing principle as well. Nothing constrains their action except perhaps their estimation of how much judicial social engineering the society will tolerate."[11]

As Justice Thurgood Marshall once told a law clerk, "You do what you think is *right* and let the law catch up."[12] Commenting on this approach, Mark Levin, a nationally syndicated talk-radio host and author, wrote, "The judiciary today behaves in the manner of an ongoing constitutional convention, unilaterally amending the Constitution almost at will."[13] When this happens, interpreting is replaced by legislating. In essence, certain justices have substituted their will for the will of the public. Alexander Hamilton addressed this exact concern in *The Federalist Papers*, no. 78: "The courts must declare the sense of the law, and if they should be disposed to exercise WILL instead of JUDGMENT, the consequence would equally be the substitution of their pleasure to that of the legislative body."[14]

Hamilton further spoke of the danger of catering to the supposed evolving standards of decency and morality of the nation: "If... the Constitution is slighted, or explained away, upon every frivolous pretext, the future spirit of government will be feeble, distrusted and arbitrary. *The rights of the subjects will be the sport of every party vicissitude. There will be no settled rule of conduct, but everything will fluc-*

tuate with the alternate prevalence of contending factions."[15] And that is exactly what the living document method of interpretation does. It substitutes God's inspired principles with man's ever-changing rules of supposed decency.

Abraham Lincoln also understood the dangers of the living Constitution method of interpretation as a means to circumvent the will of the people: "The candid citizen must confess that if the policy of the Government upon vital questions affecting the whole people is to be irrevocably fixed by decision of the Supreme Court...the people will have ceased to be their own rulers, having to that extent practically resigned their Government into the hands of that eminent tribunal."[16]

The danger of the living document methodology is that it can replace public debate, political compromise, and voting by the people (essential elements of a democracy) with judicial fiat.

Flexibility or Rigidity?

Many proponents of the living document methodology claim such a philosophy is absolutely necessary to provide flexibility in changing times, but *Roe v. Wade* (legalizing abortion) and *Obergefell v. Hodges* (legalizing same-sex marriage) provide anything but flexibility. These are social policies that the living document advocates want fixed in stone. Does anyone honestly believe that if the vast majority of society in the next few years evolved and felt that abortion and same-sex marriage were moral wrongs, that these same advocates would voluntarily say, "In compliance with the living document methodology, these cases should be reversed to be consistent with the manner in which the vast majority of society is evolving." I doubt that the argument for flexibility or evolving standards could anywhere be found among these advocates. The living document argument is useful as long as it produces the desired moral outcome. In truth, it is less a method of interpretation and more a disguise for legislating one's moral values.

Justice Gorsuch addressed the immoral and unanticipated consequences which can occur when judges decide to deviate from the original meaning of the text:

> Look, for example, at [the cases of] *Dred Scott* and *Korematsu*. Neither can be defended as correct in light of the Constitution's original meaning; each depended on serious judicial invention by judges who misguidedly thought they were providing a "good" answer to a pressing social problem of the day. A majority in Korematsu, unmoored from originalist principles, upheld the executive internment without trial of American citizens of Japanese descent despite our Constitution's express guarantees of due process and equal protection of the laws. A majority in Dred Scott, also disregarding originalist principles, held that Congress had no power to outlaw slavery in the Territories, even though the Constitution clearly gave Congress the power to make laws governing the Territories. In both cases, judges sought to pursue policy ends they thought vital. Theirs was a living and evolving Constitution. *And often enough it may be tempting for a judge to do what he thinks best for society in the moment, to bend the law a little to an end he desires, to trade just a bit of judicial integrity for political expediency.* But as Korematsu and Dred Scott illustrate, the pursuit of political ends through judicial means will often and ironically bring about a far worse result than anticipated—a sort of constitutional karma.[17]

In order to limit the power of the federal judiciary and legislative branches, James Madison, in *The Federalist Papers* no. 45, addressed the desired balance of power between the federal government and the individual states: "The powers delegated by the proposed Constitution to the federal government, *are few and defined.* Those which are to remain in the State governments are numerous and indefinite." This being the case, one might ask, "Is the power to regulate abortion or same-sex marriage included in those few powers defined in the Constitution?" At best, only a strained and unwarranted interpretation can get one there.

Madison went on to say, "The powers reserved to the several States will extend to all the objects which, in the ordinary course of affairs, concern the lives, liberties, and properties of the people, and the internal order, improvement, and prosperity of the State."[18] Are not abortion and same-sex marriage issues that concern the life, liberties, and internal order of a state? Why then is the Supreme Court ruling on these matters? Because the living document methodology gives justices the license they desire to reach beyond the four corners of the Constitution and implement laws that should be reserved for the states.

Furthermore, Madison declared in *The Federalist Papers* no. 46 that the federal government should "be disinclined to invade the rights of the individual States, or the prerogatives of their governments."[19] In seeming disregard of this caution, the Supreme Court has more than once waged an unwarranted invasion into the rights of individual states, substituting its own policy views instead. In essence, certain justices have deemed themselves the moral authority of society, both as to state and federal law. They have torn down the walls of judicial confinement so prudently established by our Founding Fathers. The living document mentality may have been intended to open the door of flexibility just a crack so that judges felt they had some leeway in interpreting the Constitution, but unfortunately, the door has now swung so wide-open that even semitrucks are driving through, hence *Roe v. Wade* (legalizing abortion) and *Obergefell v. Hodges* (legalizing same-sex marriage).

The Needed Rationalization to Reach the Desired Result

How have the judges justified their decisions in these latter types of cases?

First of all, the due process and equal protection clauses have become catchalls for any progressive right they want to declare as a natural right or inherent right regardless of centuries of history to the contrary. As a consequence, those who believe in the living document method of interpretation see few limits on their ability to interpret the Constitution. Justice Clarence Thomas pretty well summarized the position of those judges who advocate the living document methodology: "You make it up, and then you rationalize it."[20]

Robert P. George, an American legal scholar and philosopher, addressed the problem with the living method of interpretation: "I would call the attention of every American…to the first word of the first sentence of the first paragraph of the first article of the Constitution: '*All* legislative powers herein granted shall be vested in the Congress.' The word 'all' means no legislative power—none—is vested in the president or in the courts. And yet, massive amounts of legislative power are today exercised not by the Congress, but by the executive and judicial branches. What is it about the word 'all' that is so hard for them to understand?"[21]

The case of *Griswold v. Connecticut* (1965) is a prime example of this expansion of legislative power beyond the halls of Congress. The appellants challenged an 1879 state law forbidding the use of contraceptives. One might legitimately argue whether or not this should be the law of the state as determined by the people, but the US Supreme Court took matters into its own hands to decide the issue. In order to find a legal basis for their decision, the majority determined that a right of privacy was in fact a constitutional right, while conceding that such right was not directly mentioned in the Constitution. Justice William Douglas, in writing the majority opinion, coined the following creative language to derive a right, where none could be found: "The foregoing cases [referring to cases decided under such Amendments as the First, Ninth, and Fourteenth] suggest that specific guarantees in the Bill of Rights *have penumbras, formed by the emanations from those guarantees that give them life and substance.*"[22] This was the key language for the newly determined Constitutional right of privacy. After brief deference to its poetic nature and grandiloquence, this language is exposed for what it really is—a lot of froth with little, if any, substance underneath. In essence, we end up with a decision based on creativity and eloquence rather than logic and historical precedent. As a consequence, the right of privacy argument and other expansive social rights deemed to exist under the Fourteenth Amendment became a cornerstone for the decisions in cases such as *Roe and Obergefell.* No wonder that Robert Bork observed "the 'right of privacy' has become a loose canon in the law."[23]

Numerous scholars, many of whom are pro-choice, such as respected Yale legal scholar John Hart Ely, recognized how far afield the court had gone in *Roe* based on the Griswold decision: "What is frightening about Roe is that this super-protected right [the right of privacy] is not inferable from the language of the Constitution. It [*Roe v. Wade*] is bad because it is bad constitutional law, or *rather because it is not constitutional law, and gives almost no sense of an obligation to try to be.*"[24] Laurence H. Tribe, noted Harvard law professor, agreed: "One of the most curious things about Roe is that, behind its own verbal smokescreen, the substantive judgment on which it rests is nowhere to be found."[25] These are impartial assessments from recognized brilliant legal scholars commenting about jurists who made a severe departure from the original intent of the Constitution, all under the supposed penumbra of rights emanating from the living document methodology.

Robert Bork summarized the attempts to justify *Roe* with the right of privacy and similar arguments as follows: "In the years since 1973, no one, however pro-abortion, has ever thought of an argument that even remotely begins to justify *Roe v. Wade* as a constitutional decision. There is no room for argument about the conclusion that the decision was the assumption of illegitimate judicial power and a usurpation of the democratic authority of the American people. *Roe*, as the greatest example and symbol of the judicial usurpation of democratic prerogatives in this entury, should be overturned."[26] What a sad commentary on judicial activism.

Conclusion

I greatly respect all our Supreme Court justices as brilliant men and women who desire to be patriotic, regardless of their method of judicial interpretation. I likewise believe that most, if not all, have a belief in a Supreme Being. Some, however, seem so driven by their moral value system that they are willing to sacrifice judicial restraint in favor of legislating their personal social agendas. But in doing so, they often trade a short-term benefit for a long-term tragedy. The cases of *Dred Scott*, *Korematsu*, *Roe*, and *Obergefell* are classic examples. It is not the motives of these judges that I question but rather their long-range vision and unrestrained exercise of judicial power, perhaps innocently, but nonetheless incorrectly justified by their reliance on the living document method of interpretation. Is there a better method of interpretation than the living document method, not fraught with its serious weaknesses disclosed above? There is. The next chapter discusses that method.

---

1 *Trop v. Dulles*, 365 US 86, 101 (1958).

2 In Faust, "Law in a Changing Society," stanfordpolitics.org.

3 In Magnet, *Clarence Thomas and the Lost Constitution*, 61.

4 Hughes, *Addresses and Papers of Charles Evans Hughes*, 139.

5 Pursuant to Article III, Section 1 of the Constitution, federal judges shall "receive for their Services, a Compensation, which shall not be diminished during their Continuance in Office."

6 Bork, *The Tempting of America*, 6.

7 Madison, "From James Madison to Henry Lee," founders.archives.gov; spelling modernized, emphasis added.

8 Washington, "Washington's Farewell Address 1796," avalon.law.yale.edu.

9 Kyle Peterson of the *Wall Street Journal* interviewed Justice Neil Gorsuch, who spoke of the shortfalls of the living document philosophy: "To treat the Constitution as a 'living document,' [Gorsuch] says, is to regard it 'more or less as a relic,' something kept 'in the back of the church behind a screen, and you look at it as you walk by, and you move on.' But that's 'not what we the people agreed to,' he adds. 'We didn't say five judges—or nine, or whatever—sitting in Washington get to govern 330 million people. That's not a republic. It's not a democracy.'"

10 *Scalia Speaks*, 200; emphasis in original.

11 *Scalia Speaks*, 197.

12 In Levin, *Liberty and Tyranny*, 53; emphasis in original.

13 Levin, *Liberty and Tyranny*, 61.

14 Hamilton, *The Federalist Papers*, no. 78, 258. At least one person has suggested that Hamilton's language here is not meant to promote judicial restraint (see Sandefur, "misquoting Federalist 78," pacificlegal.org), but I heartily disagree. Not only are Hamilton's words clear in their intent, but so is the surrounding context: that judges should "have neither FORCE nor WILL but merely judgment" (256). It's a phrase quoted by Chief Justice Roberts in the *Obergefell* case to justify judicial restraint. Furthermore, Hamilton said, "It can be of no weight to say that the courts, on the pretense of a repugnancy, may substitute their own pleasure [will] to the constitutional intentions of the legislature" (258). Hamilton also spoke of the "integrity and moderation of the judiciary," suggesting a restraint against judicial activism, and then further said, "To avoid an arbitrary discretion in the courts [exercise of one's will rather than judgment], it is indispensable that they should be bound down by strict rules and precedents, which serve to define and point out their duty in every particular case that comes before them" (259). Hamilton meant exactly what the plain meaning of his words convey.

15 In Cousins, *In God We Trust*, 338; emphasis added.

16 In Bork, *Slouching towards Gomorrah*, 318.

17 Gorsuch, *A Republic If You Can Keep It*, 115–16. Robert Bork came to a similar conclusion: "To give in to temptation [to yield to the living document mentality], this one time, solves an urgent human problem, and a faint crack appears in the American foundation. A judge has begun to rule where a legislator should" (*The Tempting of America*, 1).

18 Madison, *The Federalist Papers*, no. 45, 155; emphasis added.

19 Madison, *The Federalist Papers*, no. 46, 157.

20 Magnet, *Clarence Thomas and the Lost Constitution*, 61.

21 George, "Return All Legislative Power to Congress," politico.com.

22 *Griswold v. Connecticut*, 381 US 479, 485 (1965); emphasis added. Justice Black, in his dissent, wrote, "The Court talks about a constitutional 'right of privacy' as though there is some constitutional provision or provisions forbidding any law ever to be passed which might abridge the 'privacy' of individuals. But there is not" (381 US 510).

23 Bork, *The Tempting of America*, 97.

24 Ely, "*The Wages of Crying Wolf*," 935, 947; emphasis added.

25 Tribe, "The Supreme Court, 1972 Term," 7.

26 Bork, *The Tempting of America*, 115–16.

C H A P T E R 7

How Should We Interpret the Constitution—Originalism?

The Benefits of Originalism

The method of interpretation known as originalism counteracts the temptation to legislate from the bench—a fatal flaw with the living document method. In essence, originalism has two major benefits. One, because it acts as a restraint against judicial activism, it provides a fixed baseline for interpretation that fosters consistency. And second, it enshrines moral laws, not just any laws, but those envisioned by our inspired Founding Fathers. Justice Scalia addressed the first benefit: "Until about the 1960s, there was general agreement in the legal culture—and among the citizenry at large—that the Constitution had a fixed and permanent meaning. It was a rock of unchanging principles to which the society was safely moored. The guarantees that it contained were limited to those expressed in its text, and the meaning of that text (which did not vary over time) could be discerned by legally trained experts (judges) on the basis of the words used, manifestations of society's understanding of the text at the time it was adopted, and subsequent constitutional traditions bearing upon the text."[1] This was a reminder that words matter—not the strained meaning given to reach a precalculated decision but the original and actual meaning intended by the authors.

Alexander Hamilton was in accord with this thinking: "Whatever may have been the intention of the framers of a constitution, or of a law, that intention is to be sought for in the instrument itself, according to the usual and established rules of construction."[2] Thomas Jefferson felt similarly: "Instead of trying what meaning may be squeezed out of the text [of the Constitution], or invented against it, conform to the probable one in which it was passed."[3] And Justice James Wilson noted, "The first and governing maxim in the interpretation of a statute is to discover the meaning of those who made it."[4] Again and again it seems the Founding Fathers were advocates of originalism as the correct method to interpret the Constitution.

Justice Neil Gorsuch stated it so succinctly: "Originalism fits with the framers' design."[5]

One constitutional scholar addressed the second benefit of originalism, namely a continuation of moral law as adopted by the Founding Fathers: "Anyone who says the American Constitution is obsolete just because social and economic conditions have changed does not understand the real genius of the Constitution. It was designed to control something which has not changed and will not change—namely, human nature."[6] Robert Bork made a similar observation: "Those who made and endorsed our Constitution knew man's nature, and it is to their ideas, rather than to the temptations of utopia, that we must ask that our judges adhere."[7] For this reason, originalism is so critical because it helps perpetuate the correct moral laws that should govern human nature as originally understood and articulated by our inspired Founders.

Justice Scalia masterfully contrasted the consequences of originalism with the living Constitution philosophy:

> If original meaning is not the criterion, what other criterion can there be that prevents judges from imposing their ideological preferences on society? Think about it. There is none. The living constitutionalist is a happy fella, because it turns out that the Constitution always means precisely what he thinks it ought to mean. That

> is indeed much of the attraction of the living Constitution. And it is an attraction not just to judges, but to the people at large. How wonderful to think that whatever you care passionately about—from abortion to the death penalty—is resolved precisely the way you think it should be *by the Constitution*. Never mind whether the people ever voted to put that in the Constitution and thus to remove it from the realm of democratic choice—only originalists care about that. It is there if it ought to be there. I urge you not to yield to that seductive and extremely undemocratic falsehood. If you believe in democracy, you are an originalist.[8]

A prime example of how the democratic process is being undermined by judges was further exposed by Scalia:

> For the constitutional evolutionist…every question is an open question, and every day is a new day. Three of the justices with whom I have sat—Justice William Brennan, Justice Thurgood Marshall, and Justice Harry Blackmun—have held that the death penalty is unconstitutional, even though it is specifically acknowledged *twice* in the Constitution: in the provisions of the Fifth Amendment that prevent the deprivation of "*life*, liberty or property without due process of law," and that require grand jury indictment for prosecution of a "*capital*, or otherwise infamous crime." Notwithstanding the clarity of these provisions, the non-originalist must ask himself, decade after decade (or is it year after year?), "Is capital punishment constitutional?"[9]

What a tragic day when a judge elevates his own personal preferences above that clearly stated in the Constitution.

Some have argued, as Gorsuch noted, "that originalism leads to bad results because the results inevitably happen to be politically conservative results." His response: "Rubbish. Originalism is a theory focused on *process*, not on *substance*. It is not 'Conservative' with a big C focused on politics. It is conservative in the small c sense that it seeks to conserve the meaning of the Constitution as it was written."[10]

But what happens when a judge is confronted with a statute that is legitimately ambiguous, where original intent cannot be readily ascertained? Justice Gorsuch addressed that issue with this sage counsel:

> It is...the judge's job to employ not his own will but the traditional tools of legal analysis—the various canons of statutory construction, rules of grammar, analogies to precedent, and the like—in an effort to discern the meaning of Congress's commands. Of course, judges sometimes disagree about which tools of legal analysis are most helpful in the art of ascertaining Congress's meaning in hard cases. They also sometimes disagree over the order of priority we should assign to these competing tools. But debates like these reflect a genuine concern with how we can best reach or approximate Congress's will, not our own.[11]

Of course, there are difficult cases to decide, and on occasion justices who employ originalism as a method of interpretation will nonetheless reach different results or exercise some personal bias in the process. That is but a reflection of human nature. Originalism is not a cure-all that leads to perfectly consistent results, but such an approach has the distinct advantage of causing one to focus on the key issue at hand, namely, the original intent of the legislators, not a desired social outcome favored by an individual judge. And in the course of doing so, it leads to greater consistency of result, a minimum of legislating by judges, and a wholesome restraint on the exercise of judicial power. On the other hand, the living document method of interpretation leads to less consistent results, more legislating by judges, and less restraint on judicial power.

A Case in Point

Perhaps no case in point is more illustrative of this division in judicial interpretation than *Obergefell v. Hodges*, in which the US Supreme Court held that same-sex marriage was a fundamental legal right that must be allowed and recognized by all states in the Union. Five justices, using the living document method of interpretation, came to such a conclusion. Four justices, using the strict constructionist method of interpretation, filed fervent and passionate dissents.

Language used by the majority to support its position included the following reasoning:

- "Changed understandings of marriage are characteristic of a Nation where new dimensions of freedom become apparent to new generations, often through perspectives that begin in pleas or protests and then are considered in the political sphere and the judicial process."[12] But what about the majority of states that sanctioned only traditional marriage? Are their perspectives now worthless? And are five justices more enlightened on social matters than the collective wisdom of these states, particularly on a matter not addressed in the Constitution and therefore within the domain of states' rights?
- "The generations that wrote and ratified the Bill of Rights and the Fourteenth Amendment did not presume to know the extent of freedom in all of its dimensions, and so they entrusted to future generations a charter protecting the right of all persons to enjoy liberty as we learn its meaning."[13] But this is a disingenuous argument. The Founding Fathers provided a way to adopt to changing circumstances:

through legislation and the amendment process, not the personal opinions of unelected jurists.

- "It is appropriate to observe these cases [of same-sex marriage] involve only the rights of two consenting adults whose marriages would pose no risk of harm to themselves or third parties."[14] Such a statement, however, seems contrary to the realities of life. Are there not many, particularly those who are subscribers of the Judeo-Christian philosophy, who believe that legal endorsement of same-sex marriage denigrates the sanctity of traditional marriage, undermines the command to multiply and replenish the earth, circumvents the divinely given endowments of a father and mother to best raise a child, promotes the name-calling of homophobe or bigot by those with differing views, and promotes same-sex relations that are prohibited by God? One does not need a vivid imagination to guess what lawsuits have been or will be filed because a religious person or group fails to cater for or perform a same-sex marriage, or doesn't allow such a marriage in their church building, or fails to allow a child to be adopted by a same-sex couple. For example, Luke Goodrich, deputy general counsel at the Becket Fund for Religious Liberty, who has tried multiple religious cases before the Supreme Court and lower courts, noted, "In Boston, Illinois, and the District of Columbia, the government decided that all adoption agencies must be willing to place children with same-sex couples. This meant that local branches of Catholic Charities, which had been placing children in adoptions for over one hundred years, would have to either violate Catholic teaching or lose their licenses. So these Catholic Charities offices were forced to end their ministries."[15] Goodrich went on to observe:

> The conflict between gay rights and religious freedom is the most significant threat to religious freedom in the United States today. If handled poorly, we can expect a variety of painful con-

> sequences. Religious business owners will suffer crippling fines. Religious counselors will lose their licenses. Religious universities will lose their accreditation. Religious hospitals, homeless shelters, adoption agencies, schools and other ministries will be attacked by lawsuits and lose millions in funding and tax exemptions. Religious individuals will lose their jobs as judges, clerks, social workers, and military chaplains. This is to say nothing of purely private forms of social ostracism.[16]

Given these possible dire consequences, both legal and social, one wonders how the court can possibly say that legalized same-sex marriage poses no risk or harm to the participants or others? It will cause monumental harm and problems to many. That is why these drastic societal changes are left best to the democratic process.

In contrast, those justices who believe in the strict constructionist method of interpretation (originalism) reached the conclusion that the Constitution does not provide a right protecting same-sex marriage, but rather that it is a decision to be made by the electorate pursuant to the democratic process of voting. Following are some of the dissenters' comments:

- Chief Justice John Roberts wrote, "Whether same-sex marriage is a good idea should be of no concern to us. *Under the Constitution, judges have power to say what the law is, not what it should be. The people who ratified the Constitution authorized courts to exercise 'neither force nor will' but merely judgment. The majority's decision is an act of will, not legal judgment...* As a result, the Court invalidated the marriage laws of more than half the States and orders the transformation of a social institution that has formed the basis of human society for millennia. It is not about whether, in my judgment, the institution of marriage should be changed to include same-sex couples. It is instead whether, in our democratic republic, that decision should rest with the people acting through their elected representatives, or with five lawyers. The Constitution leaves no doubt about the answer."[17]

- Justice Roberts continued, "The purpose of insisting that implied fundamental rights have roots in the history and tradition of our people is to ensure that when unelected judges strike down democratically enacted laws, they do so based on something more than their own beliefs. *The Court today not only overlooks our country's entire history and tradition but actively repudiates it. Those who founded our country would not recognize the majority's conception of the judicial vote. They would never have imagined yielding that right [the right to govern themselves] on a question of social policy to unaccountable and unelected judges.*"[18]
- Judge Roberts then concluded with these sobering thoughts: "By the majority's account, Americans who did nothing more than follow the understanding of marriage that has existed for our entire history—in particular, the tens of millions of people who voted to reaffirm their States' enduring definition of marriage—have acted to…'disparage,' 'disrespect and subordinate,' and inflict 'dignitary wounds' upon their gay and lesbian neighbors. It is one thing for the majority to conclude that the Constitution protects a right to same-sex marriage; it is something else to portray everyone that does not share the majority's 'better informed understanding' as bigoted. If you are among the many Americans—of whatever sexual orientation—who favor expanding same-sex marriage, by all means celebrate today's decision. Celebrate the achievement of a desired goal. Celebrate the opportunity for a new expression of commitment to a partner. Celebrate the availability of new benefits. *But do not celebrate the Constitution. It had nothing to do with it.*"[19]
- Justice Antonin Scalia noted, "It is not of special importance to me what the law says about marriage. It is of over-

whelming importance, however, who it is that rules me. *Today's decree says that my Ruler, and the Ruler of 320 million Americans, coast-to-coast, is a majority of the nine lawyers on the Supreme Court.*"[20]

- Justice Clarence Thomas commented, "The majority goes to great lengths to assert that its decision will advance the 'dignity' of same-sex couples. The flaw in that reasoning, of course, is that the Constitution contains no 'dignity' clause, and even if it did, the government would be incapable of bestowing dignity."[21] How right he is. How does a man-made court bestow dignity on an action condemned by God? Would the legalization of fornication and adultery bestow dignity upon these acts that are nonetheless immoral? Can an external decree bestow character or integrity on an individual? The court's gratuitous bestowal of dignity is but one evidence of how far these judges have strayed from judicial constraints and their duty to be interpreters of the law, not social legislators.
- Justice Samuel Alito expressed these sentiments: "I assume that those that cling to old beliefs will be able to whisper their thoughts in the recesses of their homes, but if they repeat those views in public, they will risk being labeled as bigots and treated as such by governments, employers, and schools."[22] Unfortunately, history is already confirming these dire predictions. Justice Alito gave this additional insight: "To prevent five unelected Justices from imposing their personal vision of liberty upon the American people, the Court has held that 'liberty' under the Due Process Clause should be understood to protect only those rights that are 'deeply rooted in the nation's history and tradition.' And it is beyond dispute that the right of same-sex marriage is not among those rights." And finally, Alito summed up his argument with this tragic commentary and prediction: "Today's decision shows that decades of attempts to restrain this court's abuse of its authority have failed. *A lesson that some will take from today's decision is that preaching about the proper method of interpret-*

> *ing the Constitution or the virtues of judicial self-restraint and humility cannot compete with the temptation to achieve what is viewed as a noble end by any practicable means*. All Americans, whatever their thinking on that issue [of same-sex marriage], should worry about what the majority's claim of power portends."[23] And so we should.

Five unelected judges have just taught us, in fact dictated to us, that their perspective of what the end should be justifies the means to get there, whatever the means might be. I do not believe that the justices in the majority had malevolent intent. To the contrary, I believe they decided the case the way they believed was best for society, but even well-intentioned decisions can constitute poor judgment and an abuse of power, and such I believe was the case in *Obergefell v. Hodges*. They didn't just bend the rules of judicial interpretation; they broke them. And the living document method of interpretation gave them the license to do so.

What Should Govern—Integrity or Political Agenda?

Justice Scalia went to the core of the issue when he said, "The reality is that originalism is the only game in town—the only real, verifiable criterion that can prevent judges from making the Constitution say whatever they think it should say." Then he said with tongue in cheek, "Show Scalia the original meaning, and he is prevented from imposing his nasty conservative views upon the people. He is handcuffed."[24]

And so, he was "handcuffed" when the issue of whether or not burning the American flag was protected under the First Amendment. He wrote, "The Court held...that it was unconstitutional to ban the burning of a flag. It was a 5–4 decision, and I made the fifth note." He then explained why: "You should be in no doubt that, patriotic conservative that I am, I detest the burning of the nation's flag—and if I were king, I would make it a crime. But as I understand the First Amendment, it guarantees the right to express contempt for the government, the Congress, the Supreme Court, even the nation and the nation's flag… Far from facilitating conservative opinions, originalism prevents judges, conservatives and liberals alike, from judging according to their desires."[25]

That is part of the genius of originalism. It does not lend itself to political or religious bias. It does not allow for a Republican, Democrat, Catholic, Evangelical, Muslim, or agnostic interpretation of the law. It only allows for interpretation of the law as the Founders meant it to be. If the Founding Fathers were inspired, as history confirms, then who would want to interpret the Constitution in any other way than in accordance with their inspired understanding of its meaning?

How fortunate we are to have many judges who are driven by integrity of interpretation rather than personal political philosophies and prejudices. The doctrine of originalism caters to the former; the doctrine of a living Constitution caters to the latter. Perhaps the distinction between the originalist and one who subscribes to the living document methodology is best exemplified by the conversation between William Roper and Sir Thomas More:

> *Roper*: So, now you give the Devil the benefit of law!
>
> *More*: Yes! What would you do? Cut a great road through the law to get after the Devil?
>
> *Roper*: Yes, I'd cut down every law in England to do that!
>
> *More*: Oh? And when the last law was down, and the Devil turned round on you, where would you hide, Roper, the laws all being flat? This country's planted thick with laws, from coast to coast… if you cut them down—and you're just the man to do it—d'you really think you could stand upright in the winds that would blow then? Yes, I'd give the Devil benefit of law, for my own safety's sake![26]

No matter the eloquence of speech or benevolence of goal, the underlying argument of those who subscribe to the living document method of interpretation always comes back to the same rationale—the desired social ends always justify the means, whatever those means may be.

Slouching towards Gomorrah

Suffice it to say, the living document methodology tends to endorse radical individualism, which is the supposed right to do anything that pleases you or makes you feel good, unless it physically harms or libels another person (abortion notwithstanding). As a result, the moral safeguards of society built upon Judeo-Christian laws that require some form of discipline are being compromised, eroded, and extinguished one by one. In many ways, as Robert Bork observed, "analysis demonstrates that we continue slouching towards Gomorrah."[27] And unfortunately, the living document mentality is a vehicle taking us in that direction.

Perhaps Justice Scalia summed up the issue best when he said, "A freedom-loving people respectful of the rule of law may be expected to let lawyers decide what a constitutional text means; but they cannot be expected to let lawyers decide what a constitution *ought* to say. That is not a job for lawyers, but for the people."[28] In other words, judges should interpret the law, not make the law!

Tragically, some want to change the underlying, overarching principle that forms the basis of our government from "We the People" to "We the Judges." Hopefully, we can elect and appoint judges who, regardless of political affiliation, will show the restraint and integrity to interpret the law, not make the law—who will be strict constructionists (originalists) and thus seek to preserve and foster God's moral law as understood by our Founding Fathers and as incorporated in the Constitution.

---

[1] *Scalia Speaks*, 227. Judge Gorsuch taught the same truth: "Originalism reinforces…rule-of-law values of notice and equality. Most obviously, by interpreting the text according to its ordinary public meaning and accepting that it cannot be changed outside the amendment process, originalism ensures that citizens know with some predictability the content of their constitutional rights" (Gorsuch, *A Republic, If You Can Keep It*, 125).

[2] Hamilton, "Final Version of an Opinion on the Constitutionality of an Act to Establish a Bank," founders.archives.gov.

[3] Jefferson, "From Thomas Jefferson to William Johnson," founders.archives.gov.

[4] In Barton, *Original Intent*, 28.

[5] Gorsuch, *A Republic, If You Can Keep It*, 123.

[6] Skousen, *The 5000 Year Leap*, 166; emphasis in original.

[7] Bork, *The Tempting of America*, 355.

[8] Scalia, *Scalia Speaks*, 212.

[9] Scalia, *Scalia Speaks*, 196; emphasis in original.

[10] Gorsuch, *A Republic, If You Can Keep It*, 114–15; emphasis in original.

[11] Gorsuch, *A Republic, If You Can Keep It*, 195.

[12] Anthony Kennedy, majority opinion in *Obergefell v. Hodges*, 576 US (2015).

[13] Anthony Kennedy, majority opinion in *Obergefell v. Hodges*, 576 US (2015).

[14] Anthony Kennedy, majority opinion in *Obergefell v. Hodges*, 576 US (2015).

[15] Goodrich, *Free to Believe*, 113.

[16] Goodrich, *Free to Believe*, 117.

[17] John Roberts, dissenting opinion in *Obergefell v. Hodges*, 576 US (2015); emphasis added.

[18] John Roberts, dissenting opinion in *Obergefell v. Hodges*, 576 US (2015); emphasis added.

[19] John Roberts, dissenting opinion in *Obergefell v. Hodges*, 576 US (2015); emphasis added.

[20] Antonin Scalia, dissenting opinion in *Obergefell v. Hodges*, 576 US (2015); emphasis added.

[21] Clarence Thomas, dissenting opinion in *Obergefell v. Hodges*, 576 US (2015); emphasis added.

[22] Samuel Alito, dissenting opinion in *Obergefell v. Hodges*, 576 US (2015).

[23] Samuel Alito, dissenting opinion in *Obergefell v. Hodges*, 576 US (2015); emphasis added.

[24] Scalia, *Scalia Speaks*, 211.

[25] Scalia, *Scalia Speaks*, 207.

[26] Bolt, *A Man for All Seasons*, 41–42.

[27] Bork, *Slouching towards Gomorrah*, 331.

[28] Scalia, *Scalia Speaks*, 155; emphasis added.

C H A P T E R 8

Should Free Exercise of Religion Be Encouraged in the Public Sector?

How Does the Supreme Court Interpret the First Amendment?

The First Amendment to the Constitution reads, "Congress shall make no law respecting an establishment of religion, nor prohibiting the free exercise thereof." This raises a key question: how was freedom of religion originally understood by the Founding Fathers, and how broad or restrictive should this freedom be when applied to the public sector?

For a time, the First Amendment was interpreted to encourage religion—not a specific religion but religion in general. Such an approach had a healthy effect on establishing and reinforcing moral principles. As Justice Scalia noted, "This long American tradition of official encouragement of religion, but strict neutrality among religious sects, was acknowledged by my court as recently as 1952."[1] Scalia was referring to *Zorach v. Clauson*, a case where a public school provided an early release option from its schedule so students might attend religious instruction programs. Justice William O. Douglas wrote the opinion for the court: "*We are a religious people whose institutions presuppose a Supreme Being*. When the state *encourages* religious instruction or cooperates with religious authorities by adjusting the schedule of public events to sectarian needs, it follows the best of our traditions. *For it then respects the religious nature of our people and accommodates the public service to their spiritual needs.*" He then concluded, "We find no constitutional requirement which makes it necessary for government to be hostile to religion and to throw its weight against efforts to widen the effective scope of religious influence."[2] The message of this case was clear—the Constitution encourages religion in general in order to respect the religious nature of the American people, but it does not promote one religion over another.

In 1968, however, the Court modified its position, as reflected in the case of *Epperson v. Arkansas*: "Government in our democracy, state and national, must be neutral in matters of religious theory, doctrine, and practice. The First Amendment mandates governmental neutrality between religion and religion, and between religion and nonreligion."[3] This was a significant turning point—a stunning blow to religious freedom. The Court announced that the Constitution was not designed to encourage religion in general as Justice Douglas had previously espoused. Rather, it was to remain neutral.[4]

Commenting on the precedent set by *Epperson v. Arkansas*, Justice Scalia wrote, "I do not believe in the principle of neutrality between religion and nonreligion on which it is based. Indeed, it seems to me that the First Amendment itself is a repudiation of that principle, since the Free Exercise Clause gives special favor to the free exercise of religion. The neutrality principle is also contradicted by the many national practices, dating back to the earliest times [such as military chaplains, prayers in Congress, and the motto 'In God We Trust']. The Court has changed its position on this matter once—and hopefully will change it back once again."[5]

Noticing the definite trend toward religious neutrality—or even worse, religious hostility—Charles Krauthammer wrote, "For a generation, the Supreme Court has taken the view that our public life should be not so much religion-neutral as religion-free. The result, while not exactly Jacobinic, has been impressive: a general canvassing about for religious symbols in public life and a somewhat haphazard, but effective, campaign to erase them."[6]

Unfortunately, that is the tragic goal of some—to erase from our history the influence of God in our nation and every remnant of religion from our public life.

The Reverend Paul D. Scalia concurred in this assessment: "Over the past fifty years our culture has privatized religion, sidelined it from public life."[7] Sad to say, some jurists have fallen victim to this mentality. We seem to have headed down a judicial road that for some time embraced and encouraged religion, then neutralized it, and on some occasions even sought to discourage it. Fortunately, there are some encouraging signs that the latter trend is being reversed.

Despite the clarity with which the First Amendment protects the free exercise of religion, the US Supreme Court has struggled in recent years to define a workable principle that governs freedom of religion. Should the Court encourage religion, be neutral, discourage it in the public sector, or some combination of these factors? And what tests should be applied to determine the many complex issues surrounding freedom of religion?

Since 1971 the Supreme Court has determined many cases involving freedom of religion issues under what is known as the Lemon test. It is derived from a case called *Lemon v. Kurtzman*, in which some state funds provided to church-related educational institutions were deemed unconstitutional. The Court stated, "The Constitution decrees that *religion must be a private matter* for the individual, the family, and the institutions of private choice."[8] In other words, contrary to decades of religious expression in the public sector, it was now, all of a sudden, unconstitutional as declared by judicial fiat. It doesn't take much of an imagination to realize that prayers in Congress, the financing of Congressional and military chaplains, the maintenance of a chapel in the Capitol, and property tax exemptions for religious institutions could be declared unconstitutional under such a test.

In the 1990 case of *Employment Division v. Smith*,[9] Luke Goodrich noted another test adopted by the Court: "The court said it would no longer apply the substantial-burden test [yet another test previously employed by the Court] which required the government to prove that each law burdening a religious practice was truly necessary." Instead, the court adopted a new test. It "would ask whether a law *specifically targeted* a religious practice *because* it was religious."[10] In other words, a law could limit free exercise of religion, regardless of how onerous it might be to religion, provided it was not exclusively directed at religion.

The Court has also decided other cases unfavorable to religious freedom, ruling against prayer in public forums (*Wallace v. Jaffree* and *Santa Fe Independent School District v. Doe*) and restricting government-sponsored financial support of religious schools (*Committee for Public Education v. Nyquist*).

On the other hand, in 2012, the Court made a major decision in favor of religious freedom. *Hosanna-Tabor* was a case involving a small school operated by the Lutheran church. In this case, the Supreme Court endorsed what is known as the ministerial exception test and declared, "When a minister who has been fired sues her church alleging that her termination was discriminatory, the First Amendment has struck the balance for us. The church must be free to choose those who will guide it on its way."[11] In this case, the balance weighed in favor of religious freedom. The Court also ruled in favor of religious freedom in *Hobby Lobby* and *Little Sisters*, cases discussed in a subsequent chapter having to do with abortion.

As one might imagine, cases such as the above left an uncertainty as to the Court's methodology of interpreting freedom of religion issues. The Court added further confusion when it declared a nativity scene sponsored by the government to be unconstitutional, but the public display of a Jewish menorah and Islamic star and crescent to be constitutional.[12] Robert Bork noted, "The framers and ratifiers could not conceivably have anticipated that the Supreme Court, sitting in a courtroom with a painting of Moses and the Ten Commandments [on an upper wall], would hold it an unconstitutional establishment of religion for a high school to have a copy of the Ten Commandments on a wall."[13] Such inconsistencies in decisions were a manifestation of the Court's difficulty in coming to rest with a test or tests that would provide consistency in determining religious freedom cases and be in harmony with the intent of the Founding Fathers.

Fortunately, in 2014, the Court put the prior tests aside in the case of *Town of Greece v. Galloway*. The issue was whether or not the town council could open its meetings with local clergy offering prayers that were primarily Christian in nature. The Court concluded that the test to be employed was a principle laid out in *Marsh v. Chamber* (1983), a case that decided whether or not the use of state funds by the Nebraska Legislature to hire a chaplain violated the Establishment Clause. The Supreme Court in *Marsh* decided it was not a violation. It gave this incontrovertible reasoning for its decision: "It can hardly be thought that, in the same week Members of the First Congress voted to appoint and to pay a chaplain for each House and also voted to approve the draft of the First Amendment for submission to the states, they intended the Establishment Clause of the Amendment to forbid what they had just declared acceptable."[14] In other words, the Founders' actions should be powerful evidence of how they thought the First Amendment should be interpreted.

Referring to *Marsh*, the Court in *Town of Greece* stated, "The case teaches that the Establishment Clause must be interpreted 'by reference to historical practices and understandings.' The prayer opportunity in this case must be evaluated against the backdrop of historical practice. As a practice that has long endured, legislative prayer has become part of our heritage and tradition." The Court went on to say, "Any test the Court adopts must acknowledge a practice that was accepted by the Framers and has withstood the critical scrutiny of time and political change."[15] In other words, the Court might have multiple tests for varying circumstances to determine freedom of religion issues, but if the Founding Fathers sanctioned a specific action and it has withstood the test of time, then historical reality trumps all other tests. As a consequence, the Court, referring to the *Marsh* decision, noted that previously adopted tests to determine religious freedom were "unnecessary because *history supported* the conclusion that legislative invocations are compatible with the Establishment Clause."[16]

Commenting on this case, Goodrich observed, "After many years of misguided jurisprudence, the Supreme Court appears poised to…[interpret] the Establishment Clause according to its historical meaning."[17]

What Was the Original Intent of the Founding Fathers?

Based on the rationale in *Town of Greece*, freedom of religion can best be determined under the Constitution if we can discover the original intent of the Founding Fathers on the subject, as evidenced by their "historical practices and understandings." This seems reasonable, as who would know better the intent of the First Amendment than the very men who debated and drafted its language?

Assuming this is true, did the Founding Fathers intend to support and encourage religion without fostering a given religion as Justice Douglas stated? Or were they hostile to the expression of religion in the public sector? Or as decided by the Supreme Court in 1968, did the Founding Fathers intend to be neutral, not only as to a specific sect, but as to religion in general?

As evidenced again and again, the Founding Fathers believed that Judeo-Christian morals were the basis for the Declaration of Independence and the Constitution, and furthermore, that morals are dependent upon religion. Once someone recognizes this fact, then the compelling question becomes "Why would our nation that was founded on Judeo-Christian morals, not want to nurture, foster, and encourage religion in general, particularly since religion is the prime advocate of those very foundational morals?" For this reason, the Founding Fathers and national heroes of this country not only approved of religion but even encouraged it, both in the public as well as private sector, as set forth in the following examples:

First, religion was encouraged in public education.

The Northwest Ordinance, which regulated the western expansion of the United States, was adopted by the Confederation Congress in 1787 and two years later adopted by the first United States Congress. It stated, "*Religion*, morality, and knowledge being necessary to good government and the happiness of mankind, schools and the means of education shall *forever be encouraged*."[18] Note that the government was not to discourage religion or even be neutral in this regard. Rather, it was a powerful endorsement for religion to be *forever encouraged* by government in public education! One should keep in mind that this endorsement was given by the same Congress that adopted the Constitution; hence it clearly understood the desired role of religion in the public sector.[19]

This sentiment toward encouragement of religion in education was expressed by a number of the Founding Fathers. Benjamin Rush wrote, "The only foundation for a useful education in a republic is to be laid in Religion."[20] He also understood the consequences of removing the Bible and religion from schools: "The great enemy of the salvation of man, in my opinion, never invented a more effectual means of extirpating Christianity from the world than by persuading mankind that it was improper to read the Bible at schools."[21] And Gouverneur Morris, one of the signers of the Constitution, added, "Religion is the only solid basis of good morals; therefore education should teach the precepts of religion and the duties of man towards God."[22]

It is of some interest to note that in 1787, the same year the Constitution was written, Yale University gave these instructions to its students: "All the scholars are required to live a religious and blameless life according to the rules of God's Word, diligently reading the holy Scriptures, that fountain of Divine light and truth, and constantly attending all the duties of religion."[23] No doubt the administrators of Yale University were merely echoing the sentiment of the Founding Fathers on this subject. One might ask, "Is this sentiment of the Founding Fathers found and manifested in our public schools today, and if not, why not?"

Second, religion was encouraged in all the public sector.

Many of the Founding Fathers expressed their feelings again and again that religion should be encouraged or promoted, not just in education but in all aspects of the public sector. John Witherspoon, a signer of the Declaration of Independence, stated, "To promote true religion is the best and most effectual way of making a virtuous and regular people."[24] He also said, "Those who are vested with civil authority ought…to promote religion and good morals among all under their government."[25] John Jay added, "[It is] the duty of all wise, free, and virtuous governments to countenance and encourage virtue and religion."[26]

The Continental Congress of 1778 stated, "Whereas true religion and good morals are the only solid foundations of public liberty and happiness…it is hereby earnestly recommended to the several States to take the most effectual measures for the *encouragement* thereof."[27] It would be difficult, if not impossible, to find a Founding Father or state legislature that expressed a contrary sentiment.

Jon Meacham summarized Benjamin Franklin's views on public religion as follows: "To Benjamin Franklin, history taught that 'public religion' was ultimately good for society. The concept of public religion includes a spirit of charity to others, a generous moral disposition, and rituals acknowledging a dependence on divine providence."[28] Meacham later added, "History shows that leaders in even the most difficult of crises have managed to practice public religion and preserve freedom of religion at the same time. To hope, as some secularists do, that faith will one day withdraw from the public square, if only this presidential candidate or that Supreme Court nominee comes to power, is futile. Humankind could not leave off being religious even if it tried. The impulse is intrinsic."[29]

Joseph Story, a Harvard law professor and member of the US Supreme Court from 1812 to 1845, wrote the famous *Commentaries on the Constitution of the United States*. Understanding the sentiment of the Founding Fathers and those who lived at the time the Constitution was written, he observed, "Probably at the time of the adoption of the constitution…the general, if not the universal, sentiment in America was, that Christianity ought to receive *encouragement from the state*, so far as is not incompatible with the private rights of conscience, and the freedom of religious worship. It yet remains a problem to be solved in human affairs, whether any free government can be permanent, where the public worship of God, and the support of religion, constitute no part of the policy or duty of the state in any assignable shape."[30] This was nothing less than a definitive acknowledgment of the Founding Father's desire for encouragement of religion in the public sector.

Third, our public monuments support religious expression in public.

Our public monuments honoring our Founding Fathers and other national heroes, paid for and promoted by our government, are emblazoned with statements referencing God. Among others, we read on the Washington Monument, "Laus Deo," which means "Praise God." Why would we have a permanent public pronouncement to praise God if we are only to do so in private?

On the Jefferson Memorial, we read, "God who gave us life gave us liberty. Can the liberties of a nation be secure when we have removed a conviction that these liberties are the gift of God?" How can a conviction of God's gift of liberty be maintained by our government if the Supreme Court strikes down references to God in public places?

Lincoln's Second Inaugural Address, engraved on the wall of the Lincoln Memorial, mentions God fourteen times and references the Bible four times. Does that sound like the government wanted to remove references to God and the Bible from the public domain, or rather to acknowledge Him and thank Him who was present at every significant step of our nation's founding?

One might well ask: "Why the governmental establishment, maintenance, and publicity of these monuments which support religious principles if government is not in the business of endorsing and encouraging religion in general in the public sector?"

Fourth, public prayers were offered to support religious expression in public.

Prayer has been a critical part of our nation's history. It has been the focus of presidential prayer breakfasts and the traditional beginning of each Congressional session by a clergyman hired and paid for by the government. Consequently, one must ask, did Washington, Adams, and Madison, each of whom were Founding Fathers, violate the intent of the Constitution when they sponsored national days of prayer and fasting during their service as president? Many other presidents, including Theodore Roosevelt, Woodrow Wilson, Calvin Coolidge, Franklin D. Roosevelt, Harry Truman, John F. Kennedy,

Ronald Reagan, Barack Obama, and Donald Trump, to name a few, also sponsored national days of prayer.[31]

President Truman made the National Day of Prayer an annual event and, in connection with this decision, stated, "In times of national crisis when we are striving to strengthen the foundations of peace…we stand in special need of divine support."[32] Was this not encouragement of a basic religious practice—prayer—at the highest levels of government?

Following our successful landing at Normandy, Franklin D. Roosevelt, in a nationwide radio address, led the American people in prayer: "Almighty God: Our sons, pride of our Nation, this day have set upon a mighty endeavor, a struggle to preserve our Republic, our religion, and our civilization, and to set free a suffering humanity."[33] Jon Meacham noted, "The White House released the text to the afternoon newspapers with the request that the audience—estimated at one hundred million Americans—read it along with the president. Like Lincoln before him in the fading weeks of the Civil War, *Roosevelt thought it wise to draw on the language and ritual of public religion* to do the best one could at an hour when events were beyond the control of any president."[34]

It would be hard to imagine greater endorsements of national prayer in the public settings than these. Certainly, exclusion of prayer from public places was not the intent of our Founding Fathers and other national leaders who advocated the necessity of prayer on a national and public basis in order to establish and preserve our nation.

Fifth, scripture reading was encouraged to support religious expression in public.

Franklin D. Roosevelt not only led the nation in prayer but also invited the nation to read the Bible: "I suggest a nationwide reading of the Holy Scriptures during the period from Thanksgiving Day to Christmas. Go to…the Scriptures for a renewed and strengthening contact with those eternal truths and majestic principles which have inspired such measure of greatness as this nation has achieved."[35]

Sixth, the government sponsored programs to increase our awareness of God.

Government support of religion in the public sector was not only evidenced by the Founding Fathers but by many national leaders. President Eisenhower supported the American Legion's "Back to God" Program, which was broadcast from the White House. In connection with that broadcast, he said, "As a former soldier, I am delighted that our veterans are sponsoring a movement to increase our awareness of God in our daily lives. In battle, they learned a great truth—that there are no atheists in the foxholes. They know that in time of test and trial, we instinctively turn to God for new courage. Whatever our individual church, whatever our personal creed, our common faith in God is a common bond among us."[36] Was this not encouragement of religion from the most revered and public of all government buildings?

The following year at a similar broadcast, Eisenhower stated, "Without God, there could be no American form of Government, nor an American way of life. *Recognition of the Supreme Being is the first—the most basic—expression of Americanism.*"[37] If recognition of God is the most basic expression of Americanism, why would we ever consider omitting it from the public sector? To the contrary, it should be the focus of our daily activities, both public and private, because in truth, it constitutes the heart and soul of this nation. It follows that belief in a supreme being should not only be protected but encouraged at every reasonable opportunity.

Seventh, the government sponsors many pronouncements and activities encouraging a national belief in God.

Our currency contains the words "In God We Trust." Our national anthem makes reference to God. Our pledge of allegiance—a pledge which has been made by members of the House and Senate at their daily sessions—acknowledges that we are "one nation under God." Our religious institutions are given favored income tax treatment by the government and property tax-exemptions for houses of worship.

Many of the oaths sworn in courts contain the words "so help me God." Most presidents of the nation have repeated those words when taking the oath of office with their hand on the Bible. Our Capital building has a chapel for members of Congress to worship God, and our government pays for military as well as congressional chaplains. Does this sound like a neutral position taken by the Founding Fathers and other national leaders on religion, or is it not instead a conscious and unabashed encouragement of religion in the public sector?

Eighth, the Supreme Court publicly petitions for God's help.

The Supreme Court begins each session with the words "God save the United States and this Honorable Court." How sadly ironic if this same court that regularly pleads for God's help (a form of prayer) in a governmental building should mandate governmental and public neutrality, or worse yet, even hostility against the very God from whom it seeks regular guidance.

Ninth, what the "wall of separation between Church and State" really means.

Thomas Jefferson is often quoted by the secularists and courts for his statement about a "wall of separation between Church and State."[38] This is used as evidence by them that there is no place for religion in the public sector. But did Jefferson believe that government should not encourage or even approve of religion in public life? Unfortunately, Jefferson's reference to a "wall of separation between Church and State" has been taken completely out of context by many. Jefferson was responding to a letter from the Danbury Baptists, who were concerned that the "free exercise of religion" clause might be interpreted as a government-granted right (and thus subject to change or compromise) rather than an unalienable right from God that could not be changed or compromised under any circumstances.

Based on this concern, Jefferson replied that the free exercise of religion clause was a restoration of man's "natural rights"—meaning, a right that preexisted and was independent of government, namely, a God-given right. Accordingly, Jefferson assured the concerned Baptists that there was a wall preventing government from intruding into the free expression of religion—an unalienable right, but likewise a wall that should prevent the establishment of a national religion. In other words, government was not to prohibit the free exercise of religion in the public sector (except for the establishment of a national religion)—the exact opposite of how many courts have interpreted the phrase.

Consistent with this interpretation, Jefferson gave us this clarifying statement about the federal government's ability to prohibit any religious activities: "*Certainly no power to prescribe any religious exercise*, or to assume authority in religious discipline, has been delegated to the general [federal] government. It must then rest with the States."[39] What a difference from how Jefferson is often quoted!

Furthermore, if actions speak louder than words, then Jefferson's actions should evidence his true opinion on the role of religion in the public sector. What were those actions? In his second inaugural address he invited the audience to "join with [him] in supplications [to God]" for the nation's well-being.[40] Was this not encouragement of prayer—a practice at the heart of religion, made from the nation's preeminent public pulpit? And why did he, along with Franklin, propose a national seal with these words: "God, or Providence, has favored our undertakings," knowing that such seal would become a public symbol, if they were opposed to the expression of religion in public? In addition, Jefferson, as well as James Madison, attended church services in the Capitol building—one of the most visible of government buildings. By doing so, they clearly endorsed, not condemned, the free exercise of religion in public. Jefferson, as president, also allowed church services to be held in other government buildings, such as the Treasury building and the Supreme Court,"[41] and, in addition, "authorized federal funds to pay for Christian missionaries to the Indians."[42] We might note that this was all done after the Constitution was adopted.

These actions clearly condoned religious worship in public buildings and the use of government money for religious purposes. If we are honestly looking for original intent, what better endorsement of government advocating religion in the public sector than as evidenced by these key Founding Fathers?

Nonetheless, the courts have quoted Jefferson's one-off phrase out of context in order to prohibit religious instruction, prayers, and reading of the Bible in schools, to remove displays of the Ten Commandments from public buildings and to outlaw public displays of a Christmas crèche.

No wonder Supreme Court Justice William Rehnquist opined: "The 'wall of separation between church and state' is *a metaphor based on bad history*, a metaphor which has proved useless as a guide to judging. It should be frankly and explicitly abandoned."[43]

Justice Potter Stewart was in accord: "I think that the Court's task, in this as in all areas of constitutional adjudication, is not responsibly aided by the uncritical invocation of metaphors like the 'wall of separation'—*a phrase nowhere to be found in the Constitution*."[44] That is a key observation. Jefferson's phrase is not constitutional language, and, in fact, as currently interpreted by some courts, is in opposition to most, if not all, of the Founding Fathers' observations on the subject. Likewise, it is in opposition to Jefferson's own words when placed in proper context, to his clarifying words on the subject, and to his own personal conduct endorsing religion in the public sector.

Summary of Government's Encouragement of Religion in the Public Sector

Our nation's history is saturated with references to God because His influence has been profound in the discovery, establishment, and preservation of this country. Accordingly, we pay tribute to God through the presence of religious symbols and practices in both private and public places. It is nothing less than historical fiction to think that our government has not supported and encouraged religion for over two hundred years. The initial intent of the Founding Fathers was clear—to promote and encourage religion in both the private and public sectors and, by so doing, reinforce the principles upon which our nation was built, but at the same time never establish a national religion.[45]

Our Founding Fathers would be shocked to hear some advocate that religion should be spoken only in the confines of one's home or seclusion of a private chapel—that it should be invisible in the public domain. It would be anathema to them and all they stood for.

After a clergyman expressed his hope that the Lord was on the Union's side of the Civil War, Lincoln responded, "I am not at all concerned about that, for I know the Lord is *always* on the side of the *right*. But it is my constant anxiety and prayer that *I* and *this nation* should be on the Lord's *side*."[46] How, as a nation, can we be on the Lord's side if our government is neutral in divine matters? The Savior had something to say about those who assumed a neutral position: "He that is not with me is against me" (Matt. 12:30). In essence, once government has excluded God from the public sector, it has chosen a side—the secular side. It has cast its lot with the non-religionists. There is no viable neutral position on this subject. Either God exists or He does not. Either God aided this country in its formation and preservation or He did not. Either we need God's help to fulfill our nation's destiny or we do not. The Founding Fathers clearly understood God's role in this country's origin and destiny and the need for His continued guidance. For them, it was not a debatable issue.

Unfortunately, the Supreme Court in recent years has made some decisions that compromise or even negate the Founders' intent. Justice Potter Stewart observed, "A refusal to permit religious exercises thus is seen, not as the realization of state neutrality, but rather as the establishment of a religion of secularism, or at the least, as government support of beliefs of those who think that religious exercises should be conducted only in private."[47] If we are not in favor of encouraging religion in the public sector, then we have chosen a side, and contrary to Lincoln's desire, it is not the Lord's side.

When de Tocqueville visited America, he noticed a startling contrast between France and the United States as it pertained to the role of religion in the public sector: "Upon my arrival in the United States the religious aspect of the country was the first thing that struck my attention; and the longer I stayed there, the more I perceived the great political consequences resulting from this new state of things. In France I had almost always seen the spirit of religion and the spirit of freedom marching in opposite directions. But in America I found they were intimately united and that they reigned in common over the same country."[48] This seems to be consistent with the quip of a French judge who said, "France has two religions and three hundred cheeses; the United States has two cheeses and three hundred religions."[49]

What about Those Offended by Public Expressions of Religion?

Charles Krauthammer, a Jew, responded to the argument made by those who are seemingly offended at public displays of religion:

> I'm struck by the fact that you almost never find Orthodox Jews complaining about a Christmas crèche in the public square. That is because their children, steeped in the richness of their own religious tradition, know who they are and are not threatened by Christians celebrating their religion in public. They are enlarged by it.
>
> To insist that the overwhelming majority of this country stifle its religious impulses in public so that minorities can feel "comfortable" not only understandably enrages the majority but commits two sins. The first is profound ungenerosity toward a majority of fellow citizens who have shown such generosity of spirit toward minority religions.
>
> The second is the sin of incomprehension—a failure to appreciate the uniqueness of the communal American religious experience. The United States does not merely allow minority religions to exist at its sufferance. It celebrates and welcomes and honors them.[50]

Mark R. Levin, in his book *Liberty and Tyranny*, gives some additional thoughts on the subject: "A theocracy is not established if certain public schools allow their students to pray at the beginning of the day, or participate in Christmas or Easter assemblies...or certain communities choose to construct a manger scene on the grounds of their town hall. The individual is not required to change his religious affiliation or even accept God's existence. He is not required to worship against his beliefs or even worship at all. Some might be uncomfortable or offended by these events, but individuals are uncomfortable all the time over all kinds of government activities. Some might oppose the use of their tax dollars to support these events. So what? Individuals oppose the manner in which government uses their tax dollars all the time. That does not make the uses unconstitutional."[51]

Has the Supreme Court addressed the issue of "offense" as grounds for declaring certain religious expressions unconstitutional? It has. In *Town of Greece*, claimants alleged that the town council prayers were offensive to their beliefs and therefore the prayers should be held unconstitutional. The Supreme Court acknowledged that concern and responded: "Offense, however, does not equate to coercion. Adults often encounter speech they find disagreeable; and an Establishment Clause violation is not made out any time a person experiences a sense of affront from the expression of contrary religious views in a legislative forum." Quoting an earlier decision (*Elk Grove Unified School District v. Newdow*), the Court explained, "The Constitution does not guarantee citizens a right entirely to avoid ideas with which they disagree."[52] In other words, there is no constitutional protection against being offended.

Nevertheless, it seems that many people, including some jurists, are catering to those who are offended at every public display that is somehow contrary to the particular religious or irreligious view they espouse. The words *I'm offended* are often uttered as though the words themselves constitute a valid Constitutional argument or a definitive defense that should be accepted by all, but the Court in *Town of Greece* debunked that line of reasoning. In and of themselves, those words have no evidentiary weight, no underlying rational, and no Constitutional protection.

One Christian leader, David Bednar, gave excellent counsel in this regard:

> When we believe or say we have been offended, we usually mean we feel insulted, mistreated, snubbed, or disrespected. And certainly clumsy, embarrassing, unprincipled, and mean-spirited things do occur in our interactions with other people that would allow us to take offense. *However, it ultimately is impossible for another person to offend you or to offend me. Indeed, believing that another person offended us is fundamentally false*. To be offended is a *choice* we make; it is not a *condition* inflicted or imposed upon us by someone or something else… To believe that someone or something can *make* us feel offended, angry, hurt, or bitter diminishes our moral agency and transforms us into objects to be acted upon. As agents, however, you and I have the power to act and to choose how we will respond to an offensive or hurtful situation.[53]

In other words, we make the choice to be offended. Of course, this is not an excuse to be rude or intentionally inflict harm on others. But it is good counsel for us not to take offense at every remark, activity, or display that opposes our moral underpinnings. Perhaps we could, in a more mature and civilized way, respond with greater cogency, decency, and tolerance.

Conclusion

The Founding Fathers clearly believed in God and His powerful influence for good upon this nation. They knew the need for a moral nation in order for the Constitution to be effective, and that morality was dependent upon religion.

Therefore, they supported religion in general, both in the private and public sectors, as a means to reemphasize and fortify the moral principles upon which this government was built. It was that simple and straightforward, and accordingly, it was clearly understood for the first two hundred plus years of our nation's history. Nonetheless, in recent times, some have engaged in revisionist history and unwarranted interpretations of the Constitution and have thus supplanted the original intent of our Founding Fathers with secular views that would make this a "nation without God" rather than a "nation under God."[54] This brings to mind the warning of Isaiah: "The nations and kingdoms that will not serve thee [God] shall perish; yea, those nations shall be utterly wasted" (Isa. 60:12; see also Ps. 127:1). Fortunately, it also brings to mind the converse promise as uttered by the Psalmist: "Blessed is the nation whose God is the Lord" (Ps. 33:12).

Hopefully, we will be a nation "whose God is the Lord," one that encourages religion or, as Justice Douglas said, "respects the religious nature of our people and accommodates the public service to their spiritual needs," not a specific religion but religion in general, and thus a nation that continually reinforces and reenthrones the moral principles adopted by our Founding Fathers. This would not only be consistent with their words and actions but no doubt also be extremely pleasing to the God of heaven, who is the benefactor of all blessings.

---

1 Scalia, *Scalia Speaks*, 321.

2 *Zorach v. Clauson*, 343 US 306, 313–14 (1952); emphasis added.

3 *Epperson v. Arkansas*, 393 US 103–4 (1968); emphasis added.

4 To some extent, *Everson v. Board of Education*, 330 US 1 (1947) contains similar language, but it was basically discounted or overridden by the language of *Zorach v. Clawson* in 1952 and then reenthroned in *Epperson*. The key language in *Everson* reads as follows: "Neither a state nor the Federal Government...can pass laws which aid one religion, aid all religions, or prefer one religion over another. Neither can force nor influence a person to go to or to remain away from church against his will or force him to profess a belief or disbelief in any religion. No person can be punished for entertaining or professing religious

beliefs or disbeliefs, for church attendance or non-attendance. No tax in any amount, large or small, can be levied to support any religious activities or institutions, whatever they may be called, or whatever form they may adopt to teach or practice religion. Neither a state nor the Federal Government can, openly or secretly, participate in the affairs of any religious organizations or groups and vice versa. In the words of Jefferson, the clause against establishment of religion by law was intended to erect 'a wall of separation between church and State'" (15–16; see also *Engel v. Vitale*, 370 US 421 [1961]).

5 Scalia, *Scalia Speaks*, 322.

6 Krauthammer, *The Point of It All*, 180.

7 In Scalia, *On Faith*, 10. Timothy P. Carney added this related thought: "The various assaults on religious liberty aimed at driving religion into solely the private sphere—out of the civic square, out of the marketplace, out of politics—need to end if we hope for civil society in American to have a chance" (Carney, *Alienated America*, 287).

8 *Lemon v. Kurtzman*, 403 US 602, 625 (1970); emphasis added.

9 *Employment Division v. Smith*, 494 US 872 (1990).

10 Goodrich, *Free to Believe*, 56; emphasis in original.

11 *Hosanna-Tabor Evangelical Lutheran Church and School v. EEOC*, 565, US (2012).

12 "US Supreme Court Okays Public School Ban," lifesitenews.com.

13 Bork, *Slouching towards Gomorrah*, 289.

14 *Marsh v. Chambers*, 463, US 783, 790 (1983).

15 *Town of Greece v. Galloway*, 572 US (2014); emphasis added.

16 *Town of Greece v. Galloway*, 572 US (2014); emphasis added.

17 Goodrich, *Free to Believe*, 178.

18 "An Ordinance for the Government of the Territory of the United States, Northwest of the River Ohio," 1787; emphasis added. The Northwest Ordinance provided tax dollars for schools, including religious schools. It was not a mere paper reference to religion being taught in the schools. When de Tocqueville visited the United States, he noted, "In New England, every citizen [is]...taught the doctrines and the evidences of his religion, the history of his country, and the leading features of its Constitution" (*Democracy in America*, 1:297). This was the mindset of the Founding Fathers—discussion and encouragement of religion in the public sector, of which schools were one means for doing so.

19 In the case of *McCollum v. Board of Education* (1948), Justice Felix Frankfurter opined, "Illinois has here authorized the commingling of sectarian with secular instruction in the public schools. The Constitution of the United States forbids this" (333 US 203, 212). While I recognize Justice Frankfurter as a great scholar, his opinion seems entirely inconsistent with the intent of the Founding Fathers as set forth in the Northwest Ordinance and many other expressions of the Founders' intent.

20 Rush, "Of the Mode of Education Proper in a Republic," 8.

21 In Barton, *Original Intent*, 168.
22 In Sparks, *The Life of Gouverneur Morris*, 3:483.
23 In Barton, *Original Intent*, 88.
24 Witherspoon, *The Works of John Witherspoon*, 7:118–19.
25 Witherspoon, *The Works of John Witherspoon*, 5:265; emphasis added.
26 In Lincoln, *Messages from the Governors*, 2:467; emphasis added.
27 In Barton, *Original Intent*, 331.
28 Meacham, *American Gospel*, 20, caption.
29 Meacham, *American Gospel*, 129, 233.
30 Story, *Commentaries on the Constitution of the United States*, 2:700; emphasis added.
31 Thomas Jefferson and Andrew Jackson were unwilling to designate national days of prayer but were not hesitant to request prayers in their own and the nation's behalf. Furthermore, Jefferson felt that governmental prayers should be sponsored by individual states, not the federal government.
32 Truman, "Proclamation 2978: National Day of Prayer, 1952," 160.
33 Roosevelt, "Text of Radio Address—Prayer on D-Day, June 6, 1944," fdrlibrary.org.
34 Meacham, *American Gospel*, 171; emphasis added.
35 Roosevelt, "Proclamation 2629—Thanksgiving Day, 1944," presidency.ucsb.edu.
36 Eisenhower, "Remarks Broadcast as Part of the American Legion 'Back to God' Program," Feb. 7, 1954, presidency.ucsb.edu; emphasis added.
37 Eisenhower, "Remarks Recorded for the 'Back to God' Program of the American Legion," Feb 20, 1955, presidency.ucsb.edu; emphasis added.
38 Jefferson, "To the Danbury Baptist Association," founders.archives.gov.
39 Jefferson, "From Thomas Jefferson to Samuel Miller," founders.archives.gov; emphasis added.
40 Jefferson, "Second Inaugural Address," avalon.law.yale.edu.
41 See Gingrich, *Rediscovering God in America*, 7. Furthermore, Jefferson expressed joy in the fact that four different Christian churches met in his local public courthouse, one each week of the month (see *The Writings of Thomas Jefferson*, 15:404).
42 Barton, *Original Intent*, 213.
43 *Wallace v. Jaffree*, 472 U.S. 38, 107 [1985]; emphasis added.
44 *Engel v. Vitale*, 370 U.S. 421, 445-46 (1962); emphasis added.
45 In this regard, Ben Carson noted, "It is appalling how far our country has strayed from the principles of the founding fathers" (Carson, *One Nation*, 55–56).
46 In Carpenter, *Six Months at the White House*, 282; emphasis in original.
47 Dissenting opinion in *Abington School District v. Schempp*. 374 US 201, 313 (1963). Consistent with that observation, the *Wall Street Journal* sadly noted that atheism is "the one belief to which the state's power will extend its protection" (in *Congressional Record*, 109:11089).

[48] In Metaxas, *If You Can Keep It*, 63.

[49] Scalia, *On Faith*, 100.

[50] Krauthammer, *The Point of It All*, 184–85.

[51] Levin, *Liberty and Tyranny*, 46–47.

[52] *Town of Greece v. Galloway*, 572 US (2014).

[53] Bednar, "And Nothing Shall Offend Them," 90.

[54] In this regard, Justice Scalia wrote, "How can the [Supreme] Court *possibly* assert that 'the First Amendment mandates governmental neutrality between... religion and nonreligion' and that...'adherence to religion generally' is unconstitutional? Who says so? Surely not the words of the Constitution. Surely not the history and traditions that reflect our society's constant understanding of those words. Surely not even the current sense of our society, recently reflected in an act of Congress adopted *unanimously* by the Senate and with only five nays in the House of Representatives, criticizing a Court of Appeals opinion that had held 'under God' in the Pledge of Allegiance unconstitutional. Nothing stands behind the Court's assertion that governmental affirmation of the society's belief in God is unconstitutional except the Court's own say-so, citing as support only the unsubstantiated say-so of earlier Courts going back no farther than the mid-twentieth century" (*On Faith*, 183–84; emphasis in original).

CHAPTER 9

A Case for and against Abortion

Moral Matters Facing Our Nation

When religion is encouraged in the private and public sectors, it enhances our ability to know God's will and to live it, and thus fosters a more moral society—critical to the viability of our nation's charter documents. In this spirit, the next few chapters discuss major moral issues confronting our country and what God's will is concerning each.

The Constitution and Abortion

Roe v. Wade is the landmark case on abortion. This 1973 decision overturned a Texas statute stating that it was a crime to procure an abortion except for the purpose of saving the mother's life. These are some of the conclusions reached by the US Supreme Court in that case:

- "For the stage prior to approximately the end of the first trimester, the abortion decision and its effectuation must be left to the medical judgment of the pregnant woman's attending physician."[1] The net effect, as proven by subsequent events, is that the Court approved abortion on demand for the first trimester.
- With respect to the states' important and legitimate interest in potential life, the Court stated, "The 'compelling'

> point is at viability. This is so because the fetus then presumably has the capability of meaningful life outside the mother's womb. State regulation protective of fetal life after viability thus has both logical and biological justifications. *If the State is interested in protecting fetal life after viability, it may go so far as to proscribe abortion during that period, except when it is necessary to preserve the life or health of the mother*."[2] The Court defined *viable* as "potentially able to live outside the mother's womb, albeit with artificial aid. Viability is usually placed at about seven months [28 weeks] but may occur earlier, even at 24 weeks."[3]

At first glance, it may seem that the Court reserved certain rights that allowed the states to limit abortions after twenty-four weeks, but in *Doe v. Bolton* (a case decided the same day as *Roe v. Wade*), the Supreme Court defined the health of the mother as "all factors—physical, emotional, psychological, familial, and the woman's age—relevant to the well-being of the patient."[4] In essence, this means that a woman can get a letter from her doctor (as late as the day before delivery) that continuing the pregnancy would cause her emotional or psychological stress. By doing so, she comes within the health exception defined by the Court in *Roe v. Wade*. As a consequence, we end up with abortion on demand, even in the third trimester, and the interests of the state in preserving the life of the unborn fetus are effectively nullified. That is the current state of the law as of the date of writing this book.[5]

I have no doubt that there are sincere and brilliant and good people who are pro-choice, just as there are sincere and brilliant and good people who are pro-life. Each side argues its case with passion and the powers of reason. Each side relies on its own statistics and surveys. Judges and legislators are divided on the issue. Some ecclesiastical leaders, even within the same faith, cannot reach accord. Following are some of the principal pro-choice and pro-life arguments advanced by each cause. But first, some facts on abortion to put these arguments in their proper context.

Facts about Abortion

Approximately 862,000 abortions occurred in the United States in 2017, slightly fewer than in 2014.[6] Of these, approximately 90 percent occurred in the first trimester.[7] Between 1973 (the year *Roe v. Wade* was decided) and 2017, more than sixty million legal abortions took place in the United States.[8] *This is fifty times more lives lost by Americans than in all American wars combined.*[9] To put this in further perspective, if those pregnancies had not been terminated and the children born had lived to the present time and constituted a separate country, they would have comprised the twenty-fourth largest country in the world out of 233 countries and dependent territories that existed in 2018. This "country" would have had a greater population than Italy, South Korea, Spain, Argentina, Ukraine, or Canada.[10] This is how many lives have been taken by abortion in the United States alone since *Roe v. Wade.*

Arguments for Pro-Choice

Following are some arguments often used to support the pro-choice agenda:

1. Pregnancy can adversely affect one's life.

Sarah Weddington spoke to the US Supreme Court in *Roe v. Wade* as follows: "A pregnancy to a woman is perhaps one of the most determinative aspects of her life. It disrupts her body. It disrupts her education. It disrupts her employment. And it often disrupts her entire family life."[11] Accordingly, a woman ought to be able to remove this disruption from her life.

2. Legalized abortion is necessary to achieve gender equality (socially, economically, and morally).

Men don't get pregnant and therefore do not have the responsibility to carry a baby or face the expected social norms to look after it. This inequality is resolved if women can abort their baby at any time.

3. Abortion is a safe medical procedure.

The majority of abortions take place during the first trimester. There are now sufficient qualified health facilities (at least in the US) where the procedure can be performed with little health risk to the mother. If abortions were illegal, a black market would emerge that would result in less available counseling and more back-alley surgeries that are unsafe.

4. Abortion promotes individual economic freedom and national economic growth.

Abortion frees up women so they are not confined to the home but are free to enter the job force and thus contribute to their own economic well-being, as well as the nation's economic growth.

5. Other arguments of lesser weight and counterarguments.

Other arguments for pro-choice are proposed but are of lesser weight because they have less rationale or facts to support them. Some of them are set forth below with counterarguments in response:

- A Woman Has the Absolute Right to Control Her Own Body

  At first glance, one might wonder why this was not listed first in the arguments above, since it is most frequently cited by pro-choice advocates as the prime reason justifying abortion. The reasoning goes something like this: as we maximize our choices, we maximize our opportunities for growth and happiness. Therefore, a woman should have absolute control over her own body so she can choose an abortion and thus maximize control over her future destiny and happiness. Accordingly, no government or man should be able to dictate what a woman chooses to do with her own body.[12] At first blush, this argument seems straightforward and convincing, but the problem with such argument is that it is simply not true. A woman does not have the absolute right to do anything she wants with her own body. For example, she cannot choose to hit or injure another person without just cause; she cannot choose, in most cities and states, to go unclothed in any public setting; she cannot choose to smoke in a public building; she cannot choose to take certain drugs into her body; she cannot choose to drive while drunk; and the vast majority of society believes she does not have the right to a late term abortion (such as one week before the expected due date) as evidenced by many state laws and polls on the subject. In fact, *Roe v. Wade* permits controls on a women's body by allowing state restrictions on late term abortions unless the health of the mother is in jeopardy. Why these controls? Because her choices can adversely affect other people in society, namely the unborn and society at large, who also have rights to be protected, and in these cases, rights that preempt her control over her own body. Once it becomes apparent that there exist restraints on a woman's choices concerning her body, then it undermines the argument that she has absolute control over her own body and thus the right to choose an abortion at any stage of pregnancy. The real question is not whether a woman has absolute control over her body (she doesn't) but shifts to how we can best weigh the rights of all parties affected by the woman's choice.

- Loss of Education and Health Care

The claim is made that teenagers who become mothers will end up, in most cases, with no further education, inadequate health care, and the need for public assistance. Therefore, abortion is necessary for their well-being and to avoid added burdens on society. However, those negative consequences can be avoided by putting the baby up for adoption in a home where that child will be loved and cared for.

In response, however, pro-choice advocates often argue that adoption is not a reasonable alternative to abortion because most teenagers are unwilling to give up their child. But if personal choice is so critical—the very foundation of the pro-choice argument—how is it consistent to contend that a teenager is mature enough to make the choice for an abortion but is not mature enough to make the choice for adoption of the same child, particularly after counseling with parents, spiritual leaders, and other qualified individuals on the subject?

- Exceptions for Rape or Incest

  Some claim that women who are pregnant as a result of rape or incest should have the option to have a legal abortion since their pregnancy was not a voluntary choice. To put this in perspective, the *New York Times* explained that when "abortion patients were asked why they were having an abortion, only 1 percent of the 1,900 women questioned named rape or incest. And 95 percent of those who mentioned rape or incest named other reasons as well for deciding to abort."[13] Some advocates of pro-life, after balancing the interests of all parties involved, would agree that there should be an exception for abortion in cases of rape. Others would caution, however, that this decision to abort should only be made after giving great weight to the effect this choice has on the life of the unborn child, who is innocent in this tragic set of circumstances. And others would argue that the life of the unborn baby is paramount in any case, and thus rape should not constitute an exception for abortion.

- Choice Is a Defense in and of Itself

  Some use the term *pro-choice* as a euphemism for supporting legalized abortion as though the term is a logical defense in and of itself. But such a line of reasoning is highly defective. Does pro-choice for stealing, pro-choice for drunk driving, or pro-choice for sexual abuse constitute defenses for such behavior? Choice is only one side of the equation; the other side constitutes the consequences of that choice, and the consequences of the choice to have an abortion are (1) destruction of an innocent life; (2) a guilty conscience for most, if not all, women who choose to participate; and (3) a more hardened and less compassionate society. In addition, pro-choice is a one-way street. It is argued to be good, even necessary, for the mother, but on the other hand, the father or spokesperson for the infant is deemed to have no legal choice in the matter. In truth, the term *pro-choice* is a politically correct name for the much more accurate term *pro-abortion*. It is an attempt to cover a heinous sin with a benign title. One might as well refer to adultery and fornication as consensual sex, or to lies as misstatements, or to sins as judgmental errors. Such downgrading of language is an attempt to minimize the sin, and thus, rather than acting as a restraint against such action, it encourages and promotes it.

- Unconsciousness Equates to Lack of Life

At least for the first trimester, a fetus is not fully sentient and cannot survive outside the womb. Therefore, it is not considered a viable human being or person who has separate rights to be protected. In fact, the US Supreme Court ruled in *Roe v. Wade* that a fetus (prior to established viability) is not a person who is entitled to the protection of life otherwise guaranteed under the Fourteenth Amendment. Robert Bork responded to such an argument as follows: "A newborn is not fully sentient, nor is a person in an advanced Alzheimer's disease. There are people who would allow the killing of the newborn and the senile, but I doubt that is a view with general acceptance."[14] In addition, there are human beings who are not conscious while on temporary life-support systems. What mother would allow the doctor to unplug such systems for her child and let the child die when the prognosis for future recovery is positive? In a similar sense, an unborn baby is on temporary life support systems supplied by the mother while in the womb. If left on those life-support systems for a full-term pregnancy, the prognosis for a fully conscious life is extremely high.

- A Fetus Is Part of the Mother's Body

  There are some who contend that a fetus is a part of its mother's body, and therefore she has the right to abort it under any circumstances. A fetus, however, from the moment of conception, has a separate DNA and thereafter develops separate organs from the mother, making it a separate living entity. At some future date, science, reason, and moral conscience may combine to conclude that an unborn fetus is a living human being from inception and thus entitled to the protection of a person as understood under the Fourteenth Amendment.
- Abortion Will Reduce Child Abuse, Divorce, and Illegitimate Births

  Some of the previous claims made by pro-choice advocates were that abortion would reduce child abuse (there would be fewer unwanted children), divorce (elimination of unwanted children would minimize marital stress), and illegitimate births (there would be fewer children born out of wedlock). To the contrary, since *Roe v. Wade*, statistics have shown that child abuse, divorce, and illegitimate births have increased.[15] This should not be surprising, however, because abortion fosters an immorality mentality, a loss of respect for life, and a hardened and insensitive society.

Arguments for Pro-Life

Following are some arguments often used to support the pro-life agenda:

1. Human Life Begins at Conception

What constitutes life, and when does it begin? The *American Heritage Medical Dictionary* gives this definition: "[Life is] the property or quality that distinguishes living organisms from dead organisms and inanimate matter, manifested in functions such as metabolism, growth, reproduction, and response to stimuli or adaptation to the environment originating from within the organism."[16] The cell or zygote formed at conception meets all four of these requirements.[17] If a fetus constitutes life at inception and it develops naturally into a fully developed human being, then what type of life could the fetus be other than human life? Thus, abortion is nothing short of killing that human life.

If a fetus is not a living person, then it must be nothing more than a biological mass of matter or property. That is a critical assertion of the pro-choice advocates, because if that is believed, then it is much easier to dehumanize the issue and eliminate compassion from the equation. This is not the first time in our history that some have devalued the meaning of life. For years, many argued that slaves were nothing more than the property of their owner. Fortunately, time and moral sensitivity corrected that evil.

Robert Bork explained why he changed his position from pro-choice to pro-life:

> [I] had a vague and unexamined notion that while the fetus wasn't nothing, it was also not fully human. The slightest reflection would have suggested that non-human or semi-human blots of tissue do not magically turn into human beings.
>
> From single-cell fertilized egg to baby to teenager to adult to old age to death is a single process of one individual, not a series of different individuals replacing each other. It is impossible to draw a line anywhere after the moment of fertilization and say that before this point the creature is not human but after this point it is. It has all the attributes of a human from the beginning.
>
> It is impossible to say that the killing of the organism at any moment after it originated is not the killing of a human being.[18]

Perhaps this issue is best put in perspective in this way: Suppose it is one hour before the birth of a baby. Which is the higher moral priority at that moment—the right of the mother to have an abortion for convenience's sake or the right of the baby to live? If we agree that it is the right of the baby to live, then what about one week before delivery, thirty days before, six months before, or just after fertilization and life has begun?[19] Where does one draw the line once he or she agrees that at some point, the life of the unborn baby takes precedence over the convenience of the mother? If a baby is a person one hour after birth, is it not also a person one hour before birth and thus entitled to Constitutional protection? And if a person one hour before birth, why not a person the moment that same life commenced at fertilization?

If there is any doubt about whether or not an unborn baby constitutes a human life or a person, as defined in the Constitution, and thus is entitled to protection of life under the Fourteenth Amendment, would we not always want to weigh any possible doubt in favor of life, particularly since the alternative has irreversible catastrophic consequences?

For those opposed to abortion, the right to life outranks any reason for abortion with the possible exception of cases when the mother's life is in jeopardy, or there is rape or incest, or the baby cannot survive beyond birth. Even in those circumstances, an abortion should be performed only after proper counseling and prayerful reflection.

2. Respect for Life

If people believe that the convenience or personal challenges of the mother takes precedence over the life of an unborn infant, then society's respect for life is diminished. If that is the case, then what morally stops that mother from killing her newborn infant immediately after birth? After all, it may be inconvenient to care for this infant, or this newborn may cause emotional trauma or stretch economic resources or prevent the mother from getting a job or pursuing her education. In other words, what is the moral difference if the baby is killed one hour before delivery or one hour after delivery? In both cases, the baby *cannot* survive on its own, and in both cases, it *can* survive with the help of another. Or what about parents taking the life of severely ill or handicapped children who are dependent upon parents for their support because it is inconvenient or costly or an emotional struggle to care for them? Or what prevents children from taking the life of dependent parents who are inconveniencing them because of the time and effort it takes to provide for them, the substantial economic burden it imposes, and the resulting toll of emotional stress it causes?

Unfortunately, society is losing its respect for life. President Ronald Reagan spoke of "a young pregnant woman named Victoria, who said, 'In this society we save whales, we save timber wolves and bald eagles and Coke bottles. Yet, everyone wanted me to throw away my baby.'"[20] Who believes that a bald eagle or Coke bottle is more important than an unborn baby?

Abortion teaches a disregard for the sacredness of human life—one who is a child of God. If a society chooses abortion, it can become a slippery slope—a stepping stone to euthanasia, mercy killings, terminating the life of the disabled, assisted suicide, and the like.[21] I am bewildered when I see people who are rabid opponents of capital punishment, even for the most heinous of crimes—who protest, petition, and vote for its abolition—yet with equal vigor promote capital punishment by way of abortion for the innocent, unborn child.

Charles Krauthammer told of a Planned Parenthood official, caught on video, speaking in a casual, even jocular tone "while haggling over the price of an embryonic liver [from an abortion]. 'If it's still low, then we can bump it up,' she joked, 'I want a Lamborghini.'" Krauthammer then added, "Abortion critics have long warned that the problem is not only the obvious—what abortion does to the fetus—but also what it does to us. It's the same kind of desensitization that has occurred in the Netherlands with another mass exercise in life termination: assisted suicide. It began as a way to prevent the suffering of the terminally ill. It has now become so widespread and wanton that one-fifth of all Dutch assisted-suicide patients are euthanized without their explicit consent."[22]

Women may seek abortions for a variety of reasons, but one must eventually ask the soul-searching question, "Do those concerns outweigh the right of an innocent and defenseless child to have the opportunity for a happy and full life?" Unfortunately, statistics have repeatedly shown that the vast majority (well over 90 percent) of all abortions are for the personal convenience of the mother—unrelated to preserving her life or in response to rape or incest.[23] Have we now become so consumed in self-gratification that personal convenience takes precedence over human life?

Robert Bork shared the following experience: "One evening I naively remarked in a talk that those who favor the right to abort would likely change their minds if they could be convinced that a human being was being killed. I was startled at the anger that statement provoked in several women present. *One of them informed me in no uncertain terms that the issue had nothing to do with the humanity of the fetus but was entirely about the woman's freedom*."[24] It would be hard to think of a much more selfish comment than that. In truth, the issue has a great deal to do with the life of the unborn and society in general.

President Reagan noted, "Abortion concerns not just the unborn child, it concerns every one of us. The English poet, John Donne, wrote: 'Any man's death diminishes me, because I am involved in mankind; and therefore, never send to know for whom the bell tolls; it tolls for thee.'"[25] And thus, the bell tolls for all of us each time an abortion is performed.

3. Many State Homicide Laws Recognize the Fetus as a Living Human Being

On April 2, 2018, the National Right to Life Committee set forth "a summary of the laws of 38 states that recognize the unlawful killing of an unborn child as homicide in at least some circumstances."[26] Many of these laws refer to the unborn as a "person" or "human being" or "member of the species *Homo sapiens*." In other words, contrary to the decision in *Roe v. Wade*, these states felt that an unborn fetus was a person—a living human who deserved legal protection. This means that someone who committed a violent act in these states that resulted in the death of an unborn child could be charged with homicide. But after *Roe v. Wade*, a woman who voluntarily chose an abortion, resulting in the exact same consequence (homicide of an unborn child) would be crime-free.

4. Adoption Is a Viable Alternative

As noted by Linda Lowen, a former radio and television broadcast journalist, "With 1.5 million American families wanting to adopt a child, there is no such thing as an unwanted child."[27] Who is not touched by these words of Mother Teresa, a woman of God? "Please don't kill the child. I want the child. Please give me the child. I am willing to accept any child who would be aborted and to give that child to a married couple who will love the child."[28] If a pregnant woman is unable to provide a meaningful life for her baby, then the greatest and most loving gift she can give her child is the right to life through an adoption by loving and caring parents.

5. Abortion Can Trigger a Guilty Conscience—Shame, Remorse, and Embarrassment

Some claim that there is no evidence of "post-abortion traumatic stress syndrome," a term that is not recognized by the American Psychological Association and the American Psychiatric Association.[29] If this is meant to say that no one experiences guilt, shame, embarrassment, or other psychological damage after an abortion, then this would be contrary to the account of thousands of others who are witnesses that there is a heavy emotional and psychological price to be paid.

Carol Everett is one powerful witness in this regard. She owned two abortion clinics and managed four others. She shared her observation of how women react immediately after having abortions:

> There are two reactions in the recovery room. The first one is: I've killed my baby. And even then, it amazed me that that was the first time they called it a baby and the first time they called it murder. But, you know, as bad as that sounds, that's probably the healthiest reaction.

> The second reaction is: I am hungry, you kept me in here for four hours and you told me I'd only be here for two; let me out of here. Now that woman is doing what I did. She's running from her abortion… When I finally did deal with it [my own abortion], I cried nonstop for five months because, you see, I killed my baby, and I'm still not through that. *I believe that every woman, even if she's not physically harmed, is harmed by abortion.*[30]

At some point, one must ask the soul-searching question: If abortion is morally correct (a reflection of God's will) why have thousands, even millions, who have undergone an abortion experienced so much lasting guilt, regret, and pain associated with such an event? Because freedom of choice does not result in freedom from consequence. David Horowitz, a Jewish agnostic and author, noted that what pro-choice advocates "are actually demanding is not, in fact, the freedom to choose. They are demanding to be free from responsibility for their choices."[31] But no secular law can free them from the consequences of breaking God's moral law. For that, the day of accountability will inevitably come.

Pro-life proponents have provided the following confirming evidence of the emotional and spiritual complications a woman feels following an abortion: "The website *afterabortion.com* established by a woman who had 5 abortions provides a place for women to help each other cope with the aftermath of their abortions. There are nearly 2.5 million posts. They tell stories of how they were coerced into aborting their children by boyfriends, husbands, friends, and family. They describe how abortion was far from being a choice. They speak of overwhelming guilt, nightmares, excessive drinking, drug abuse, promiscuity, an inability to form or maintain relationships, difficulty bonding with later children, and other ways in which they are suffering."[32]

Abortion is not some inconsequential procedure that is tucked in the distant recesses of one's mind and heart and then quickly forgotten. It has moral consequences that can haunt a woman for years, even a lifetime. Rationalization may dull the senses for a time, but in moments of self-reflection and honesty, the guilt and remorse will return. It is a time bomb waiting to explode.

Before being baptized into a Christian faith, an eighty-four-year-old woman confessed that she had had an abortion some forty-six years earlier. As part of this confession, she said, "I have carried the burden of having aborted a child every day of my life for forty-six years. The pain, the guilt, the suffering would never go away. Nothing I did would take the pain and guilt away. I was hopeless until I was taught the true gospel of Jesus Christ. I finally came to know that I could be forgiven if I truly repented of my sins."[33]

As a leader in a Christian church, I conducted scores of personal interviews of people who wanted to be baptized. Many of those I interviewed had participated in abortions before they had received Christ's gospel. In almost every case, they felt intense remorse. They acknowledged they had felt guilt, depression, sorrow, and a loss of the Spirit from the moment the tragic event occurred. It was not the powers of reason alone that told them it was wrong. It was much more. It was their moral conscience as illuminated by the Spirit. And now as the Spirit had become even more prevalent in their life, it accentuated all the more the need for repentance and the desire to avail themselves of the healing powers of Christ's Atonement.

6. Abortion Produces a Calloused and Desensitized Society

A mother's love for her child is the most natural of all affections. It is God-given. When I discussed this subject with my wife, she said, "I felt that love and affection for our little babies the moment I knew I was pregnant. It was instantaneous." While I was writing this book, a young couple called me, sobbing on the phone. They had just lost their little baby during the second trimester of pregnancy. They asked me if I would speak at the graveside service. I did. I saw their eight-year-old daughter crying uncontrollably as they placed dirt on the casket of her tiny brother. I contrast this natural, even heavenly, affection for an unborn child with those who willingly sacrifice the life of their own unborn child for convenience purposes. When that love between mother and child and father and child is cast aside, it leads to a calloused and desensitized society.

7. Abortion Is a Horrific, Inhumane Act

Justice Clarence Thomas dissented from the majority opinion in *Stenberg v. Carhart* (2000), a case having to do with the legality of a law outlawing partial-birth abortions. In it, he described the horrors of the primary form of abortion used after sixteen weeks of gestation. Referring to the testimony of various physicians, he said that the "procedure requires the physician to dilate the woman's cervix and then extract the fetus from her uterus with forceps. Because of the fetus's size at this stage, the physician generally removes the fetus by dismembering the fetus one piece at a time. In other words, the physician will grasp the fetal parts and 'basically tear off pieces of the fetus and pull them out.' When all of the fetus' limbs have been removed and only the head is left in utero, the physician will then collapse the skull and pull it through the cervical canal. At the end of the procedure, the physician is left, in [Dr. Carhart] words, with a 'tray full of pieces.'"[34]

I have never witnessed an abortion, nor do I desire to do so, but if Justice Thomas's description is accurate or even close to it, then such a procedure is a barbaric, savage, horrific act of inhumanity. It should shock every conscience and be repulsive to every compassionate cell in our bodies. Does one honestly believe that the convenience of a woman (cases where the life of the mother is not in jeopardy) outweighs this heinous treatment of an innocent and unborn baby? Mother Teresa put this in perspective: "The greatest misery of our time is the generalized abortion of children."[35]

8. Pro-Abortion Activists Are Attempting to Restrict Freedom of Religion

You would think that the pro-abortion activists would be content with their victory in *Roe v. Wade*, but they are not. They not only want legal protection for abortion but also moral approval by everyone. And if they can't get that, then compulsory acceptance.

There is a concerted effort to force hospitals and physicians to perform abortions even though it is contrary to their religious beliefs in order to support the perceived higher moral ground of pro-choice. Fortunately, in *Doe v. Bolton*, the Supreme Court decided that religious freedom prevails. Luke Goodrich summarized the current state of the law as follows: "Women may have a constitutional right to abortion, which means the government can't stop them from having one. But doctors [and hospitals] also have the right of religious freedom, which means the government can't force them to participate." Nonetheless, Goodrich noted that "a leading ACLU attorney has acknowledged that her goal is to establish a norm that declining to perform an abortion is an illegal act of sex discrimination."[36] In addition, others are still seeking to require doctor and hospital participation in abortions based on grounds of sex discrimination, necessary emergency care, or medical negligence.

Pro-choice activists want to require businesses to provide health insurance that covers abortions and contraceptives, even though such businesses and their owners are religiously opposed to it. Fortunately, in the cases of Hobby Lobby (an art and crafts store) and Little Sisters (a Catholic organization which serves the elderly poor), this issue was decided under federal law in favor of religious freedom.

Unhappy with these decisions, pro-choice activists are now striving to achieve their goal by relying on state rather than federal law. Currently, four states require businesses to provide health insurance that covers abortions, with no exception for one's religious beliefs.[37]

The Storman family of Olympia, Washington, owned a small grocery story and pharmacy. They were sued for being unwilling to sell the morning-after pill that can cause early abortions, even though it was against their religious belief. One might question the motive of such suit when the fact was disclosed that "within a five-mile radius of the Stormanses' pharmacy, over *thirty* pharmacies sold the morning-after pill."[38] In addition, overnight delivery of such pill was available. The trial court decided in favor of the Stormans, but on appeal, the Ninth Circuit reversed the decision. The case was appealed to the Supreme Court, and shortly thereafter, Justice Scalia died. Accordingly, the appeal was never taken up because only three justices (one short for the appeal to proceed) voted in favor of it. Justice Alito wrote a strong dissent, joined by Chief Justice Roberts and Justice Thomas: "This case is an ominous sign. If this is a sign of how religious liberty claims will be treated in the years ahead, those who value religious freedom have cause for great concern."[39]

Some jurisdictions have passed laws that prohibit pro-life counselors from participating in peaceful conversations with future abortion candidates if done within a certain distance of abortion clinics. This is true even though such conversations take place on public property. Other laws attempt to restrict pro-life organizations from only hiring people who support their mission.[40]

How ironic, even tragic, that these pro-choice advocates of abortion seek to deny that same right of choice to those who desire not to perform abortions or dispense abortion related drugs, or to those who desire to give pro-life counseling to abortion candidates. In other words, they are pro-choice for abortion and *no choice* for those with opposing religious beliefs. For them, tolerance has become a one-way street.

9. Other Arguments of Lesser Weight and Counterarguments

Other pro-life arguments are proposed but are of lesser weight because they have less rationale or facts to support them. Some of them are set forth below with counterarguments in response:

- The Use of Contraceptives and Moral Restraint

  Some pro-life adherents argue that there are solutions, other than abortion, to the issue of not wanting a child, such as contraception and abstinence. Critics counter, however, that only 8 percent of women who have abortions have failed to use contraceptives in some way.[41] This response, however, fails to address the issue of discipline and moral restraint, particularly in nonmarital relations which are the source of the vast majority of abortions. In other words, if the foregoing statistics are correct, then women should be aware in advance that contraceptives are not an effective substitute for moral restraint for multiple reasons.

- Tax Funding

  Some have argued that abortion should be outlawed because tax money should not be used to support an immoral act. While this is arguably a valid concern, it does not address the core issue. For example, if someone funds her own abortion without the aid of tax money, does that abortion now become morally acceptable?

A Moral Issue

How does the honest searcher of truth sort through this maze of arguments and counterarguments? As noted by Charles Krauthammer, "A curious thing has happened to the abortion debate. It remains politically hot, but it is intellectually spent. Everyone seems to know both sides of the argument backward and forward."[42] Nonetheless, knowledge alone has not brought about a consensus on this issue.

Certainly, pro-choice advocates believe they have the rationale and facts supporting their case just as pro-life advocates believe they have the rationale and facts supporting their case. Each side claims moral superiority. Who then is right? And what should be the governing policy for our nation? Because this is a moral issue, it cannot be solved by reason alone, as demonstrated by the divisiveness on this issue in our country, even among the brightest of people. For example, Justice Antonin Scalia was an advocate of pro-life; on the other hand, Justice Ruth Bader Ginsburg was an advocate of pro-choice. Both have been brilliant intellectual stars, and both have done much good for society. Accordingly, the answer to the abortion debate is not to be determined by brilliance alone but requires a moral mandate from Him who is the author of all moral law—God. And thus, one should ask, "Has God spoken on this issue?"

Some years ago, my father, who was an attorney, was trying a lawsuit in a California state court. For his authority, he cited only one case—a California Supreme Court case, issued many years before. His opponent cited a number of lower court decisions of much more recent vintage. The judge finally said to my father, "Mr. Callister, don't you have a more recent case than this?"

My father looked at the judge and replied, "Your Honor, may I remind you that when the Supreme Court speaks on a matter, it only needs to speak once." The judge nodded with approval. He was reminded that the Supreme Court trumps all lower court decisions, however numerous or recent or rational they may be.

Likewise, God only needs to speak once on an issue of morality, and that one declaration trumps all the opinions of the lower courts, whether uttered by the US Supreme Court, state legislatures, psychologists, counselors, politicians, friends, parents, or would-be moralists of the day. What then has God said on the issue of abortion? The next chapter addresses that question.

---

1 *Roe v. Wade*, 410 US 113, 114 (1973).

2 *Roe v. Wade*, 410 US 113, 163–64 (1973); emphasis added.

3 *Roe v. Wade*, 410 US 113, 160 (1973).

4 *Doe v. Bolton*, 410 US 179, 192 (1973).

5 Justice Byron White wrote the following critical dissent in *Doe v. Bolton*: "With all due respect, I dissent. I find nothing in the language or history of the Constitution to support the Court's judgment. The Court simply fashions and announces a new constitutional right for pregnant mothers and, with scarcely any reason or authority for its action, invests that right with sufficient substance to override most existing state abortion statutes. The upshot is that the people and the legislatures of the 50 States are constitutionally disentitled to weigh the relative importance of the continued existence and development of the fetus, on the one hand, against a spectrum of possible impacts on the mother, on the other hand. As an exercise of raw judicial power, the Court perhaps has authority to do what it does today; but in my view its judgment is an improvident and extravagant exercise of the power of judicial review that the Constitution extends to this Court" (*Doe v. Bolton*, 410 US 179, 222 [1972]). The bottom line is that seven individuals on the US Supreme Court unilaterally usurped the right of millions of Americans who had already made a decision on the moral and legal implications of abortion in their own respective states.

6 See Guttmacher Institute, "Induced Abortion in the United States," Sept. 2019, guttmacher.org.

7 See Centers for Disease Control, "Abortion Surveillance—United States, 2016," cdc.gov. According to the CDC, 623,471 abortions were reported in 2016. However, clinics are not required to report abortions; in fact, no abortions were

reported from California, Maryland, New Jersey, or the District of Columbia. Consequently, the actual number is much higher.

8 See National Right to Life Committee, *The State of Abortion in the United States*, 5.

9 An estimated 1.1 million Americans have been killed in war. See Crigger and Santhanam, "How Many Americans Have Died in U.S Wars?" pbs.org.

10 Worldometers, "Countries in the World by Population (2020)," worldometers.info.

11 In Torricelli and Carroll, *In Our Own Words*, 303.

12 Some pro-choice proponents fear that if the government can prohibit abortion, it could also have power over other reproductive choices, such as using contraception or undergoing sterilization.

13 Lewin, "Rape and Incest: Just 1% of All Abortions," A17.

14 Bork, *Slouching Towards Gomorrah*, 176.

15 See Coolidge, "Five Promises Abortion Couldn't Keep," care-net.org.

16 *American Heritage Medical Dictionary* (2008), "life."

17 This confirmation of life is further verified by a world-famous heart surgeon who wrote, "In the course of my studies as a medical doctor, I learned that a new life begins when two special cells unite to become one cell, bringing together 23 chromosomes from the father and 23 from the mother. These chromosomes contain thousands of genes. In a marvelous process involving a combination of genetic coding by which all the basic human characteristics of the unborn person are established, a new DNA complex is formed. A continuum of growth results in a new human being" (Russell M. Nelson, "Abortion: An Assault on the Defenseless," 35–36). Lest there be any question, this newly created zygote has a DNA code separate and apart from that of its mother and father, further evidencing it is an independent, living organism.

18 Bork, *Slouching Towards Gomorrah*, 173, 175.

19 Recently, a presidential candidate was asked a thought-provoking question by someone in the audience. The audience member said that he was born on September 8. He then asked in essence, "Did my life have no value on September 7th, the day before I was born?" The candidate responded that what really matters is the choice of the woman (in other words, the life of the unborn is insignificant compared with the choice of the mother). I was shocked to hear loud cheers and clapping from the audience in response to that answer.

20 Reagan, *Abortion and the Conscience of the Nation*, 59.

21 If one questions the reality of this possibility, just read this observation of President Reagan: "What more dramatic confirmation could we have of the real issue [the value of human life] than the Baby Doe case in Bloomington, Indiana? The death of that tiny infant tore at the hearts of all Americans because the child was undeniably a live human being—one lying helpless before the eyes of the doctors and the eyes of the nation. The real issue for the courts was *not* whether Baby Doe was a human being. The real issue was whether to protect

the life of a human being who had Down's Syndrome, who would probably be mentally handicapped, but who needed a routine surgical procedure to unblock his esophagus and allow him to eat. A doctor testified to the presiding judge that, even with his physical problem corrected, Baby Doe would have a 'non-existent' possibility for 'minimally adequate quality of life'—in other words, that retardation was the equivalent of a crime deserving the death penalty. The judge let Baby Doe starve and die, and the Indiana Supreme Court sanctioned his decision" (Reagan, *Abortion and the Conscience of the Nation*, 43–45). President Reagan further observed, "As the New Jersey Supreme Court said two decades ago, in a decision upholding the sanctity of human life, 'a child need not be perfect to have a worthwhile life'" (Reagan, *Abortion and the Conscience of the Nation*, 57).

22 Krauthammer, *The Point of It All*, 116–17.

23 Finer and others, "Reasons U.S. Women Have Abortions," 112.

24 Bork, *Slouching Towards Gomorrah*, 183.

25 Reagan, "Abortion and the Conscience of the Nation," 39.

26 National Right to Life Committee, "State Homicide Laws That Recognize Unborn Victims," nrlc.org.

27 Lowen, "Key Arguments from Both Sides of the Abortion Debate," thoughtco.com.

28 Mother Teresa, *Where There is Love, There is God*, 98.

29 See Cohen, "Abortion and Mental Health: Myths and Realities," 8.

30 In Terzo, "After an Abortion: A Look into the Recovery Room," liveaction.org; emphasis added.

31 Horowitz, *Dark Agenda*, 106.

32 Ruse and Schwarzwalder, "The Best Pro-Life Arguments for Secular Audiences," frc.org.

33 In Andersen, *The Divine Gift of Forgiveness*, 25.

34 *Stenberg v. Carhart*, 530 US 914, 984–85 (2000).

35 In Reagan, *Abortion and the Conscience of the Nation*, 40.

36 Goodrich, *Free to Believe*, 91, 98.

37 See Goodrich, *Free to Believe*, 100–102.

38 See Goodrich, *Free to Believe*, 93–94.

39 In Goodrich, *Free to Believe*, 95.

40 See Nicole Ault, "New York Tries Again to Muzzle Pro-Life Groups," *Wall Street Journal*, January 18–19, 2020, A13.

41 Kaye and others, *The Benefits of Birth Control in America*, 10.

42 Krauthammer, *The Point of It All*, 112.

CHAPTER 10

What Has God Said about Abortion?

What Is God's Moral Law Concerning Abortion?

Because the issue of abortion is a moral one, it requires the same God who spoke on Mount Sinai and delivered the Ten Commandments to speak with moral authority on this matter today. Without this moral direction and other commands given by God, there would be no reliable reference points for society—no checks and balances against the powers of passion and selfishness and rationalization. As a consequence, each individual might live according to his or her own carnal desires with little regard for its effect on society and his or her relationship to God.

Although not all moral wrongs are punishable under our modern legal system (for instance, fornication and adultery), the role of the true believer in God is to live not only a legal life but also a moral life. The true believer must ask, "Has God spoken on the moral issue of abortion, and if so, what has He said?" This is a critical point because once God has spoken on an issue, the debate is over. It is no longer about the pros and cons of abortion, but rather it is about our acceptance or rejection of God's will on the matter. In essence, the real issue is not whether we are pro-choice or pro-life, but whether we are pro-God.

During the Civil War, the North believed God was on their side; the South believed He was on their side. Regardless of their passion and reason, at least one side was wrong. Under such circumstances, Lincoln observed (as quoted earlier), "I know the Lord is *always* on the side of the *right*. But it is my constant anxiety and prayer that *I* and *this nation* should be on the Lord's *side*."[1] That is the crux of the matter on every issue on which God has spoken—are we on the Lord's side?

Lest there be any question, God has addressed the issue of abortion through Jewish law, the Bible, early Christian writers, the Reformers, and through modern Christian leaders. Part of the power and persuasiveness of these declarations is found in their remarkable consistency and repetition. In this manner, God has declared His side of the matter with unmistakable clarity. The issue becomes whether we will be on God's side regardless of our personal sympathies and prejudices or whether we will become a moral law unto ourselves. In other words, what will govern our lives, God's will or ours?

Jewish Law

Flavius Josephus, the first-century Jewish historian, wrote concerning Jewish law, "The law, moreover, enjoins us to bring up all our offspring, and forbids women to cause abortion of what is begotten, or to destroy it afterward; and if any woman appears to have done so, she will be a murderer of her child, by destroying a living creature, and diminishing human kind."[2] The Roman historian Tacitus (c. AD 56–120) confirmed this attitude of the devout Jews. Of their beliefs, he said, "It is a deadly sin to kill a born or unborn child."[3]

The Bible

Before citing the Bible on this subject, I note the following tragic commentary made by Charles Krauthammer:

> Every manner of political argument is ruled legitimate in our democratic discourse. But invoke the Bible as grounding for your politics, and the First Amendment police will charge you with breach-

> ing the sacred wall separating church and state. [Stephen] Carter [a Yale law professor] notes, for example, that one is allowed to have any view on abortion so long as it derives from ethical or practical or sociological or medical considerations. But should someone stand up and oppose abortion for reasons of faith, he is accused of trying to impose his religious beliefs on others. Call on Timothy Leary or Chairman Mao, fine. Call on St. Paul and all hell breaks loose.[4]

Understanding those ramifications, I nonetheless proceed. I do so, however, with the comforting assurance that 71 percent of Americans, as revealed by a 2017 Gallup poll, believe the Bible to be divinely inspired.[5]

The Bible, both Old and New Testaments, are in accord with Jewish law on this subject. The psalmist said, "Lo, children are an heritage [gift] of the Lord: and the fruit of the womb is his reward. As arrows are in the hand of a mighty man; so are children of the youth. Happy is the man that hath his quiver full of them" (Ps. 127:3–5). In other words, children are a blessing from heaven.

Furthermore, the Bible explicitly addresses the rights of an unborn child to live: "If men strive, and hurt a woman with child, so that her fruit [child] depart from her…he shall be surely punished" (Exod. 21:22; see also Ps. 139:13–19). In this scripture, the fetus is referred to as a child that has the right to be protected from the harm of others. Certainly, that would include the right to be protected from an abortion. On one occasion, the Lord told Jeremiah that "before *thou* camest forth out of the womb I sanctified *thee*, and ordained thee a prophet unto the nations" (Jer. 1:5; emphasis added). Why would God refer to the fetus as *thou* and *thee* if it were just a mass of biological tissue? Furthermore, if Jeremiah was not yet a living soul before birth, how could the Lord have ordained him a prophet?

When Elizabeth, the mother of John the Baptist, was in her sixth month of pregnancy, she was visited by Mary. Elizabeth said to her, "As soon as the voice of thy salutation sounded in mine ears, *the babe leaped in my womb for joy*" (Luke 1:44; see also verse 41). How could John, an unborn babe, leap for joy if he was not a conscious, emotional living human being?

Most abortions are attributable to intimate relations occurring outside the bonds of marriage. According to the Center for Disease Control, approximately 86 percent of women who obtained abortions in 2016 were not married.[6] This was the case in spite of the Lord's command on multiple occasions to abstain from sexual relations outside of marriage (see Matthew 5:19; Acts 15:20; 1 Corinthians 6:9; 1 Thessalonians 4:3). Many people, even Christians, do not like to hear this moral standard of the Lord because it stifles their fun or bridles their passions, but if that moral law were obeyed, the number of abortions would drastically decline. The real truth is, an individual who chooses to be immoral and thereafter becomes pregnant has already exercised her right of choice. Unfortunately, some engage in a second sin of abortion in an unsuccessful attempt to erase the consequences of the prior sin—fornication or adultery. At some point, we have to face the central issue of Christianity—is it our will or God's will? If it is God's will, then abortions, except in very limited circumstances, would be entirely eliminated.

The Bible speaks of perilous times that shall come in the last days and then enumerates some of the evils that will accompany those times: "For men [speaking of men and women] shall be lovers of their own selves…without natural affection…lovers of pleasure more than lovers of God" (1 Tim. 3:2–4). One must wonder, does this have some applicability to those who love their own selves more than they love their unborn child? Does this apply to future mothers whose natural affection for their unborn child is abandoned on the abortion table? Does this apply to those whose fornication and adultery led to abortion because they were lovers of immediate pleasure more than lovers of God?

Fortunately, where there have been mistakes and sins, even serious ones, the Savior in His mercy is able to provide complete and full forgiveness if we repent. So complete and expansive are the Lord's forgiving and cleansing powers that He is able to take our lives, even when in the depths of despair and sin, and give us "beauty for ashes" (Isa. 61:3). That is the miraculous gift of the Atonement of Jesus Christ. But the choice is ours. Will we repent or rationalize? Choose God's will or our will? Christ is our great exemplar. Just as He submitted His will to the Father's (see Luke 22:42), the true Christian is willing to submit his will to the Father and Son.

Early Christian Writers

In addition to the Bible, we are fortunate that the early Christian writers preserved the position of the primitive Christian church on abortion. They spoke clearly, unequivocally, and repeatedly on this sensitive topic. There is no ambiguity in their language, no whitewashing of the issue, no rationalization of the doctrine, but rather a remarkable unity and directness on the subject. It is surprising to me that in deciding *Roe v. Wade*, the US Supreme Court, who reviewed the history of abortion both politically and religiously, referred to none of these writers who preserved Christian doctrine on this matter. For example, *The Didache* (AD 80–140), a church manual of early Christianity, instructed, "Do not murder a child by abortion or kill a new-born infant."[7] *The Constitutions of the Holy Apostles* (c. third or fourth century) records a similar warning: "Thou shall not slay thy child by causing abortion, nor kill that which is begotten."[8]

Tertullian (c. AD 140–230) wrote to the Roman emperors and defended the Christians against the false assertion they were murderers by using the following logic: "In our case, murder being once for all forbidden, we may not destroy even the fetus in the womb, while as yet the human being derives blood from other parts of the body for its sustenance. To hinder a birth is merely a speedier man-killing; *nor does it matter whether you take away a life that is born, or destroy one that is coming to the birth. That is a man which is going to be one; you have the fruit already in its seed.*"[9]

Clement of Alexandria (c. AD 160–215) wrote of the callousness caused by abortion: "These women who in order to hide their immorality, use abortive drugs which expel the child completely dead, abort at the same time their own human feelings."[10]

Hippolytus (c. AD 170–236) taught, "Women, reputed believers, began to resort to drugs for producing sterility, and to gird themselves round, so to expel what was being conceived on account of their not wishing to have a child either by a slave or by any paltry fellow. Behold, into how great impiety that lawless one has proceeded, by inculcating adultery and murder at the same time!"[11]

Marcus Minucius Felix, a third-century Christian lawyer, was one more witness of the unified Christian view on this subject in the early Church: "There are some women among you [the Romans] who by drinking special potions extinguish the life of the future human in their very bowels, thus committing murder before they even give birth."[12]

What adds credibility to the testimony of the early Christian writers is the remarkable consistency in their stand against abortion even though many lived at different times and in different countries.

The well-respected *Encyclopedia of Early Christianity* notes of the early Christian church: "Christians viewed the fetus as God's creation. They insisted that the destruction of the fetus was murder."[13] In other words, there was no timeline when abortion was acceptable—no exception for first trimester abortions.

Historian Will Durant made this observation regarding early Christian history: "Abortion and infanticide, which were decimating pagan society, were forbidden to Christians as the equivalents of murder."[14] The position of the early Christian church on this matter, as set forth in the Bible and further confirmed and preserved by the early Christian writers, was unmistakable.

Reformers

Reformers reaffirmed this opposition to abortion. In 1540, Martin Luther proclaimed, "The beginning of children is wonderfully pleasing to [God]. How great, therefore, the wickedness of human nature is! How many girls there are who prevent conception and kill and expel tender fetuses, although procreation is the work of God!"[15] John Calvin added, "If it seems more horrible to kill a man in his own house than in a field, because a man's house is his place of most secure refuge, it ought surely to be deemed more atrocious to destroy a fetus in the womb before it has come to light."[16]

Modern Christian Leaders

C. S. Lewis, one of the most respected Christian authors of the twentieth century, explained the immorality of trying to correct one sin with another: "It [is] certainly *not* wrong to remove the natural consequences of sin provided the means by which you remove them are not in themselves another sin (E.g. it is merciful and Christian to remove the natural consequences of fornication by giving the girl a bed in a maternity ward and providing for the child's keep and education, but wrong to remove them by abortion or infanticide)."[17]

In 1994, Mother Teresa, one of the most respected of modern Christian leaders, was invited to speak at the National Prayer Breakfast in Washington, DC. Following is a portion of her remarks, for which she received a standing ovation:

> The greatest destroyer of peace today is abortion, because it is a war against the child, a direct killing of the innocent child, murder by the mother herself. And if we accept that a mother can kill even her own child, how can we tell other people not to kill one another? How do we persuade a woman not to have an abortion? As always, we must persuade her with love and we remind ourselves that love means to be willing to give until it hurts. Jesus gave even His life to love us. So, the mother who is thinking of abortion, should be helped to love, that is, to give until it hurts her plans, or her free time, to respect the life of her child. The father of that child, whoever he is, must also give until it hurts.
>
> By abortion, the mother does not learn to love, but kills even her own child to solve her prob-

> lems. And, by abortion, that father is told that he does not have to take any responsibility at all for the child he has brought into the world. *Any country that accepts abortion is not teaching its people to love, but to use any violence to get what they want. This is why the greatest destroyer of love and peace is abortion.*
>
> The beautiful gift God has given our congregation is to fight abortion by adoption. I can't tell you what joy, what love, what peace those children have brought into those families. It has been a real gift of God for them and for us. I remember one of these little ones was very sick, so I sent for the father and the mother and I asked them: "Please give me back the sick child. I will give you a healthy one." And the father looked at me and said, "Mother Teresa, take my life first than take the child." So beautiful to see it—so much love, so much joy that little one has brought into that family.

Mother Teresa concluded, "America can become a sign of peace for the world. From here, a sign of care for the weakest of the weak—the unborn child—must go out to the world. *If you become a burning light of justice and peace in the world, then really you will be true to what the founders of this country stood for, God bless you*!"[18] Her reference to the Founding Fathers is noteworthy. She understood their values were based on Judeo-Christian morals, and hence abortion would be anathema to these God-fearing men.

In October 2018, Pope Francis commented on abortion as follows: "Is it right to 'take out' a human life to solve a problem? Is it right to hire a hit man to solve a problem? You cannot, it is not right to kill a human being, regardless of how small it is, to solve a problem."[19]

The General Board of American Baptist Churches in the USA adopted the following resolution:

"As American Baptists we oppose abortion,

- as a means of avoiding responsibility for conception,
- as a primary means of birth control,
- without regard for the far-reaching consequences of the act."[20]

Following is a statement by Russell M. Nelson, president of The Church of Jesus Christ of Latter-day Saints, on the subject of abortion: "As a servant of the Lord, I dutifully warn those who advocate and practice abortion that they incur the wrath of Almighty God who declared, 'If men…hurt a woman with child, so that her fruit depart from her…he shall be surely punished' (Exod. 21:22)."[21]

There is no question that abortion has been consistently denounced by God and many religious leaders for centuries.

A Personal Story of Awakening

Abby Johnson had served as director of a clinic in Texas that provided medical services for women, including abortions. Although she had had two abortions of her own, she wanted to help women avoid unwanted pregnancies and thus reduce the number of abortions that took place. She felt she was rendering a great service to women in need.

Then one day her world turned upside down. For the first time, she was called into the exam room to assist in an ultrasound-guided abortion. She felt uncomfortable but nonetheless participated. She was startled to see on the ultrasound the baby about to be aborted—"the profile of the head, both arms, legs, and even tiny fingers and toes. Perfect." She then heard the nurse, after taking measurements, call out "thirteen weeks," announcing the fetus's age.

As the doctor moved the cannula or suction tube nearer to the baby, Abby thought, *The fetus doesn't feel pain*. I had reassured countless women of this as I'd been taught. *The fetal tissue feels nothing as it is removed. Get a grip, Abby. This is a simple, quick medical procedure.*

To her surprise and horror, she then noted, "As the cannula pressed in, the baby began struggling to turn and twist away. It seemed clear to me that the fetus could feel the cannula and did not like the feeling."

As the suction tube approached closer to the baby, she was shocked to hear the doctor say lightheartedly to the nurse, "Beam me up, Scotty"—meaning, turn on the suction to extract the fetus. Then the truth hit Abby like a massive missile to the heart. She noted in horror, "I could see the tiny body violently twisting" in response to the invasion of the suction tube. "For the briefest moment it looked as if the baby were being wrung like a dishcloth, twisted and squeezed. The little body crumpled and began disappearing into the cannula before my eyes. The last thing I saw was the perfectly formed backbone sucking into the tube... The image of the tiny body, mangled and sucked away, was replaying in my mind."

Then the moment of truth came. *That was a human baby—fighting for life!... What I have told people for years, what I've believed and taught and defended is a lie... I had believed a lie.* She then said that she "had blindly promoted the 'company line'" that this was not a baby but rather a mass of cells that felt no pain whatsoever. "I felt so guilty."

Abby then sadly noted that the road she had been walking was "paved with regret, pain, brokenness, shame, and even blood on my hands."

As Abby reflected upon one of her own abortions she wrote: "I hear the faulty thinking that plagues every woman considering an abortion—thinking expressed in the phrase *if I have this child*. If I have this child? Why wasn't it obvious to me that I already had a child, who was growing inside of me? Once you are pregnant there is no if. That child, though tiny and in an early stage of development, already exists! But I didn't see that."

In reflection Abby honestly confessed, "*I didn't search God's Word for His will* or seek counsel from other believers. As with so many other troubling thoughts, I let it pass out of my conscious awareness.

I was leading an unexamined life, filled with inconsistences." When she did search God's will and let her conscience prevail, she transformed from pro-choice to pro-life.

As Abby's new vision unfolded, she reflected upon the perspective of the pro-life group that had been so comforting and helpful to her, namely "that their vision to truly care for a woman went far beyond her immediate circumstances. They cared about each woman as a whole person—*an eternal person*—in the context of her family, her spiritual needs, her long-range physical and emotional health. They offered solutions that would enhance a woman's life over the long term."

While seeking the comfort and counsel of some friends at the pro-life center who had always been kind to her in spite of their differences of opinion, she said, "A dam deep inside of me had broken, and a torrent of guilt, grief, pain, remorse, shame, secrets, and fear was bursting out of me with every sob. It was a horrible, wonderful, frightening, cleansing gush of raw emotion."

In short, Abby was repenting. She was experiencing the miraculous gift of the Savior's Atonement—His cleansing, purifying, and healing powers soothing another human soul who had sinned but wanted to be right with God. And in His mercy, He would make it possible. No wonder she exclaimed, "I felt the presence of God—felt the connection I'd been longing for over the past few years. I knew I was in the presence of the Almighty God, and once again tears flowed—more deep, cleansing tears. But they were not tears of grief and remorse this time. They were tears of relief, of awe, tears of relief that are available to all who seek God's mercy."[22]

The Need for Moral Law

I understand that there are those who do not believe in God, but for those who do, particularly the Judeo-Christian God, His position on abortion is crystal clear. God has spoken repeatedly and powerfully on the subject. There can be no misunderstanding of His position on this moral issue.

Ben Carson summarized the moral dilemma as follows: "From the Creation story to the Ten Commandments to the Gospels to the

Epistles, the Bible provided an explanation for the meaning of life and instructed us in moral principles. We held to a Judeo-Christian standard while respecting the beliefs of those who didn't share them, and that standard saved us from confusion. Today, fewer people believe in the Bible, or even in absolute truth, and our rejection of an objective moral standard has thrown our society into disarray. If in fact we do really believe in God and His word, many of the moral 'gray' issues of today become black and white."[23] And so it is with abortion.

Some may mistake my directness on this subject with lack of compassion, but that it is not my intent. In truth, I believe that the greatest love I can offer to others is to teach God's will in a clear and undiluted fashion, without ever diminishing my love for the individual. I recall the words of a friend who used to say, "Sometimes we are so worried about offending people, that we never ever save them."

Is *Roe v. Wade* Irreversible?

In light of God's unequivocal stance on abortion, some might ask whether *Roe v. Wade* is reversible, or is it cast in stone as some believe? Fortunately, we have some historical precedent that gives us hope for its reversal. *The Dred Scott* case of 1857—decided by a 7–2 majority in the US Supreme Court (the same majority as in *Roe v. Wade*)—decided that a black slave, even if freed, could not be an American citizen and therefore could not have standing to sue in a federal court. Fortunately, the conscience of the American people became more aligned with God's will, namely that we are all children of God (see Romans 8:16–18), and in 1868, that decision was legally nullified by the adoption of the Fourteenth Amendment to the Constitution.

In 1896, the US Supreme Court in *Plessy v. Ferguson*, upheld in a 7–1 decision the constitutionality of racial segregation for public facilities as long as they were equal, but this time it took over fifty years before the US Supreme Court, in *Brown v. Board of Education* (1954), overruled and reversed *Plessy v. Ferguson* in a 9–0 decision. It took that many years for the justices to realize that the Constitution had been interpreted incorrectly.

Hopefully, the conscience of the American people will continue to align with God's will, and *Roe v. Wade* will be either overturned by Constitutional Amendment or reversed by the Supreme Court, based on the correct judicial interpretation of the Constitution. This reversal might declare an unborn child to be a person and thus protected under the Fourteenth Amendment or conclude that the Court does not have the power to make any law, let alone laws on abortion, and thus leave to each individual state the power to legislate the legality of abortion.[24] If the latter occurs, then some states may rule in favor of abortion and others against it, but at least the will of the people, not the majority of nine jurists, will decide this moral issue, consistent with the letter and spirit of the Constitution.

Summary of Moral Considerations

If one does not believe in God, then his or her argument may focus on when human life or viability begins, because hopefully, all people would admit that the life of a human being should be protected. Some may acknowledge that life begins at conception but argue that life alone is not enough to grant a fetus protection. Plants have life and animals have life, but neither constitute human life, and thus they are not designated as persons protected by the Constitution. Accordingly, some may argue that a fetus does not constitute human life (even though it naturally develops into a full human life) until the first heartbeat, until the first evidence of brain activity, until it possesses "a functioning rational activity,"[25] until the fetus can survive outside the mother's womb (albeit with external support), until the spirit first enters the body, or until some other moment of reasoned determination. But who is to say which of these arguments is correct? For the nonbeliever, there is no definitive answer. That is why it is essential to have God's input on the matter, which input outweighs and supersedes man's reasoning, however logical, compelling, or persuasive it may seem. Why? Because He is omniscient, omnipotent, and perfect, and thus has the absolute final say on all moral matters.

God has made His position clear on abortion as collectively found in early Jewish sources, the Bible, early Christian writers,

Reformers, and many modern-day Christian leaders. His message has not changed. Abortion is an egregious sin. God has decreed it, and history will confirm it.

Consistent with God's law, there are some who have justifiably undergone abortions for valid health reasons or in cases of rape or incest. No doubt, however, there are many other people (religious and non-religious) who have undergone abortions for other reasons—some who were pressured, some who were confused or embarrassed, and some who knowingly but willingly proceeded, believing that personal convenience trumped the life of another. Particularly in these latter cases, abortion needs to be called for what it is—a pernicious evil. No amount of rationalization can justify it. It results in guilt, remorse, and the loss of life of the most innocent of all—an unborn baby. It is a scourge on our society that produces a more hardened, calloused people. It is contrary to the most fundamental of Judeo-Christian principles that serve as the basis for the laws of our nation, and it strikes at the moral conscience of everyone receptive to light, believer or not. Why?

Because it is in direct opposition to God's moral law.

After fully considering all aspects of abortion, President Reagan gave this inspired and visionary counsel: "I have often said we need to join in prayer to bring protection to the unborn. Prayer and action are needed to uphold the sanctity of human life. I believe it will not be possible to accomplish our work, the work of saving lives, 'without being a soul of prayer.'"[26]

What does this all mean? It means that even though God has spoken clearly against abortion, the moral principles underlying a pro-life viewpoint are being sacrificed by many on the altars of secularism and radical individualism. It means that some may need to choose between God's will and his or her own will, however difficult that may be. That is the real and ultimate pro-choice issue. Will we choose God's laws of morality or the moral relativism of the world?

Everyone has a conscience or moral compass to help them choose God's way.

Thomas Jefferson gave this counsel to his daughter Patsy: "If ever you are about to say any thing amiss or to do any thing wrong, consider before hand. You will feel something within you which will tell you it is wrong and ought not to be said or done: this is your conscience, and be sure to obey it. Our maker has given us all, this faithful internal Monitor, and if you always obey it, you will always be prepared for…death."[27] What inspired counsel from one of our imperfect but noble Founding Fathers.[28]

Just before Alexander Hamilton was killed in his duel with Aaron Burr, he wrote his wife, Eliza, the following poignant lines: "I charge you to remember that you are a Christian. God's Will be done! The will of a merciful God must be good."[29]

This is a test of our discipleship. Will it be God's way or the world's way? Adherence to personal convenience and secular ideology or adherence to moral conscience as enlightened by God? God Himself has promised, "Blessed is the nation whose God is the Lord" (Ps. 33:12). Hopefully our nation will make God its Lord by following His moral laws. If we do so, God has further promised, "If my people, who are called by my name, shall humble themselves, and pray, and seek my face, and turn from their wicked ways; then will I hear from heaven, and will forgive their sin, and will heal their land" (2 Chron. 7:14). And what a healing we need. Hopefully, we will be pro-life in saving the unborn and pro-choice in choosing God's will.

---

1 In Carpenter, *Six Months at the White House*, 282; emphasis in original.

2 Josephus, *Against Apion*, 2:25.

3 In Smith, *Into the World of the New Testament*, 129.

4 Krauthammer, *The Point of It All*, 187.

5 Saad, "Record Few Americans Believe Bible is Literal Word of God," news.gallup.com.

6 Centers for Disease Control, "Abortion Surveillance—United States, 2016," cdc.gov.

7 *The Apostolic Fathers*, 148.

8 *The Ante-Nicene Fathers*, 7:466.

9 In *The Ante-Nicene Fathers*, 3:25; emphasis added.

10 In "The Fathers on Abortion," Aug. 8. 2005, catholicism.org.

11 In *The Ante-Nicene Fathers*, 5:131.

12 In Bercot, *Will the Real Heretics Please Stand Up*, 27.

[13] *Encyclopedia of Early Christianity*, "Abortion," 7. The Encyclopedia further noted, "Augustine differed as to when life began, but he found intentional abortion of the formed fetus to be murder. John Chrysostom also viewed deliberate abortion as murder."

[14] Durant, *The Story of Civilization*, 3:598.

[15] Luther, *Luther's Works*, 4:304.

[16] Calvin, *Commentaries on the Four Last Books of Moses*, 3:42.

[17] Lewis, *The Collected Letter of C. S. Lewis*, 3:91.

[18] Mother Teresa: "An Address at the National Prayer Breakfast," catholic.org; emphasis added.

[19] In Pullella, "Pope Compares Having an Abortion to 'Hiring a Hit Man,'" reuters.com.

[20] "American Baptist Resolution Concerning Abortion and Ministry in the Local Church," religiousinstitute.org.

[21] Nelson, "Reverence for Life," 13.

[22] Johnson, *Unplanned*, 1-8, 19, 45, 64, 147, 156, and 185.

[23] Carson, *One Nation*, 192–93.

[24] President Ronald Reagan observed, "*Roe v. Wade* has become a continuing prod to the conscience of the nation" (*Abortion and the Conscience of the Nation*, 39).

[25] Bissell, "A Calm Look at Abortion Arguments," reason.com.

[26] Reagan, *Abortion and the Conscience of the Nation*, 61–62.

[27] Jefferson, "From Thomas Jefferson to Martha Jefferson," founders.archives.gov.

[28] Some criticize Jefferson because he had slaves. Slavery is wrong, but Jefferson's involvement in slavery does not discount the incredible good he did in helping establish the underlying principles of this nation. Such criticism is a form of presentism in which one imposes his or her current cultural values on past ages. While easy to do, it tends to distort the historical context in which such events occurred. Perhaps Jefferson didn't live up to every ideal he espoused, but that does not lessen the worth or truth of such ideals.

[29] Hamilton, "From Alexander Hamilton to Elizabeth Hamilton," founders.archives.gov.

CHAPTER 11

Has God Spoken about Same-Sex Relations and Marriage?

Introduction

If a moral people is an ongoing condition to the viability of the Constitution and its enumerated liberties as proclaimed by the Founding Fathers, then one must ask, "Has God spoken on the issue of same-sex expression and marriage? And if so, what has He said?" And if we are to be a moral people, what should be our stand on this issue, popular or unpopular as it may be?

I have friends and family whom I deeply love who have experienced same-sex attraction and, in some instances, same-sex relationships. I have only one desire for them and others in similar circumstances—what is best for them as ordained by God, what is best for society, and what I can do to further those objectives.

Unfortunately, same-sex relations and marriage is a sensitive topic about which many will not tolerate any debate. Some, on both sides of the issue, are so emotionally charged that they attack those with opposing views with derisive terms or labels. As a consequence, many conversations about same-sex relations have regrettably lacked reason, honest discussion, and simple respect for one another.

Hopefully, these types of encounters can be replaced with respectful dialogue and decent human kindness, and ultimately a desire to know and live God's will.

What We Know and Don't Know

Perhaps a good starting point is to have an accurate understanding of both sides of the issue. Following are some significant points that I believe we need to acknowledge as known facts, along with questions which need to be asked and, where possible, answered. I have tried to express the following fairly, but if I have erred, it has not been done intentionally or maliciously:

Our fundamental identity is as a child of God.

People with same-sex attraction believe their identity is more than just a sexual preference for those of the same sex. One such person described same-sex attraction as "a way of being, an existence, an identity, a way of relating to the world and expressing one's existence."[1] Keeping that in mind, we must never forget, however, that our fundamental identity is as a child of God, and whether we have same-sex attraction or heterosexual attraction, or any other notable characteristics, these are but subcomponents of our true and complete identity as a child of God.

And because each of us is a child of God, He loves us immensely regardless of our sexual attractions. As a consequence, He expects that each of us will love our brothers and sisters in a similar way.

We do not know with certainty what causes same-gender feelings.

Many people feel that their same-sex attraction is rooted in biological causes. As a result, they believe they were born this way and, consequently, experienced same-sex feelings at an early age. Others believe that everyone is born heterosexual and that same-sex attraction is somehow voluntarily (or involuntarily) nurtured or developed as a result of one's environment and life experiences. Those who hold this latter belief often point to the fact that with rare exceptions, we are each born with male or female organs that were divinely designed to be used with someone of the opposite sex so that we can become "one flesh" (Mark 10:8). Likewise, they point out that with rare exception, every cell in our bodies designates us as either male or female. To this latter assertion, some counter that our genes may determine our sex, but they do not necessarily determine our gender identity. I don't think anyone honestly knows why someone experiences same-sex attractions. Numerous theories have been offered, such as DNA composition, hormonal exposure during pregnancy, environmental effects, and the like, but none have been proven with certainty.[2]

There are differences of opinion as to whether or not same-sex attractions can be transformed to heterosexual attractions.

There is a difference of opinion about whether or not someone can change homosexual attractions to heterosexual feelings through prayer, fasting, and therapy, or whether someone can retain some same-sex preferences while also developing some heterosexual tendencies. It seems that most people who experience same-sex attraction feel that a complete or substantial transformation is unlikely if not impossible. In connection with this, many believe that reported cases of such transformation are temporary in nature or testimonials triggered by social or religious pressure. On the other hand, there are documented cases of people who, with God's help, have experienced diminished same-sex attraction for sustained periods and are either living happy single lives or have developed sufficient heterosexual feelings to have successful marriages with a partner of the opposite sex (some examples are discussed in the next chapter).

Being born with a certain condition does not automatically make it good.

Many people with same-sex attraction believe that God would not give them or allow them to have these feelings without the opportunity to express them within a same-sex relationship, including same-sex marriage. In other words, they believe these feelings come from God and therefore must be good. But being born with a certain condition does not necessarily make it good. If so, we would all be perfect at birth. To the contrary, we are all imperfect. We all have dispositions and characteristics of some type, such as pride or impatience or anger, that we must strive to master or overcome during our mortal life or in the life hereafter. This is part of what the scriptures call the natural or carnal man (see Romans 7:14; 1 Corinthians 3:3; 1 Corinthians 15:44). Accordingly, we might acknowledge that certain conditions in and of themselves are not good, but what we can learn from them might be very good.

How does God view same-sex relations?

Perhaps the most burning question of all is, "How does God view same-sex relations." The real issue is not what a man thinks or even what a church's stand is but what is God's stand on the issue. And once we know that answer, are we willing to follow it?

Biblical References about Sexual Relations Between People of the Same Sex

First and most importantly, God has expressed His love on multiple occasions for all His children—regardless of race, religion, sexual orientation, gender, or the like. In truth, "God is no respecter of persons" (Acts 10:34). Accordingly, He expects us to follow His example and likewise be no respecter of persons. Christ declared, "This is my commandment, that ye love one another, as I have loved you" (John 15:12).

Because God loves us, He has given us certain moral laws that, when obeyed, bring us consummate joy in this life and in the life to come. These laws include the command for males and females to marry and to refrain from any sexual relationships, heterosexual or homosexual, that are outside this approved marriage relationship. When individuals, as well-meaning as they may be, advocate for and engage in same-sex relationships, they set themselves up as higher tribunals than God as to what is right and wrong, and in the process, lose the right to a fulness of joy. It should be clarified and emphasized, however, that there is no sin in having same-sex attraction, only in exercising it.

There is no question that the Lord has repeatedly condemned same-sex relations. One of the reasons Sodom and Gomorrah were destroyed by fire was because homosexuality was so prevalent among its citizens (see Genesis 19:5–9; Jude 1:7). Additionally, in the Old Testament, the law of Moses prescribed, "If a man also lie with mankind, as he lieth with a woman, both of them have committed an abomination" (Lev. 20:13).[3]

New Testament church leaders continued to teach against sexual relations between those of the same sex. Paul wrote of "vile affections: for even their women did change the natural use into that which is against nature: and likewise also the men, leaving the natural use of the woman, burned in their lust one toward another; men with men working that which is unseemly" (Rom. 1:26–27).

Paul warned the people of Corinth that those guilty of certain sins would not inherit the kingdom of God: "Neither the sexually immoral, nor idolatrous nor adulterers nor men who have sex with men" (1 Cor 6:9 NIV). In a letter to Timothy, Paul also spoke against those who "defile themselves with mankind" (1 Tim. 1:10), or as the New International Version says, "for those practicing homosexuality." The injunction was clear and repeated—same-sex relations are a sin in God's eyes.

Some have contended that the sexual acts referred to above were done in the context of deviant worship to idols. As a consequence, they have attempted to rationalize away those scriptures, suggesting they refer specifically to men who lusted after other men as part of idol worship, not men who loved other men. Such an interpretation, however, is simply not justified in the scriptures. For example, the context of 1 Timothy 1:10 cited above has nothing to do with idol worship. In addition, there are no scriptures of which I am aware expressly supporting same-sex relations or same-sex marriage under any conditions.

Some have claimed that Christ did not command against same-sex relations but only that the Law of Moses and Paul the apostle established such prohibitions. The Savior, however, commanded that marriage was to be between a man and woman (see Mark 10:6–8), not those of the same sex. Furthermore, such an argument is disingenuous since the Law of Moses was given by God, and in addition, the apostles were commanded to teach "whatsoever I [Christ] have commanded you" (Matt. 28:20). In fact, Paul specifically referred to God as condemning the act of men who lusted "one toward another" (see Rom. 1:26–27). Likewise, Paul testified, "My preaching was not with enticing words of man's wisdom, but in demonstration of the Spirit and the power" (1 Cor. 2:4).

Recognizing the clarity and frequency of these scriptures, some seeking justification for their position have suggested that "times have changed" since the Bible was written and that current social conditions warrant same-sex relations and same-sex marriage. But who has the right to change God's laws? A politician, a judge, a philosopher, an academician, a social activist? If none of these, then what evidence do we have that God has changed this law in modern times? None.

Absolutely none.

No wonder Ben Carson noted, "As a Bible-believing Christian… I believe God loves homosexuals as much as he loves everyone, but if we can redefine marriage as between two men or two women or any other way based on social pressures as opposed to between a man and a woman, we will continue to redefine it in any way that we wish, which is a slippery slope with a disastrous ending, as witnessed in the dramatic fall of the Roman Empire. I don't believe this to be a political view, but rather a logical and reasoned view with long-term benefits to family structure and the propagation of humankind. God obviously knew what he was doing when he ordained the traditional family, and we should not denigrate it in order to uplift some alternative."[4]

German theologian Wolfhart Pannenberg, former professor of theology at the University of Munich, ably summarized this point as follows: "If a church were to let itself be pushed to the point where it ceased to treat homosexual activity as a departure from the biblical norm, and recognized homosexual unions as a personal partnership of love equivalent to marriage, such a church would no longer stand on biblical ground but against the unequivocal witness of Scripture."[5] In essence, it would transform its worship from a God of absolute morals to a God of moral relativism.

Early Christian Writers

The early Christian church continued for some time to teach a prohibition against same-sex relations. Polycarp, a second-century bishop, wrote, "Refrain from lusts in the world, for every *lust warreth against the Spirit, and neither whoremongers nor effeminate persons nor defilers of themselves with men shall inherit the kingdom of God*."[6] Tertullian (c. AD 140–230), a Christian convert evidently educated in Rome, admonished, "The Christian [man] confines himself to the female sex."[7]

Cyprian (c. AD 200–258), a bishop in Carthage, spoke disapprovingly of those souls who have a "madness of vice…men with frenzied lusts rushing upon men."[8] Aristides the Athenian (c. AD 125), who wrote a defense of Christianity, spoke of those who "practiced foul things in sleeping with males."[9] Athenagoras (c. AD 70–132), an Athenian philosopher who converted to Christianity, condemned those "who do not abstain even from males, males with males committing shocking abominations, outraging all the noblest and comeliest bodies in all sorts of ways, so dishonouring the fair workmanship of God."[10] And Origen (c. AD 185–255), the most prolific of the early Christian writers, noted, "Those who call themselves wise have despised these virtues [purity and integrity], and have wallowed in the filth of sodomy, in lawless lust, 'men with men working that which is unseemly'" (1 Rom. 1:27).[11]

Any sexual relationship between man and man, or woman and woman, was considered unnatural and condemned by the early Christian leaders. This was not new doctrine being taught by these early Christian leaders but a preservation of the original doctrine taught in the Old and New Testaments.

The world-renowned historian Will Durant observed that among the early Christian leaders, "homosexual practices were condemned with an earnestness rare in antiquity."[12] The *Encyclopedia of Early Christianity* came to the same conclusion: "The church fathers universally condemned male homosexual behavior. They clearly regarded it as contrary to the created constitution and function of men and women. *All the evidence indicates that the teaching mind of the early church unreservedly condemned homosexual activity.*"[13] Note the wording—not some of the evidence or the majority of the evidence or even the preponderance of the evidence, but rather "All the evidence…unreservedly condemned homosexual activity."

So errant were same-sex relations that the early Church leaders "deemed it an index of the moral disorder of humanity."[14] There was no exception for men who claimed to love other men, or women who claimed to love other women, in spite of some assertions to the contrary.

No amount of rationalization or submission to political correctness or claims of tolerance can change God's decree as taught by the Bible and early Christian leaders. This doesn't mean that such a person is bad or unloved by God. In fact, we all sin in different ways. Perhaps the real test of our discipleship is not to rationalize our conduct but to square up to it and to do all within our power to overcome our wrongful behavior. In this spirit, the Savior said to the woman caught in adultery, "Go, and sin no more" (John 8:11).

Statements by Modern Christian Leaders

C. S. Lewis gave the following insights on this topic:

> The homosexual has to accept sexual abstinence just as the poor man has to forgo otherwise lawful pleasures because he would be unjust to his wife and children if he took them. That is merely a negative condition.
>
> What should the positive life of the homosexual be? Perhaps any homosexual who humbly accepts his cross and puts himself under Divine guidance will…be shown the way. I am sure that any attempt to evade it (e.g., by mock-or quasi-marriage with a member of one's own sex even if this does not lead to any carnal act) is the wrong way.[15]

The Church of Jesus Christ of Latter-day Saints believes that "the experience of same-sex attraction is a complex reality for many people. The attraction itself is not a sin, but acting on it is. Even though individuals do not choose to have such attractions, they do choose how to respond to them. With love and understanding, the Church reaches out to all God's children, including [those with same-sex attraction]."[16]

There are some Christian faiths that embrace and endorse same-sex marriage despite the numerous denunciations in the Bible and writings of the early Christian leaders. Some Christian leaders have adopted the attitude that it is somehow uncharitable, un-Christ-like not to condone homosexuality. In essence, such proponents have become revisionist theologians in that they have ignored the primary sources—the Old Testament, the New Testament, and the early Christian writers—and in the process have attempted to supersede God's moral law with the world's. In so doing, they become divided between two masters—the world on same-sex matters and God on other moral issues. But God has spoken directly on this dilemma and the eventual outcome: "No man can serve two masters: for either he will hate the one, and love the other; or else he will hold to the one, and despise the other. Ye cannot serve God and mammon" (Matt. 6:24).

I can understand how someone might endorse same-sex relations if he or she does not believe in God. Certainly, there are feelings of compassion and tolerance that might lead one in that direction. But if someone believes in God, particularly the Judeo-Christian God and His scriptural Word, then it would be hard to honestly deny that He has spoken against same-sex relations, clearly and repeatedly.

Chief Justice Warren Burger, ruling on the constitutionality of a state law outlawing sodomy, wrote that "to hold that the act of homosexual sodomy is somehow protected as a fundamental right would be to cast aside millennia of moral teaching."[17] Suffice it to say, there have been millennia of moral teachings on the subject of sexual relations between those of the same sex, and God's stance on this issue has never changed.

Traditional Marriage

When one realizes that same-sex relations are contrary to God's moral law, then it should not be difficult to understand why many in the Judeo-Christian community are opposed to same-sex marriage, since it is intended to place a label of moral acceptance on an immoral relationship. In essence, the legalization of same-sex marriage is intended to superimpose God's moral law with a legally acceptable veneer.

In the Old Testament, we read, "Therefore shall a man leave his father and mother, and shall cleave unto his wife: and they shall be one flesh" (Gen. 2:24). So there would be no misunderstanding about God's sanction of traditional marriage, He repeated the command in the New Testament (see Mark 10:6–10).

Traditional marriage is the only marriage relationship that is sanctioned by God. If we keep God's word and are married in His way, then husbands and wives have the opportunity to receive God's blessing and thus maximize and perfect their love for each other. This does not mean that two men and two women cannot love each other, but that love cannot be fully blessed by God in a sexual relationship.

Men and women are equal in God's sight, but they are not identical. They are counterparts that complement and supplement each other, that make for a more perfect whole. We see counterparts in nature that likewise make for a more perfect whole. For example, the sun and moon. But what if there were no moon and instead two suns? One for the day and one for the night. The implications would be devastating—burned crops and an overheated earth. Or what if there was no sun but instead two moons? One for the day and one for the night. There would be no sunlight for crops or trees or plants to grow. Food would disappear or be drastically reduced, and famine would be rampant. Fortunately, these counterparts—the sun and moon—work in perfect harmony to provide a livable, sustainable, and enjoyable universe.

Likewise, males and females are necessary counterparts in God's plan. Each is necessary to multiply and replenish the earth (see Genesis 2:28). Two women or two men cannot fulfill that divine command. When joined together in marriage, men and women constitute the ideal foundation for the family setting. Women generally have a God-given nurturing skill. This is consistent with the law of nature that only women can be pregnant and bear children. On the other hand, men generally have a protective and providing nature.

This partnership of a woman as wife and mother and a man as husband and father is the best combination to raise children in a stable and righteous environment. It is not just a question of love (as important as love is); it is also a matter of divine endowments, which God has uniquely given to men and women to perfect and complement each other in the marriage relationship.

Marriage is among the most sacred and holy of human relationships. It has been defined by God as a covenant relationship between a man, a woman, and God (see Genesis 2:24–25; Ephesians 5:31–33). It has been the moral law for centuries, even millennia. It is intended to maximize the physical, emotional, and spiritual bonding between a man and woman in a holy communion. Any other marriage relationship falls short of receiving God's endorsement and thus His fullest blessings.[18]

The Consequences of Legalizing Same-Sex Marriage

The consequences of legalizing same-sex marriage, as was done by the US Supreme Court in *Obergefell v. Hodges*, are monumental. To begin with, it endorses and promotes immorality as acceptable behavior in our society. Second, it demeans the sacred ordinance of marriage as defined by God, by granting a counterfeit marriage the same legal protection and sanction. Third, it runs counter to one of the main purposes of marriage—to have children in the natural way provided by God to the extent possible. Fourth, it dispenses with the ideal environment—raising a child in a home with a mother and father who have been endowed by God with different but mutually compatible gifts to maximize the chances of successful parenting. And fifth, it opens the door to a variety of lawsuits and hostility between those with different opinions. Of course, there are some exceptions to the foregoing, but they are just that, exceptions.

The Choice Comes Down to Obedience or Disobedience

I can understand one's argument for same-sex expression: "Just as you have feelings for someone of the opposite sex, I have feelings for someone of the same sex. Therefore, let us each express our feelings in the way that is natural and rewarding to us." That has a compelling logic to it and invokes a natural compassion for those with such feelings. But logic and compassion are not the end of the story.

They are trumped by a higher source of truth.

God has spoken clearly, forcefully, and repeatedly against same-sex relations, including same-sex marriage. As hard as one might contend for same-sex relations, there is no compelling argument that can override God's command. And so, the choice comes down to one of two alternatives: obey or disobey God's moral law. The prophet Joshua put the choice as clearly and succinctly as it can be stated: "Choose you this day whom ye will serve; but as for me and my house, we will serve the Lord." Fortunately, the people responded, "God forbid that we should forsake the Lord, to serve other gods" (Josh. 24:15–16). The god of secularism condones same-sex marriage; the God of heaven condemns it.

I think there is a human tendency to readily believe in God as to those things that agree with our personal philosophy but to minimize or rationalize those divine directives that seem inconsistent with our personal prejudices. In other words, it is much easier to believe in a God of convenience and concurrence than a God of inconvenience and incongruity. Perhaps there is no greater example of this quandary than the choice that must be made concerning same-sex expression. For many, God's decree against such behavior may run counter to one's genuine sympathy for those who experience same-sex attraction or run contrary to one's notion of fairness, but at some point, there will always be a disconnect between our powers of reason and God's will. It may come with the unexpected loss of a loved one, or financial distress, or failing health, or betrayal by a spouse, or lack of understanding of God's doctrine on a particular subject, but such moments will invariably come. Then comes the acid test—are we committed to God's will even though we don't fully understand the rationale behind it, or do we abandon God and put our trust in man? Some may consider the former state of mind to be naïve, but for the believer, it is an act of faith. The position we take on same-sex expression is one of those pivotal moments in life when we must choose between faith in God or faith in man—trust in God or trust in the world.

Faith may be minimized by some, even discounted by others, but for many, it is an incredible source of power. It is what gave Job the strength to suffer and endure without ever abandoning God. It is what gave Abraham the courage to lift the dagger and be willing to plunge it downward to spill the lifeblood of his beloved son. It is what motivated Shadrach, Meshach, and Abednego to enter the fiery furnace without hesitation, and enabled Daniel to enter the lions' den without fear. It is what drove Moses to the edge of the Red Sea with the Egyptian army in hot pursuit, unwilling to wave the white flag, knowing that somehow, beyond his powers of reason, God would deliver His covenant people. It is what gave the widow of Zarephath the confidence to give her last portion of meal and oil to a prophet of God. In each case, reason was lacking, but faith was flourishing. For those requiring an underlying reason for every command of God, faith will be an unreachable quest. Sometimes God requires us to obey His commands without the intellectual comfort of knowing why. That is when our faith is exposed for what it really is.

God put faith in its proper priority when He invited us to live in the world but not be of the world. In fact, the apostle Paul taught, "The wisdom of this world is foolishness with God" (1 Cor. 3:19). On the other hand, faith in God is a manifestation of the highest form of intelligence. It is putting aside our pride (a deterrent to learning) and submitting our heart and intellect to that one being who knows all. As a consequence, faith both expedites and maximizes our search for truth.

God's laws require us to be different, to stand out and be apart from the world even though it may be unpopular or uncomfortable. That is part of the price of being a Christian. The Savior said, "My kingdom is not of this world" (John 18:36).

Ultimately, we must choose which kingdom we will live in, which will govern our life—the reasoning of the world or the will of

God. Both have their paydays—one in the fleeting currency of the world and the other in eternal blessings experienced both on earth and in heaven. The apostle John spoke to this point: "And the world passeth away, and the lust thereof: but he that doeth the will of God abideth for ever" (1 John 2:17).

A Christian leader made this significant observation: "The submission of one's will is really the only uniquely personal thing we have to place on God's altar. The many other things we give to God, however nice that may be of us, are actually things He has already given us, and He has loaned them to us. But when we begin to submit ourselves by letting our wills be swallowed up in God's will, then we are really giving something to Him. And that hard doctrine lies at the center of discipleship."[19] And so it does. In other words, are we willing to submit our will to God's, even when it runs contrary to our personal desires and passions? If so, then we are disciples of Christ, not only in name but in deed.

Some engage in immorality such as fornication, adultery, and same-sex relations with no attempt to justify themselves. They know that what they are doing is morally wrong, but personal weaknesses and passions have temporarily won the day. Others attempt to justify their actions: "We are two consenting adults who love each other. Therefore, why should we not engage in conduct that is pleasurable to us?" There is a simple answer to this question, as difficult as it may be to accept. It is that God has consistently commanded against fornication, adultery, and homosexual conduct. In the end, however difficult the decision may be, a person with same-sex attraction must choose whether to obey or disobey God's command, just as a single heterosexual must. God gave the measuring rod to determine our love for Him: "If ye love me, keep my commandments" (John 14:15).

Does this obedience to God mean that one must grit one's teeth and gut out a mortal life without physical enjoyment compatible with one's sexual attraction, or is there divine help available so one can experience peace and joy even while not acting on these feelings? The following chapter is an attempt to address that question.

---

[1] Christofferson, *That We May Be One*, xix.

[2] A *Wall Street Journal* article summarized a recent study of more than 470,000 people concerning factors that affect sexual orientation as follows: "When the researchers pooled all of the identified markers to create a score for an individual person, the genetic variation explained less than 1%, making it practically impossible to predict a person's sexual orientation or behavior based on his or her genome" (Abbott, "Genetics Tied to Same-Sex Behavior," A3).

[3] "Hellenistic Jewish writers denounced homosexuality as frequently as any sin," *Encyclopedia of Early Christianity*, 542.

[4] Carson, *America the Beautiful*, 182.

[5] Pannenberg, "Revelation and Homosexual Experience," 37.

[6] In *The Apostolic Fathers*, 179; emphasis in original.

[7] In *The Ante-Nicene Fathers*, 3:51.

[8] In *The Ante-Nicene Fathers*, 5:278.

[9] Aristides, *The Apology of Aristides*, 51.

[10] *The Ante-Nicene Fathers*, 2:147.

[11] *The Ante-Nicene Fathers*, 4:631.

[12] Durant, *Caesar and Christ*, 598.

[13] *Encyclopedia of Early Christianity*, 542–543; emphasis added.

[14] *Encyclopedia of Early Christianity*, 543.

[15] Lewis, *The Collected Letters of C. S. Lewis*, 3:472; spelling standardized; emphasis in original.

[16] Ballard, "The Lord Needs You Now!" 29.

[17] *Bowers v. Hardwick*, 478, US 186, 197 (1986).

[18] Sir William Blackstone, a contemporary of the Founding Fathers and noted jurist and commentator on the laws of England, wrote, "Man, considered as a creature, must necessarily be subject to the laws of his creator. This will of his Maker…is of course superior in obligation to any other. It is binding over all the globe in all countries, and at all times: no human laws are of any validity, if contrary to this" (*Commentaries on the Laws of England*, 1:39, 41).

[19] Maxwell, "Sharing Insights from My Life," speeches.byu.edu.

CHAPTER 12

Is There Divine Love and Help for Those with Same-Sex Feelings?

Can Someone's Sexual Orientation Ever Change?

Some have asserted that it is impossible for one's sexual attraction to permanently change. In other words, that it is an irreversible part of one's eternal identity. An angel of God addressed this type of assertion: "For with God nothing shall be impossible" (Luke 1:37). On another occasion, the Savior said, "Verily I say unto you, if ye have faith as a grain of mustard seed...nothing shall be impossible unto you" (Matt. 17:20). And the apostle Paul taught, "I can do all things through Christ which strengtheneth me" (Phil. 4:13). What mortal has the right to make an exception to these divine declarations and thus attempt to limit God's power? Admittedly, a change in sexual orientation may not occur fully, or even partially, in mortality, but God is not limited to mortality. He has eternity to work with our natures. Both in this life and the next, He can help us fulfill His command to "be ye therefore perfect, even as your Father which is in heaven is perfect" (Matt. 5:48).

For years, people claimed it was physically impossible to run a sub four-minute mile. They believed the human body was not built for such speed and endurance.[1] Today, world-class runners break that mark routinely. In fact, well over a thousand different runners have broken the four-minute mile that was once deemed an impossible feat.[2]

Lee DeForest, inventor of the vacuum tube, declared in 1957 that a "man-made moon voyage will never occur regardless of all future scientific advances."[3] The impossible happened twelve years later. Suffice it to say, I am wary when people claim something is impossible, particularly in light of God's statements in direct contradiction of such claim.

Some have contended that their sexual attraction can never change because it is part of their eternal identity. Such a position, however, at least in the eternal sense, is inconsistent with God's command against same-sex expression and His declaration that with Him, nothing is impossible.

Can a Person Be Happy without Expressing His or Her Same-Sex Feelings?

I realize that I am an outsider and cannot fully empathize with those who experience same-sex attraction. So I turn to the insights of those who have had or continue to experience such feelings. Below are some of their experiences and how they have found happiness without acting on their same-sex attraction:

"I needed to leave it an open question and to trust in God."

Ty Mansfield, now a marriage and family therapist, experienced same-sex attraction but also wanted to live Christ's teaching on the subject. He said, "I wanted to believe that peace, at the very least, was possible since 'change' [of sexual orientation] didn't seem to be happening as quickly as I would like." As a consequence, he "started to more openly explore the possibility of a gay relationship." However, at a church meeting, he said he "felt enveloped by the Spirit as it taught me that whether I ever married or achieved my desired transformation in this life, I was infinitely loved and accepted of God. My responsibility was to continue to live one day at a time while seeking and following the guidance of the Spirit. I felt a hope and joy and freedom in Christ that I hadn't felt in years."[4]

Mansfield decided he would surrender himself to Christ and live day by day without engaging in any same-sex activities. He made this thought-provoking observation: "The call of Christ is to become *holy* before it is to become heterosexual."[5] He then added, "I still have much to learn about the Savior's Atonement, but according to my experiences thus far in life, the promise of the Atonement is as much a promise of peace and sustaining grace *during* our mortal challenges as it is a promise of deliverance through and from them."[6] In other words, the Savior can support, comfort, and give joy to those experiencing same-sex attraction even while exercising restraint not to express those feelings.

Mansfield also made this spiritually mature observation: "Through all that I've learned, same-gender attraction has become less my 'struggle,' my 'problem,' or my 'cross.' Rather, it has become more my teacher and my friend. I no longer hate my attractions as an enemy to be conquered; I honor them as a mentor—as a divinely orchestrated spiritual tutor—and one of the greatest blessings the Lord has granted me. *Without that mentor, I would never have been brought to my knees as I have been or brought to know Him as my Savior and Redeemer as I do*."[7]

Mansfield's feelings seem compatible with those of the apostle Paul, who prayed repeatedly for an infirmity to be removed, but without success. Finally, he realized that this infirmity could help make him strong:

> There was given to me a thorn in the flesh, the messenger of Satan to buffet me, lest I should be exalted above measure.
>
> For this thing I besought the Lord thrice, that it might depart from me.
>
> And he said unto me, My grace is sufficient for thee: for my strength is made perfect in weakness. Most gladly therefore will I rather glory in my infirmities, that the power of Christ may rest upon me.

> Therefore I take pleasure in infirmities, in reproaches, in necessities, in persecutions, in distresses for Christ's sake: for when I am weak, then am I strong. (2 Cor. 12:7–10)

Paul recognized that the Lord was not going to miraculously remove his thorn in the flesh, but like Ty Mansfield, he knew that that thorn—that perceived weakness—could make him strong spiritually. Both the apostle Paul and Mansfield recognized that the cup of affliction would not immediately pass from them. Ella Wheeler Wilcox poignantly wrote of this as follows:

> All paths that have been, or shall be
> Pass somewhere through Gethsemane.
> All those who journey soon or late,
> Must pass within the garden's gate;
> Must kneel alone in darkness there,
> And battle with some fierce despair.
> God pity those who cannot say:
> "Not mine, but thine," who only pray,
> "Let this cup pass;" and cannot see
> The *purpose* in Gethsemane.[8]

The apostle Paul and Mansfield recognized the need to cope with their challenge, the purpose in it, and to seek the Savior's healing and strengthening powers that emanated from His suffering in Gethsemane (see Isaiah 53:3–5).

Mansfield provided several personal and helpful insights on the divine help he received in connection with his same-sex feelings:

Speaking of those who believe a change in sexual orientation is impossible, he wrote, "They do not allow for the possibility that for some individuals, sexual orientation may be sufficiently fluid or flexible to allow for satisfying, heterosexual relational intimacy."[9] Mansfield is a living example. He said, "As much as I felt I wouldn't marry, I tried to leave it an open question and to trust in God." Thereafter, he attended a church meeting in which he had a feeling of divine love. He said, "There was a feeling of what I perceived as pure celestial love and desire to be with a daughter of God in the most holy, connected, and uniting of ways. *With that feeling came the words, 'Just stay with me. If you do, this is the feeling you will someday feel—and it will be a permanent part of your being.'*"[10]

Mansfield continued, "While growth and change are inevitable when we submit our lives to the Lord, we cannot hold the Lord hostage to an arbitrary timetable or qualify our faith in Christ...upon some dangerously narrow characterization of what change should look like."[11]

While acknowledging that he still retains some same-sex feelings, Mansfield has been happily married to Danielle since 2010 and is the proud father of their two children.

"I had been putting something ahead of God."

Sarrah (pseudonym) is gay. In college, she played Division 1 soccer on a full scholarship. However, she felt a void in her relations with others. She wrote, "I just assumed that the emptiness I felt would one day magically be filled by my future husband. That was when I met *her*."[12] She then tells of her ongoing physical relationship with Brenda (also a pseudonym). During this time, she reflected, "I knew...my actions were in direct conflict with my undeniable testimony of the gospel of Jesus Christ. I felt guilty, shameful, and unworthy. I wanted to stop, but it seemed impossible to let her go."[13]

One day, Sarrah became unconscious at soccer practice. She found herself opening her eyes in a hospital bed. Recognizing the seriousness of her condition, she had a burning desire to be right with the Lord. She wrote, "*I knew that what seemed impossible to me was not impossible for the Lord. In that moment I committed in my heart to change.* Thus began my journey of becoming."[14] Thereafter she started to develop a friendship with a boy named Kyle (pseudonym). She said, "I was earnestly working to turn my heart to God," but at night she said that she would "hide away in the shadows with Brenda."[15]

In her effort to follow Christ, Sarrah said, "When I realized that I had been putting something ahead of God, I understood that the ultimatum was not deciding between her [Brenda] and Kyle. Rather, the choice was between my relationship with Brenda and my relationship with God. I needed to fill this painful void with Christ before I could truly be one with Kyle."[16]

After repeated struggles with her mixed feelings, Sarrah finally married Kyle.

It took time to adjust emotionally and physically. She acknowledged, "I may have occasional [same-sex] attractions for the rest of [my life]. But over time, and with a hope in the resurrection, [my] feelings will change and fade."[17] In conclusion, she observed, "I experienced firsthand that faith always precedes the miracle. The miracle I now enjoy daily is an incredible relationship with Kyle that fulfills me in every way. I am absolutely in love with him. I am filled with peace, joy, and happiness that are more powerful than any unwanted attraction I may experience."[18]

"I will have the marriage and family I have prayed for."

Kirk (pseudonym) is single and gay. He is in his fifties. He was married to a woman for three years, but his marriage ended in divorce. He has been active in his church as a teacher and leader. He believed that if he was obedient and served well, his feelings would change, but this didn't happen. At one point, he said, "The jolting disappointments of life had awakened me to the realization that I had been handling life's problems by my own power. I had not been using the energy and power of Christ's Atonement that had been all around me." Among other things, he said, "My prayers got a spiritual overhaul."[19]

Then one day, he had a sacred experience. He said that as he left a holy house of God, "I was suddenly aware that my attractions had shifted slightly. I don't know if I can describe it more accurately because it was an immediate awareness that something significant had changed in a small way. That magical, mystical mechanism that controls physical attractions had moved. After all my years of trying to force it or maneuver it, suddenly it had moved. I also knew that it was nothing I had done; rather it was the Lord's work." He then added, "It was as if the Lord was saying to me, 'Remember that I, and only I, can truly heal you. Today I have shown you a small degree of what I will do.' My actions are now driven by the sure hope that there is another side of the veil and that I will have the marriage and family I have prayed for."[20]

"I've been privileged to witness firsthand profound changes."

Rich Wyler tried to hide his homosexual feelings for years. As a consequence, he married a woman and struggled for the first nine years of their marriage. He sought therapy and joined a men's organization that helped him bond with men in a nonphysical way. He said, "Through all of this, I felt a deep transformation taking place. I had tried so many times to stop the sinful behavior. But without the godly substitute—the pure love of Christ, true brotherhood, and the charity spoken of in scripture—I had always fallen back to the cheap imitations of intimacy that ultimately caused even more pain."[21]

He then explained, "The further I turned from my past sins, the more driven I felt to share my testimony of change with others." Accordingly, in 2000, he began a website titled "People Can Change" for those "struggling with unwanted same-sex attractions with little hope those feelings could be diminished or eliminated."[22] After years of operating this site, Wyler wrote, "I've been privileged to witness firsthand profound changes in the lives of many hundreds of men."[23]

Wyler's wife, Marie, died in 2006, in the nineteenth year of their marriage. Wyler shared this beautiful observation: "I thank my Heavenly Father that Marie did not pass away until after He had brought about in me the mighty change of heart that enabled me to remain completely faithful to her during the second half of our marriage…and to become the husband she always deserved. Our earthly marriage ended at the high point of our relationship: completely in love, completely trusting and mutually devoted to serving the Lord."[24] Wyler married another woman in 2010.[25]

While acknowledging the foregoing stories, I am aware that people can and sometimes do revert to former habits. I am also aware that on occasion, people with same-sex attraction have entered into heterosexual marriages that ended in divorce for a variety of reasons. Unfortunately, some treat such returns to a former life or divorces almost gleefully, as if to say "That failure proves I am right—people should not attempt to bridle nor can they diminish or eliminate their same-sex attraction under any circumstances. In addition, they can't develop heterosexual feelings and sustain them. Therefore, I am justified in my same-sex relations." This justification, however, is built upon a faulty premise—that because some have temporarily failed or experienced a setback, it must mean that no one can succeed. The testimonies of the foregoing and many others are proof to the contrary.

What Is to Be Learned?

What is to be learned from these and other stories of people experiencing same-sex attraction? There are certain common elements. Each of these people found that if they truly turned themselves over to God and obeyed His law, then the Savior could provide them with peace and happiness even during their restraint of same-sex feelings, often even generating some feelings for the opposite sex that allowed for happy lives. And in some cases, they even enjoyed heterosexual marriages. In addition, God gave them the hope and assurance that divine feelings of love between a man and woman will be realized, if not in this life then in the life to come.

Some mentioned that same-sex attraction was a mentor or catalyst that brought them to Christ in new and deeper ways. In this regard, one married man wrote, "Same-gender attraction has brought me to a path that has led me to turn more fully to our Savior with a broken heart, which is our ultimate reason for entering mortality. For this, I am grateful."[26]

Tom Christofferson, who lived with a gay partner for nineteen years, wrote, "Because I am gay, there came a time when I had to *know*, not merely believe, that Jesus Christ lives, that I will be resurrected as He was, and that through the power of His Atonement I can gain strength and power to become His worthy disciple."[27]

That knowledge eventually came.

As a result, Christofferson wrote an insightful and tender book entitled *That We May Be One*. In it, he explained that his parents, siblings, friends, and fellow church members were not judgmental about his gay lifestyle but loved him and embraced him with open arms. It was this love and respect that brought him back to Christ. As a result, he separated from his partner, whom he loved and respected, and was rebaptized into his church.

About a year after these events occurred, a dear friend asked him why he couldn't find a way to be with his partner again. He thought about her question and replied, "Because the way I feel now, the way I experience the influence of the Holy Ghost, is powerful and delicious to me, and I don't ever want to live without it again. I pray that someday he [my previous partner] will know—and all who do not today share that awareness will know—the sweetness of communion with Heavenly Father and His Son through the Holy Spirit."[28] Living God's moral law brings a sweet, beautiful spirit which transcends any feelings that may come from living another lifestyle, however passionate those feelings may be.

Such comments remind me of something a friend of mine said after the untimely death of his wife: "I have never complained because I know it was His [God's] will." He then made this profound statement: "I have never asked why but rather what is it that He wants me to learn from this experience."[29] Perhaps that is a lesson for us all in whatever struggles or challenges we face in life.

One other note: the testimony of these men and women who faced same-sex challenges, as well as others I have read, were so sincere, so honest, so heartfelt, and so Christlike that I felt the need to be more supportive, more comforting, more loving, and more inclusive of them in my life. That was one witness to me that they spoke by the Spirit—their words inspired in me a desire to be a more Christlike person, more thoughtful and more compassionate, particularly to those who face such difficult struggles. I hope these feelings are reciprocal—that those who are engaged in same-sex relations will not have contempt but rather respect for those who honestly believe that such actions are prohibited under God's moral law but who also understand that none of us are perfect and that everyone is a beloved son or daughter of God and deserves to be treated as such. I also would add that there are those in the gay and lesbian communities who have made substantial contributions to advancing the liberties enunciated in the Constitution, by way of media commentary and otherwise, for which I am most grateful.

Why Does God Require Such a Sacrifice?

We may not understand why God would ask someone with same-sex attraction to do such a hard thing—to refrain from expressing his or her sexual desires—but we can take comfort in knowing that God is perfect in His love and consistent with that love. He requires all mortals to do difficult things. Some face poverty and hunger every day of their lives. Some have physical disabilities that prevent them from engaging in physical activities or getting married. Others have emotional or social incapacities that hinder their ability to make friends and fully function in society. And the list goes on and on. Requiring us to face difficult tasks in life does not make God unfair or uncompassionate. He has not singled out one group unfairly. He knows that what we have to endure in this life is but a dot on the eternal spectrum, and if we can be obedient here and remain faithful to Him, regardless of the degree of difficulty, we can have eternal life and a fulness of joy in His presence forever. It is somewhat like giving someone this option: you can either sin and have a hundred dollars today or be obedient and have a trillion dollars tomorrow. Which would you choose?

Linda Reeves, a religious leader, put in perspective the trials we face in life compared to the incomparable glorious rewards of the world to come: "I do not know why we have the many trials that we have, but it is my personal feeling that the reward is so great, so eternal and everlasting, so joyful and beyond our understanding that in that day of reward, we may feel to say to our merciful, loving Father, 'Was that *all* that was required?' What will it matter…what we suffered here if, in the end, those trials are the very things which qualify us for eternal life and exaltation in the kingdom of God with our Father and Savior?"[30] The apostle Paul likewise spoke of this need for an eternal perspective as we face our trials: "For our light affliction, which is but a moment, worketh for us a far more exceeding and eternal weight of glory" (2 Cor. 4:17). So glorious is that reward that Paul wrote, "Eye hath not seen, nor ear heard, neither have entered into the heart of man, the things which God hath prepared for them that love him" (1 Cor. 2:9).

On one occasion, the Savior gave a remarkable sermon known as the Bread of Life. In that sermon, He explained that His mission in life was "not to do mine own will, but the will of him that sent me" (John 6:38). The Savior then explained that those who were listening needed to accept Him and His Atonement and lifestyle or they would have "no [eternal] life" (John 6:53) in them. Many of his disciples responded, "This is an hard saying; who can hear it?" Some of them murmured, and to those who did, the Savior asked, "Doth this offend you?" The scriptures record, "From that time many of his disciples went back and walked no more with him." What a tragedy! They had been offended by the truth that would save them. The Savior then asked His twelve apostles, "Will ye also go away?" Peter responded with the answer that should be spoken by every mouth and resound in every heart: "Lord, to whom shall we go? thou hast the words of eternal life. And we believe and are sure that thou art the Christ, the Son of the living God" (see John 6:60–69).

The words spoken by the Savior and His prophets on same-sex relations are a hard saying for many. But this is one of those moments in life when we must make a difficult, even critical, choice of eternal consequence. Will we turn away from Christ because His saying is hard, or, like Peter, turn to Him, knowing there is no other path to salvation and eternal joy?

True Love and Compassion

Unfortunately, there are many who advocate for same-sex expression, including same-sex marriage, on the grounds of love and tolerance and compassion. Perhaps some do so, failing to understand God's commandment on the subject. They may not understand that the lifestyle they are promoting or endorsing can thwart an individual's spiritual progress and counter the purposes of God. Others may be aware of God's commandments but elevate their own wisdom and ideology above His. Or perhaps some have fallen prey to the social pressures of the day, just as they have fallen prey to accepting sexual relations outside the bonds of marriage.

Whatever the reason may be, no reason is good enough to justify the violating of God's commandment.

God has taught the true nature of compassion and love. He hates sin but loves the sinner. We can disapprove of fornication and adultery but still love the individual who committed them. Likewise, we can disapprove of same-sex relations but deeply love the individuals involved. The act and the person are totally separate. We can love our children even though we may disapprove of some of their choices.

The world would have us believe otherwise—if you disapprove of the act, you must despise the person. That is the great lie authored by the evil one. We can and should love those with same-sex attraction without embracing or endorsing a homosexual lifestyle.

The Supreme Court in the United Kingdom understood this distinction between the act and the person. A gay rights activist ordered a cake from a bakery with the request that it be decorated with the message "Support Gay Marriage." The owners of the bakery objected to doing so based on their evangelical Christian beliefs. The Court held that there was no discrimination based on sexual orientation. Instead, the Court made this significant statement: "The objection was to the message, not the messenger."[31]

The real question we should ask ourselves is, "What is true love?" Is it to encourage and applaud an act that is contrary to God's law under the false impression we are supporting and helping such individuals, or rather is it to kindly and patiently encourage them to return to the path that leads to God? Who is more loving—the parent who never disciplines a child or the parent who kindly and patiently, but honestly, points out what that child is doing wrong and helps him or her get back on the right track? To support someone in actions that lead him or her away from God is a pseudo-compassion, a false love, a misplaced loyalty. But that is exactly what we do if we endorse or encourage same-sex relations or marriages.

Those who truly love their friends will never encourage them to commit immoral actions under the pretense of compassion or tolerance.[32] Instead, with true love, and sometimes needed courage, they will do everything in their power to reverse the destructive course and bring their friends and loved ones back to God. In Proverbs, we find this wise counsel: "My son, despise not the chastening of the Lord; neither be weary of his correction: For whom the Lord loveth he correcteth" (Prov. 3:11–12). The epistle to the Hebrews teaches the same principle: "If ye endure chastening, God dealeth with you as with sons. Now no chastening for the present seemeth to be joyous, but grievous: nevertheless afterward it yieldeth the peaceable fruit of righteousness unto them which are exercised thereby" (Heb. 12:7, 11). In other words, humility and receptivity to correction bring the fruit of peace in one's life.

Suppose a friend were about to jump from a cliff. All he could envision was the exhilarating joy of the free fall for the next ten seconds. Would you encourage him in that pursuit and yell, "Jump! Jump!" Or would you exercise all the love and persuasion you could muster to dissuade him, to turn him from his course, to explain to him that his actions have dire and drastic consequences, that there is also an eleventh second, known as impact, that will bring prolonged pain and suffering, maybe even death?

Likewise, there are spiritual cliffs and actions, such as fornication, adultery, pornography, abortion, and same-sex relations, that may seem to bring temporary pleasure or relief, but they, too, have their eleventh second—their moment of impact, their prolonged pain and suffering, even spiritual death if there is no repentance. One is not justified because his or her actions may be legal. The true test is and always will be whether or not they are moral. And certainly, God has spoken clearly and unmistakably on His opposition to same-sex relations.

Some people will disagree with the position stated above. I understand that, but in truth their disagreement is not with me but with God. Moses faced such a situation. The Israelites were murmuring to

Moses and Aaron because they had no bread. Moses replied: "[Y]our murmurings are not against us, but against the Lord" (Exod. 16:8).

I desire to be respectful of others' honest opinions, but I cannot, in good conscience, dismiss God's expressed will on the subject as evidenced by the holy scriptures and by many early and modern Christian leaders. We must always love the individual but never embrace or endorse same-sex relations simply because it is socially in vogue or politically correct or seems like the tolerant thing to do. It always has been and always will be in opposition to God's plan for eternal joy. At some point, we have to choose what will govern our life—our reason and prejudices or God's will. In the meantime, we might all take counsel from these words of Abraham Lincoln during the heated debate on slavery: "We are not enemies, but friends. We must not be enemies. Though passion may have strained, it must not break our bonds of affection."[33] In the end, we are all children of God, all spirit brothers and sisters who deserve and need each other's love and respect.

Do We Place Our Trust in God or Man?

When I see people protesting against churches or schools or court decisions because they favor same-sex marriage or abortion, I realize that their real protest is not against an earthly institution or decision but against God. They have chosen to counsel God rather than take counsel from Him, to elevate their wisdom above His. In this regard, Lincoln taught, "The fear of the Lord is the beginning of wisdom."[34]

Alexis de Tocqueville, a brilliant intellect, nonetheless submitted his intellect and will to that of God's: "I am unacquainted with [God's] designs, [meaning he didn't understand all of His purposes], but I shall not cease to believe in them because I cannot fathom them, and *I had rather mistrust my own capacity than his justice.*"[35] What a humble, magnificent thought. Likewise, we might ask, "Is our motto 'in man we trust' or 'in God we trust'?" We will all face crossroads in life when we must make that choice—the choice that will ultimately determine our eternal destiny.

The Savior said of His own disciples, "They are not of the world, even as I am not of the world" (John 17:16). Sometimes being a disciple of God requires an uncomfortable separation from the world, even ridicule, but perhaps it is our ultimate test. Do we have the courage to stand for God's ways in contrast to the world's ways, or do we yield to the peer pressure of a secular society?

Conclusion

All of us sin in one way or another. When we do, we have a choice—to either rationalize or repent. When we rationalize, we delay our return to God. When we repent, we hasten our return to Him and invite His Spirit and healing powers into our lives, which know no limits or bounds. We act, as Lincoln said, in accord with "the better angels of our nature."[36]

Whatever our beliefs, we must never forget that everyone is a child of God.

Accordingly, we should love those engaged in same-sex relations and—with patience, kindness, and understanding—encourage them to live God's law. In addition, we should do all within our power to see that the laws of the land concerning marriage comport with the laws of God. In the end, this will produce the best spiritual and social result for each of us as individuals as well as for society at large. Then we will be entitled to the fullest measure of liberties provided under the Constitution because we are a moral people—the necessary condition to such a blessed state of affairs.

---

1 See Litsky and Weber, "Roger Bannister," nytimes.com.

2 See Taylor "What Breaking the 4-Minute Mile Taught Us," hbr.com.

3 In Associated Press, "Famed Scientist Dismisses Possibility of Space Travel," 6.

4 Mansfield, "A Seal of Living Reality," 4–5.

5 Mansfield, "A Seal of Living Reality," 10; emphasis in original.

6 Mansfield, "A Seal of Living Reality," 11; emphasis in original.

7 Mansfield, "A Seal of Living Reality," 14; emphasis added.

8 Wilcox, "Gethsemane," 88; emphasis in original.

[9] Mansfield, "A Seal of Living Reality," 16.
[10] Mansfield and Mansfield, "Living with Same-Sex Attraction," ldsliving.com; emphasis added.
[11] Mansfield, "A Seal of Living Reality," 18.
[12] Reynolds, "Becoming," 59; emphasis in original.
[13] Reynolds, "Becoming," 60.
[14] Reynolds, "Becoming," 61; emphasis added.
[15] Reynolds, "Becoming," 61.
[16] Reynolds, "Becoming," 62–63.
[17] Reynolds, "Becoming," 66.
[18] Reynolds, "Becoming," 66.
[19] Reidman, "The Gift of Hope," 71.
[20] Reidman, "The Gift of Hope," 76.
[21] Wyler, "A Mighty Change of Heart," 82.
[22] Wyler, "A Mighty Change of Heart," 83.
[23] Wyler, "A Mighty Change of Heart," 85. In the spirit of full disclosure, one of Wyler's former therapists, a cofounder of People Can Change, has returned to a gay lifestyle.
[24] Wyler, "A Mighty Change of Heart," 86.
[25] See Wyler, "A Mighty Change of Heart," 77.
[26] Richards, "Learning the True Gospel: The Transforming Power of the Atonement," 177. The words of Victor Frankl seem appropriate here: "We must never forget that we may also find meaning in life even when confronted with a hopeless situation, when facing a fate that cannot be changed. For what then matters is to bear witness to the uniquely human potential at its best, which is to transform a personal tragedy into a triumph, to turn one's predicament into a human achievement" (*Man's Search for Meaning*, 135). Or we might add, to turn a seeming personal tragedy into a spiritual victory.
[27] Christofferson, *That We May Be One*, 37.
[28] Christofferson, *That We May Be One*, 125–26.
[29] Scott, "Temple Worship," 45.
[30] Reeves, "Worthy of Our Promised Blessings," 11; emphasis in original.
[31] *Lee v. Ashers Baking Company* (2018) UKSC, case 49, para. 22.
[32] *Tolerance* can be a slippery word. When employed to justify one's support of same-sex marriage, it may be nothing less than a camouflage to disguise one's disobedience to God.
[33] Lincoln, "First Inaugural Address," avalon.law.yale.edu.
[34] In Wolf, *The Almost Chosen People*, 120; quoting Psalm 111:10.
[35] De Tocqueville, *Democracy in America*, 1: xx; emphasis added.
[36] Lincoln, "First Inaugural Address of Abraham Lincoln," avalon.law.yale.edu.

CHAPTER 13

Is Zero Population Growth a Solution for Environmental Concerns?

What Obligation Do We Have to the Environment?

Because the Founding Fathers taught that a moral people were essential to preserving the liberties enumerated in the Constitution, it raises the question, Do we have a moral obligation to preserve our environment? And if so, what is the nature of that obligation?

The Bible teaches that God created the earth in six days (or periods) and then rested on the seventh. His creation is breathtaking. We can witness the stunning sunrises and sunsets, the cascading waterfalls, the winding rivers, the heaven-bent redwoods, the wildflowers in all their brilliant glory, the snowcapped mountains, the seemingly endless prairies of golden grain, and the boundless variety of animals. The beauty of nature surrounds us everywhere. It is wondrous to behold.

But the earth is not only exquisitely beautiful; it is also incredibly functional. It has fertile soil to produce seemingly endless food supplies; snow, rain, and fresh water to quench the thirst of the masses; sufficient oil to provide energy for billions; solar energy and wind to provide supplemental and alternative power sources; and metals and basic elements for technology purposes to satisfy the never-ending craving to extend our lives and facilitate our daily enjoyment and advancement. It is hard to believe, as some claim, that all this happened by chance from some chaotic mass. It is much easier and credible to believe that an intelligent being—God—created it so that His children would be blessed with the necessary elements and aesthetic beauty to enjoy a rich and productive life. This, in turn, would prepare them for a more glorious life in the world to come.

Because God created the earth for us, we have a divine stewardship to care for it, to protect its beauty, and manage its resources wisely. No doubt we can and should do better in this regard. Fortunately, there are simple and practical things each of us can do to assist in this regard, such as beautifying our homes, conserving electricity, gas, and water, cleaning up our cities, recycling, and even planting trees where possible. I commend those who are engaging in such activities and offering other practical solutions.

Zero Population Growth Is Not the Answer

That said, some have proposed zero or negative population growth as a principal solution to solving our environmental issues. Dr. Paul R. Ehrlich, a well-known Stanford scientist and environmentalist, and considered by many to be the expert and champion of zero population, mentions it numerous times in his best-selling book *The Population Bomb*. Below are some of the predictions he made in 1968 (when global population was about 3.5 billion, about half the current population), based on his belief that the earth was grossly overpopulated and unable to sustain more growth:

First, "We [the United States] are today involved in the events leading to famine; tomorrow we may be destroyed by its consequences."[1] Ehrlich predicted, "Unless the population size in the United States is reduced rapidly, it too will be facing massive famine by the year 2000."[2] The population in the US in 1968, when Ehrlich's book was written, was 201,000,000. It was 282,000,000 in 2000. The population increased dramatically, but there was no US famine. The prediction was dead wrong.

Second, Ehrlich predicted, "The battle to feed all of humanity is over. In the 1970's, the world will undergo famines—*hundreds of millions of people are going to starve to death.*"[3] He then added, "We already know that it is impossible to increase food production enough to cope with continued population growth."[4] Contrary to Ehrlich's prediction, famines have significantly decreased, and food production has increased to meet a growing population.

Joe Hasell and Max Roser, writing for an organization known as Our World in Data, explained, "It is...very clear that in recent decades the presence of major life-taking famines has diminished significantly and abruptly as compared to earlier eras. The parts of the world that continue to be at risk of famine represent a much more limited geographic area than in previous eras, and those famines that have occurred recently have typically been *far* less deadly."[5] They also explained that many of the famines that have occurred are not due to a lack of food or overpopulation but are "attributable to political causes, including non-democratic government and conflict."[6] One notable example of this is when Venezuelan dictator Nicolas Maduro withheld humanitarian food and other essential supplies from his people for political reasons. Another reason there are some famines is due to the inability or unwillingness to allocate and distribute excess food supplies to the needed locations in a timely manner, not because there exists a worldwide shortage of food.

The following, a summary of a chart prepared by Hasell and Roser,[7] graphically demonstrates the reduction in deaths by famine over the past few decades, contrary to Ehrlich's dire prediction:

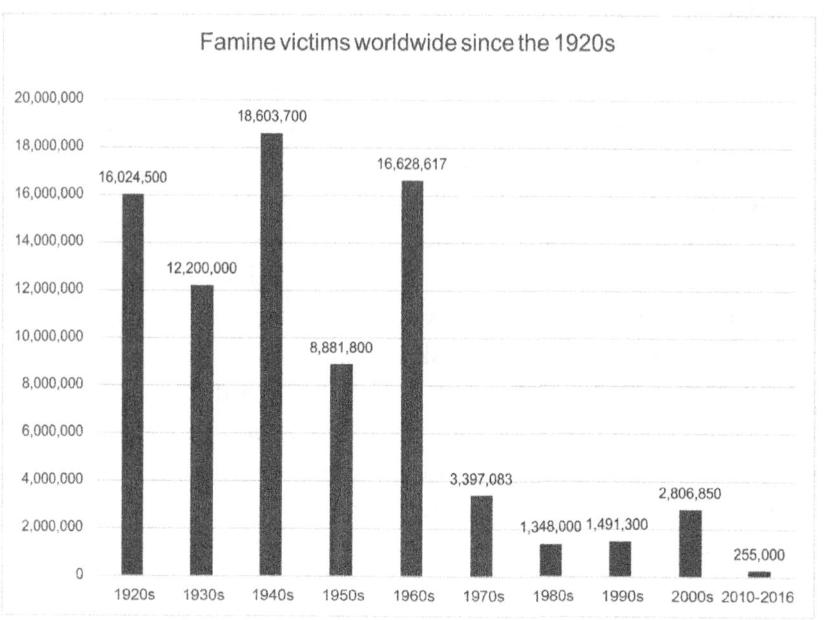

But why this dramatic decrease in deaths by famine? Hasell and Roser noted that this occurred because of "increasing agricultural yields [Ehrlich predicted there would be insufficient increases]; improvements in health care and sanitation; increased trade; reduced food prices [Ehrlich predicted they would increase] and food price volatility; as well as reductions in the number of people living in extreme poverty [Ehrlich predicted these numbers would rise]."[8]

As to this latter prediction, Jordan Peterson noted, "Between the year 2000 and the year 2012 [while world population increased], the rate of absolute poverty in the world fell by 50%. The poor in the world are getting rich at a rate that is absolutely unparalleled in all of human history."[9]

Hasell and Roser concluded, "Thus, overall, we can see in the rapid decline of famine mortality one of the greatest accomplishments of our era, representing technological progress, economic development and the spread of stable democracies."[10] It is important to remember that such accomplishment was generated at a time of rapid population growth, not decline.

Third, Ehrlich further wrote, "No sane society wants to promote larger population size today."[11] He then explained that nations are weakened when their populations are large, reporting "that Russia and China have realized this and are moving to limit their populations."[12] Obviously, Ehrlich did not envision the drastic consequences of China's one-child policy (in truth a self-destructive policy), which was reversed in 2016. The consequences were devastating—a declining population, the burden of the young attempting to support a disproportionate aging population, newborn babies abandoned, especially females, and a top-heavy surplus of males. In 1983 alone, there were 14.4 million abortions (compared to 21 million births) and 20.7 million sterilizations in China. This is all noted in an article by Feng Nang, Baochang Gu, and Yong Car: "China's one-child policy will be remembered as one of the costliest lessons of misguided public policymaking. The costly lessons to be learned are not only in politics and public policymaking, but also in how parts of the academic community informed and misinformed public policymaking."[13] Unfortunately, we see that same misinformation being spread today.

Once a nation adopts a zero population policy, it is almost impossible to reverse the course. Chao Deng, writing an article for the *Wall Street Journal* in January 2020, noted, "China's birthrate fell to its lowest level in the country's modern history. In hopes of relieving demographic pressures on the economy, the government began allowing families to have two children in 2016, *after economists warned that the strict one-child birth-planning program implemented in 1980 was creating a demographic time bomb*. The country's workforce began shrinking eight years ago. The move hasn't had the expected impact: While Chinese newborns increased in 2016, they have dropped steadily since."[14]

A fourth prediction from Ehrlich: "Buy natural resources stocks; their price is sure to go up. Why? Exploding population and finite resources."[15] Ehrlich's rationale was that if you have a fixed supply of resources and an increasing demand for them as necessitated by a growing population, then prices must increase. It was but a simple application of the law of supply and demand. Once again, he was wrong.

Many may recall the famous bet between Ehrlich and Julian Simon, an economist. As Tim Worstall noted in a contribution to *Forbes* magazine, "Ehrlich insisted that commodities would become more expensive: they were running out in the face of the population explosion. Simon asserted the opposite: more people meant more brains meant better methods of extraction and lower usage per unit of production. Thus prices should fall."[16] Ehrlich picked five commodities: nickel, copper, chromium, tin, and tungsten, and he predicted their prices would rise in the next ten years. Simon bet they would decrease, as adjusted for inflation. Ten years passed, and Simon won the bet. The real price of these commodities dropped more than 50 percent.

Marian L. Tupy and Gale Pooley of HumanProgress.org cited a study by the Cato Institute in Washington, DC, of forty-two natural resources from 1960 to 2016. The study concluded that "after adjusting for the appreciation in GDP per person, commodity prices fell by 53 percent." Tupy and Pooley then went on to say: "*Humanity is creating faster than it is consuming. That is an astonishing verification of Simon's prophecy.*"[17] Ehrlich was wrong because he underestimated man's creativity, ingenuity, and ability to adapt to changing circumstances. This proved to be a recurring fatal flaw in his reasoning.

Because Ehrlich's predictions were consistently wrong, his proposed solutions were also wrong, some of which are set forth below:

- "We must have population control at home, hopefully through a system of incentives and penalties, *but by compulsion if voluntary methods fail.* Population control is the only answer [to saving mankind and the environment]."[18] Words and phrases such as *compulsion*, *population control*, and *the only answer* ought to be a red flag that our liberties are about to be curtailed.
- "Abortion is a highly effective weapon in the armory of population control."[19] But Ehrlich fails to understand that God's goal is *not* population control but rather to "multiple and replenish [fill] the earth" (Gen. 1:28). In addition, as discussed below, population control is a policy and procedure that is highly detrimental to a nation's survival.

- To control population growth, he suggested "the addition of temporary sterilants to water supplies or staple food," giving "responsibility prizes...to each man who accepted irreversible sterilization [vasectomy] before having more than two children," mass sterilization, and "a federal law guaranteeing the right of *any* woman to have an abortion if it is approved by a physician [he got that one in *Roe v. Wade*]." He then concluded by saying, "Of course, this enlightened atmosphere does not exist today."[20] Suffice it to say, once God is taken out of the equation (Ehrlich was an avowed atheist), the disease of intellectual superiority quickly fills the void.
- Ehrlich spoke of the burgeoning population in India and endorsed a proposal to sterilize "all Indian males with three or more children." Commenting on this compulsory program, he said, "*Coercion? Perhaps, but coercion in a good cause.*"[21] This was nothing less than endorsement of a dictatorship over democracy, the use of force over persuasion, and the exaction of compulsion over agency. In other words, he argued that the ends justify the means, however immoral the means may be. With this line of reasoning, one might argue that it would be appropriate to break down a door without a search warrant and then justify such unlawful action because two ounces of an illegal substance were found in a bathroom drawer. Fortunately, our current law recognizes that the unlawful search is more immoral than the crime of drug possession, and thus any evidence obtained is not permitted as evidence in court. In other words, the ends do not justify the means.
- "Complain bitterly about any positive treatment of large families. Attack the publicizing of 'mothers of the year' unless they have no more than two children."[22] If this were the case, then Mary (the mother of Jesus), Martha Washington, Abigail Adams, Coretta Scott King (the wife of Martin Luther King), Queen Victoria, and many other noble and distinguished women would not be eligible for consideration as mother of the year. What a tragedy!

- "Give your child an IUD to take to 'show and tell.'"[23] Is there no sensitivity, decency, and good judgment left?

It is remarkable that one can be wrong so many times in pages so few. No wonder Charles Krauthammer commented, "The late '60s featured Paul Ehrlich's huge best-seller, *The Population Bomb*, an astonishingly wrongheaded prediction of the End brought on by overpopulation—by 1983."[24] And no wonder Jonathan Last, a journalist and best-selling author, called *The Population Bomb* "one of the most spectacularly foolish books ever published."[25]

Even with Ehrlich's multitude of mispredictions, he declared as recently as 2011 that if he were to rewrite *The Population Bomb*, "My language would be even more apocalyptic."[26] Lest some argue that the zero population growth agenda is past history, one needs only to realize that the same end goal is currently being sought, only couched in the more acceptable terms of *climate emergency*.

In November 2019, over eleven thousand scientists from 153 countries signed their names to an article entitled "World Scientists' Warning of a Climate Emergency" that contains these words: "Profoundly troubling signs from human activities include sustained increases in both human and ruminant livestock populations. Economic and population growth are among the most important drivers of increases in CO_2 emissions from fossil fuel combustion; therefore, *we need bold and drastic transformations regarding economic and population policies* [sounds like a euphemism for population control]. Still increasing by roughly 80 million people per year, or more than 200,000 per day, *the world population must be stabilized—and, ideally, gradually reduced*. There are proven and effective policies that strengthen human rights while lowering fertility rates and lessening the impacts of population growth."[27]

Some claim these authors were misreported as proposing population control, but it is hard to read the simple meaning of their words and not come to that conclusion. How do you use proven and effective policies to gradually reduce the world's population without a population control agenda? In addition, we have millennials now signing petitions not to have children under the banner of environmental concerns. Unfortunately, the zero population mentality is alive and thriving, but now coming under the cover of more politically correct names and causes.

Think of the kings and queens of the eighteenth, nineteenth, and twentieth centuries. How comfortable was life for them? Since those days, we have had a population explosion. Has the standard of living decreased? Is there less food, fewer living essentials, fewer conveniences? How many of those kings and queens enjoyed the essentials and conveniences of most common men today in those same countries where they once reigned—good health care, running water, heated homes, electricity, televisions, computers, phones, supermarkets, cars, trains, planes, online shopping, and delivery? The increased population resulted in more people, and thus a greater capacity for ingenuity to produce the technology and inventions that made this higher standard of living possible.

The Facts of Zero Population Growth

What are the facts concerning population decline? Jonathan Last wrote an entertaining and highly informative book entitled *What to Expect When No One's Expecting: America's Coming Demographic Disaster*. Following are some facts about population decline and the related consequences—not false predictions but actual historical facts and consequences, each of which come from Last's book:

- "In order for a country to maintain a steady population, it needs a fertility [or birth] rate of 2.1—remember this is the Golden Number. If the rate is higher, the country's population grows; lower, and it shrinks. Which means that the Japanese and Italians (with fertility rates of about 1.4) are on the verge of downsizing their countries. Their cities are dwindling; some small towns are on the cusp of simply closing. The average person in Japan and Italy will soon have no brothers, sisters, aunts, or uncles."[28] In fact, so desperate has Italy become for population growth that CNN has reported, "Two Italian destinations, hoping to revive declining communities by luring new residents" are selling "homes priced at a little over a dollar."[29]

- "If current fertility rates remain constant in Europe, the total population of the continent will go from 738 million in 2010 to 482 million by the end of the century. That's a scary scenario, but there's spookier stuff out there. Remember, just 3 percent of the world's population lives in countries that are not seeing fertility decline."[30] Accordingly, the Europeans are not begging for zero population. Why? Because, as Last observes, "None of the 27 EU member states is above replacement level in fertility and only 8 of them are even near it."[31]
- "Even today, thanks to Ehrlich, many people still believe that 'overpopulation' is a looming problem. But in reality, from Africa to Asia, from South America to Eastern Europe, and from Third World jungles to the wealthy desert petro-kingdoms, nearly every country in every region is experiencing declines in fertility."[32] The prime reason there is still an increase in annual world population is due to a decrease in infant mortality, improved health treatment, and increasing life expectancies.
- "From a combined TFR [total fertility rate] of 3.7 in 1960 (the end of the Baby Boom), the fertility rate in the United States dropped to 1.8 in 1980, a 50 percent decline in a single generation. Our TFR went as high as 2.12 in 2007 before slumping back to 2.01 in 2009."[33] In 2018, it was 1.72, a record low. If it were not for immigration, the United States would be one more nation with a declining population.

The Consequences of Zero Population Growth

What, then, are the consequences when a nation starts to fall below a birthrate of 2.1 and thus fails to repopulate itself?

- Last writes, "Throughout recorded human history, declining populations have *always* followed or been followed by Very Bad Things. Disease. War. Economic stagnation or collapse."[34]

- Last noted that Russia had 149.6 million people in 1995, but that decreased to 138 million in 2013. He projected that "by 2050, its population will be nearly a third smaller than it is today." He then went on to quote Vladimir Putin, who warned "his countrymen that they were 'facing the serious threat of turning into a decaying nation.'"[35] With reality setting in, Russia has realized the devastating effect of a zero or negative population mentality and even declared a national day of conception on September 12 of each year.
- Population decreases often result in economic decline. Why? Because there are fewer skilled and common laborers, fewer consumers, and fewer innovators to provide solutions to the challenges that confront society, as so dramatically illustrated in the bet between Paul Ehrlich and Julian Simon. As Massimo Livi Bacci, an Italian professor of demography, observed, "Historically, areas depopulated or in the process of losing population have almost always been characterized by backward economies."[36] Adam Smith corroborated this in *Wealth of Nations*: "The most decisive mark of the prosperity of any country is the increase of the number of its inhabitants."[37] Last further added, "No nation has experienced long-term prosperity in the face of contracting population."[38] Why then would anyone propose zero population growth?
- A contracting population results in fewer youth to support retirees. Last points out that "in 1975 Japan had eight workers for every one retiree. By 2005, that ratio fell to 3.3 workers for each retiree. In 2055, it will be a thoroughly unsustainable 1.3 workers for every one retiree."[39]
- Quoting demographer David Reher, Last noted, "'In a few short decades there is a good chance that labor shortages will become a problem affecting most of the world and not just one of the developed nations.' And from there, the problems cascade. With fewer people working, the tax base declines just as demands on the government (in the form of pensions and medical coverage) increase."[40]

Singapore is a prime example of the irreversible course that can be set when a zero population growth mentality is foisted on its people. In 1960, Singapore had a fertility rate of 5.45, which decreased to 4.7 in 1965. The government then enacted a set of measures to further reduce this rate. This involved national propaganda, with frequent ads stating, "Girl or Boy, Two is Enough." Abortion and sterilization were encouraged, and parents with more than two children were penalized with actions such as higher hospital charges. The campaign worked. By 1976, the fertility rate had dropped to 2.1, right at replacement level. But little did anyone expect that the propaganda train had become a runaway disaster.

The fertility rate didn't stabilize at 2.1. It kept dropping—to 1.74 in 1980, to 1.48 in 1999, to 1.41 in 2001, to 1.24 in 2004, and to a devastating 1.11 in 2013, before rising to a meager 1.16 in 2017. Almost every incentive known to man was implemented to reverse the course. The old slogan "Two is Enough" was replaced by "Have Three or More Children if You Can." Huge tax breaks for those with additional children were implemented, a matchmaking service for college graduates was begun, preferences for entry to the finest schools was given, a "baby bonus" program offering $18,000 for a third child was adopted, there were government matching savings accounts for two or more children, increased maternity leave, the sterilization bonus was eliminated, abortion was discouraged, etc. How did it fare?

As Jonathan Last noted, "Despite all the incentives, all the public campaigns, all the perks and payouts, the average woman in Singapore can barely be bothered to have a single child."[41] The implementation of zero population growth is often an irreversible and devastating course leading to serious economic, social, and spiritual declines.

In 2014, the Singapore government issued this warning about its country's population decline:

> At current birth rates and without immigration, [Singapore's] citizen population will begin to shrink around 2025. As workers retire and as

> fewer young Singaporeans enter the workforce, Singapore's citizen old-age support ratio—the ratio of citizens in the working ages to each elderly citizen—is projected to fall from 5.9 to 2.1 between 2010 and 2030.
>
> With our growing number of senior citizens, healthcare and long-term care spending is expected to increase. As a result, the smaller base of economically active citizens may have to pay higher taxes to support the aging population and their growing needs.
>
> Singapore is a key hub for many businesses serving the Asia markets. They may consider moving out of Singapore if manpower needs are not met. As businesses scale back, job opportunities for Singaporeans will be limited. With less attractive job opportunities in Singapore, more highly-skilled Singaporeans will start to seek opportunities elsewhere. This may cause a vicious cycle, further shrinking the size of the workforce.
>
> As the economy stagnates, it will be difficult to garner fiscal resources to invest in physical infrastructure for instance, or to address the needs of lower-income Singaporeans. Without economic growth, social and welfare programmes can quickly become unsustainable.[42]

The runaway train—zero population—was wreaking its havoc, with no reversible course in sight.

God's Plan Versus Man's Plan

I do not know Ehrlich's motives. Perhaps they were well-intentioned but nonetheless misguided. What I do know is that Ehrlich not only failed to take into account the remarkable adaptability and creativity of man, but he also failed to recognize and understand the purposes and designs of God. Consequently, he came up with his own plan that was a disaster because it was counterproductive to God's.

How then does God feel about zero population growth? First, the Lord said to Adam and Eve, "Be fruitful, and multiply, and replenish the earth" (Gen. 2:28).

The Hebrew word that was translated as "replenish" also means "fill"—meaning God wants us to fill the earth. Suffice it to say there is a lot of unfilled space on earth today for further population growth.

Russell M. Nelson, president of the Church of Jesus Christ of Latter-day Saints, shared this eye-opening fact: "At the fifth World Congress of Families, in 2009, [my wife] and I heard a scholar present a paper in which he made a stunning statement. He said that if each man, woman, and child now living upon the earth were allotted a quarter of an acre of land, all 6.8 billion people would fit in the country of Brazil, with 20 percent of Brazil still left unoccupied. Does that sound like the earth is overcrowded? I checked that calculation. It is correct."[43]

The Psalmist said, "Lo, children are an heritage of the Lord: and the fruit of the womb is his reward. As arrows are in the hand of a mighty man; so are children of the youth. Happy is the man that hath his quiver full of them" (Ps. 127:3–5).

This is certainly a divine endorsement of having many children.

After Abraham showed his extraordinary obedience by being willing to sacrifice his son Isaac, the Lord said to him, "I will bless thee, and in multiplying *I will multiply thy seed as the stars of the heaven, and as the sand which is upon the sea shore.* And in thy seed shall all the nations of the earth be blessed" (Gen. 22:17–18, emphasis added). Abraham's reward from God for his extraordinary obedience was to have a posterity as numerous as the stars in heaven and the sand upon the seashore that would bless all nations. Does this sound like God was encouraging a zero population mentality?

But will there come a time when the earth will be overpopulated and there are inadequate earthly resources to support the growing numbers? If one does not believe in God, then this might be a concern for the distant future, but there is a God who knows the end from the beginning.

The apostle Paul tells us that God knows exactly how many people have been designated to come to this earth: "[God] hath determined the times before appointed [when we will come to earth], and the bounds of their habitation [where we will be born]" (Acts 17:26). This makes sense. God is not winging it with regards to populating this earth. Because He is omniscient, He knows exactly when and where each of His children will come to this terrestrial sphere.

This earthly experience is necessary for God's spirit children to grow and develop and become more like Him (see Matthew 5:48). That is why a zero population growth agenda (including abortion) is counterproductive to God's plan because it prevents or delays God's spirit children from entering mortality.

Since God is omniscient and thus knows the exact number of His children who will come to this earth, He has provided ample resources to care for them. On one occasion, the Savior shared the following parable: "Which of you, intending to build a tower, sitteth not down first, and counteth the cost, whether he have sufficient to finish it? Lest haply, after he hath laid the foundation, and is not able to finish it, all that behold it begin to mock him, saying, This man began to build, and was not able to finish" (Luke 14: 28–30). Given this parable, can one imagine God building or creating anything without counting the cost? So it was when He created the earth.

He counted the cost beforehand. He knew exactly how many resources would be needed for those who would inhabit the earth, and so He provided those necessary resources, plus a surplus. Otherwise, it might be said of Him, "This man began to build, and was not able to finish [provide the necessary resources for his creations]."

The earth was created for a purpose—that God's children would have a place to be tested in mortality and receive the opportunity to return to God's presence in a glorified state. Any program that attempts to frustrate that purpose, such as zero population growth, is in direct opposition to God's will to fill the earth. Zero population growth, and any programs or philosophies that support such an agenda, are not a solution to our environmental concerns. God does not want us to solve environmental problems by frustrating the prime purpose for which the earth was created—namely to inhabit it with His children.

Conclusion

The back cover of Jonathan Last's book *What to Expect When No One's Expecting* summarizes the fallacy of the zero or negative population growth mentality:

> For years, we have been warned about the looming danger of overpopulation: people jostling for space on a planet that's busting at the seams and running out of oil and food and land and everything else.
>
> It's all bunk. *The 'population bomb' never exploded. Instead, statistics from around the world make clear that since the 1970's, we've been facing exactly the opposite problem: people are having too few babies* (emphasis added). Population growth has been slowing for two generations. In Japan, people buy more adult diapers than they do diapers for babies. In Italy, there are already more deaths than births every year.
>
> And all of this is coming to America, too. In fact, it's already here. Middle-class Americans have their own, informal one-child policy these days. And an alarming number of upscale professionals don't even go that far—they have dogs, not

> kids. In fact, if it weren't for the wave of immigration we experienced over the last thirty years, the United States would be on the verge of shrinking, too. What happened? Everything about modern life...has pushed Americans in a single direction, making it harder to have children. And making the people who still do want to have children feel like second-class citizens.
>
> *What to Expect When No One's Expecting* explains why the population implosion happened and how it is remaking culture, the economy, and politics both at home and around the globe. It concludes with this warning: "if America wants to continue to lead the world, we need to have more babies."

Arthur Brooks noted in his well-documented book on charity, "All serious studies to date tell us that the net benefits to American society from childbearing are large and positive."[44] So often God's laws seem counterintuitive to conventional thinking or worldly wisdom. For example, when we are mistreated, the Savior tells us to turn the other cheek (Matt. 5:39), "love your enemies" (Matt. 5:44), and "bless them that curse you" (Matt. 5:44). Likewise, the arguments against population control may seem counterintuitive to some. But if we live the moral law to "multiply and replenish the earth," then in ways both expected and unexpected, God is more likely to help us solve the environmental concerns and other moral issues facing our nation today.

---

1 Ehrlich, *The Population Bomb*, xi.
2 Ehrlich, *The Population Bomb*, 76.
3 Ehrlich, *The Population Bomb*, xi.
4 Ehrlich, *The Population Bomb*, 108; emphasis added.
5 Hasell and Roser, "Famines," ourworldindata.org; emphasis in original.
6 Hasell and Roser, "Famines," ourworldindata.org.
7 Hasell and Roser, "Famines," ourworldindata.org.

8 Hasell and Roser, "Famines," ourworldindata.org.
9 In Wood, "An Expert Told Us What Draws People to Socialism," nationalinterest.org.
10 Hasell and Roser, "Famines," ourworldindata.org.
11 Ehrlich, *The Population Bomb*, 137.
12 Ehrlich, *The Population Bomb*, 186.
13 Wang and others, "The End of China's One-Child Policy," brookings.edu.
14 Deng, "China's Birthrate Hits a New Low," A7.
15 Ehrlich, *The Population Bomb*, 149.
16 Worstall, "But Why Did Julian Simon Win the Paul Ehrlich Bet?" forbes.com.
17 Tupy and Pooley, "How Julian Simon Won a $1,000 Bet with 'Population Bomb' Author Paul Ehrlich," fee.org.
18 Ehrlich, *The Population Bomb*, xi; emphasis added.
19 Ehrlich, *The Population Bomb*, 88.
20 Ehrlich, *The Population Bomb*, 135, 138–39, 142.
21 Ehrlich, *The Population Bomb*, 165–66; emphasis added.
22 Ehrlich, *The Population Bomb*, 179.
23 Ehrlich, *The Population Bomb*, 182.
24 Krauthammer, *The Point of It All*, 134.
25 Last, *What to Expect When No One's Expecting*, 7.
26 In Haberman, "The Unrealized Horrors of Population Explosion," nytimes.com.
27 Ripple and others, "World Scientists Warning of a Climate Emergency," 10–11; emphasis added.
28 Last, *What to Expect When No One's Expecting*, 3.
29 Marchetti, "Buying a $1 Italy Dream House Just Got Even Easier," cnn.com.
30 Last, *What to Expect When No One's Expecting*, 97; emphasis in original.
31 Last, *What to Expect When No One's Expecting*, 148.
32 Last, *What to Expect When No One's Expecting*, 8.
33 Last, *What to Expect When No One's Expecting*, 15.
34 Last, *What to Expect When No One's Expecting*, 7; emphasis in original.
35 Last, *What to Expect When No One's Expecting*, 25.
36 Livi Bacci, A *Concise History of World Population*, 95.
37 Smith, *Wealth of Nations*, 74.
38 Last, *What to Expect When No One's Expecting*, 136.
39 Last, *What to Expect When No One's Expecting*, 142.
40 Last, *What to Expect When No One's Expecting*, 100.
41 Last, *What to Expect When No One's Expecting*, 154–55.
42 Singapore Human Resources Institute, "Singapore," apfhrm.com/docs/Singapore-Country-report.pdf.
43 Nelson, "Youth of the Noble Birthright: What Will You Choose?" broadcasts.ChurchofJesusChrist.org.
44 Brooks, *Who Really Cares*, 99.

CHAPTER 14

Capitalism Promotes Liberty, Freedom of Speech, and Initiative

Introduction

There is an ongoing debate about capitalism versus socialism. There are good people on both sides of the issue. The purpose of this and the next chapter is not to question one's motives for advancing either theory but to discover whether there are certain moral principles that will help us determine which system should be adopted by a people who desire to be in accord with God's moral law and which system brings greater joy to its people.

What are Capitalism and Socialism?

In brief, capitalism is an economic and political system in which production of goods and services is controlled by private owners for individual profit in a free-market society. This is done for the purpose of maximizing individual wealth based on hard work, ingenuity, expertise, vision, and other like talents.

On the other hand, socialism is the elimination of private ownership in favor of state ownership and control of property, goods, and services for the purpose of distributing income equally among an entire population and eliminating all class distinctions. Some try to distinguish between socialism and communism, but the difference is one of degree, not kind. In fact, they have similar DNA. Communism is the father; socialism is the child. Adam Buick, speaking on behalf of the Socialist Party of Great Britain, confirmed this: "As far as we are concerned, socialism and communism are exact synonyms."[1]

Various degrees of socialism have been adopted in different countries. At one end of the spectrum is the Karl Marx, Frederic Engels style known as communism.

Lesser forms are sometimes referred to as European-style socialism or democratic socialism.[2]

Most countries have adopted some socialistic policies. For example, the United States, which is considered a capitalist country, has adopted a social security system for retirement purposes and Medicare for health benefits. In fact, most countries are a hybrid of capitalism and socialism. Accordingly, the labels *capitalism* or *socialism* are not nearly as important as the underlying principles that govern each respective economic system. Hence the emphasis in this chapter and the next is to focus on these principles and their moral influence on society.[3]

What Are the Moral Principles Underlying Capitalism and Socialism?

Socialism has a worthy goal: to eliminate poverty and class distinctions. In essence, to achieve economic equality. There is nothing wrong with this end goal; it is laudable and often driven by people who are compassionate. The problem is the means used to get there. On the other hand, capitalism does not have such an end goal; neither is its goal inequality. Rather, its goal is to provide a system of opportunities and choices that allows everyone to strive for a better economic life if they so choose. This, too, is a laudable goal. John Meacham summarized it well when he said, "We cannot guarantee equal outcomes, but we must do all we can to ensure equal opportunity."[4]

Referring to colonists who desired a better economic life by escaping a monarchy and aristocracy, Arthur Schlesinger wrote,

"Here it was man alone, not his ancestors, who counted. Even the humblest folk could hope to better their condition, and the equality of opportunity that had now become theirs meant as well the opportunity to be unequal."[5] Simply put, it was capitalism the colonists desired.

The Founding Fathers felt that socialism was both morally evil and unconstitutional. Samuel Adams noted, "The Utopian schemes of levelling [redistribution of wealth], and a community of goods [central ownership of the means of production and distribution], are as visionary and impractical as those which vest all properties in the Crown are arbitrary, despotic, and, in our government, unconstitutional."[6] In other words, the Constitution was meant to define and protect equal rights, not mandate the distribution of equal things.

Will and Ariel Durant, in their comprehensive work *The Lessons of History*, spoke of the historical incompatibility between opportunity and equality: "*Freedom and equality are sworn and everlasting enemies, and when one prevails the other dies. Leave men free, and their natural inequalities will multiply almost geometrically*, as in England and America in the nineteenth century under *laissez-faire*. Only the man who is below the average in economic ability desires equality; those who are conscious of superior ability desire freedom; and in the end superior ability has its way. *Utopias of equality are biologically doomed*."[7] In other words, the freedom to have a market economy on one hand, but mandatory equality of income and wealth on the other, are simply incompatible goals.

F. A. Hayek, winner of the Nobel Memorial Prize in Economics and recipient of the Presidential Medal of Freedom, exposed the immorality of socialism: "A movement [socialism] whose main promise is the relief from [individual] responsibility cannot be but antimoral in its effect, however lofty the ideals to which it owes its birth."[8]

Despite the foregoing, there exists a current debate in our society today: which system—capitalism or socialism—will do more to benefit society by promoting personal liberty, spiritual growth, reducing poverty, and accelerating discoveries to enhance man's cultural, scientific, and intellectual development? The following is designed to answer that and other related questions. In doing so, I have not discussed the environmental issues which are important. There is no question that some capitalists have a disregard for the environment in order to maximize profits, and this is certainly a huge negative. But on the other hand, history isn't kind to the socialists' treatment of the environment, as evidenced by countries such as Cuba, Venezuela, Russia, and China, who have adopted many socialistic policies.

Suffice it to say, both systems could do much better in this regard.

Capitalism Maximizes Freedom and Thus Our Opportunity for Personal and Spiritual Growth

Perhaps the most fundamental right of man is the freedom to make and carry out choices. Our choices are what lead to our growth or decline, to our happiness or unhappiness. Without the freedom to make choices, we are merely puppets of some higher power. If we are seeking personal and spiritual growth in our life, as God would have us do, then it is our internal choices, not external forces, that will maximize that growth. In other words, growth comes from within, not from without. Capitalism provides us the opportunity to be a participant or spectator, to take risks or play it safe, to succeed or fail, but underlying it all is the right to choose. Some will use this freedom for good, others for evil. That choice is inherent in capitalism and thus consistent with our God-given rights of life, liberty, and the pursuit of happiness.

To the contrary, socialism, in whatever form it is enacted, always strips some rights of choice from the individual and transfers them to a state-controlled entity. It may be the lost right to choose a private insurance plan or doctor or to own or work for a private enterprise (because government has nationalized that industry) or a restriction on religious liberty and freedom of speech as exists in North Korea and Cuba, or excessive taxes that result in less discretionary income and thus less freedom to fund social policies of one's choice. But there is always some personal loss of freedom in direct opposition to our God-given right to life, liberty, and the pursuit of happiness.

Socialism is a freedom robber and power grabber. It is a system which is designed to mandate "goodness" by government decree based on the false belief that a forced change in behavior will bring about a voluntary change in human nature. No doubt there is some ostensible moral reason for granting greater governmental control, but one must always count the cost in loss of personal freedom. Some rationalize that cost, saying that it contributes to the "greater good," and accordingly, in that particular case, the end justifies the means. But the end never justifies an immoral means.[9]

Socialism not only siphons off power from individuals and then transfers it to the state, but in the process, it also creates a new power not previously in existence. It creates the most powerful monopoly of all. While socialism decries the abuse of private monopolies, it ironically creates the ultimate monopoly as it takes over private means of production. For example, when government expropriates the health, transportation, media, or energy sectors, it not only controls planning, production, and distribution, as is the case in the private marketplace, but it also controls all related rulemaking and rule-enforcing. All the powers related to health, transportation, media, and energy are centered in one set of hands—the government. It is both batter and umpire combined in one. It has destroyed the diffusion of power and competition that previously existed in the free market. There is simply no check and balance system left, and that is when power runs wild.

Many advocates of socialism see government, not God, as the ultimate redeemer and savior of social injustices. They have replaced the omniscience of God with the wisdom of man and, in the process, replaced the freedom of man with the force of government—all in the name of social justice. Forced equality has taken priority over choice, and where there is no choice, happiness quickly shrivels and misery blossoms.

Justin T. Haskins, senior editor and research fellow at the Henry Dearborn Institute for Liberty, confirmed this conclusion: "The main reason I oppose socialism is because regardless of the outcomes a socialized country might experience, I believe a socialist system *requires* certain freedoms to be eliminated—freedoms so essential to humanity that they ought to be considered unalienable human rights. Socialists have a tendency to obsess over economic equality, but they almost always fail to assign any importance at all to freedom, which, as has been proven since the dawn of history, has real and substantial *value* for most people."[10]

There is an eternal principle in operation that cannot be camouflaged or circumvented—the greater the freedom, the greater the opportunity for spiritual and intellectual growth. Democracy, including capitalism, maximizes that opportunity. Socialism minimizes it. Alexis de Tocqueville gave his concurring opinion: "Democracy extends the sphere of individual freedom, socialism restricts it. Democracy attaches all possible value to each man; socialism makes each man a mere agent, a mere number. Democracy and socialism have nothing in common but one word: equality. But notice the difference: while democracy seeks equality in liberty, socialism seeks equality in restraint and servitude."[11] De Tocqueville hit the nail on the head. Democracy, including capitalism, advocates and promotes equal and full human liberty. Socialism is willing to sacrifice that liberty for the sake of forced equality. But with that forced equality comes increased governmental intervention—and in the process, a loss in individual freedom.

Understanding this loss of freedom, Hayek cautioned, "Although we had been warned by some of the greatest political thinkers of the nineteenth century, by Tocqueville and Lord Acton, that socialism means slavery, we have steadily moved in the direction of socialism." No wonder his book on the evils of socialism is titled *The Road to Serfdom*.[12] Suffice it to say, every step forward toward socialism is a step backward in personal freedom and spiritual growth.

Capitalism Promotes Free Speech

Milton Friedman, a world-renowned economist, observed, "It is a mark of the political freedom of a capitalist society that men can openly advocate and work for socialism."[13] The United States is a classic example. Our capitalistic society allows for full freedom of speech concerning socialistic ideas. In fact, such ideas are propagated on a daily basis in schools, on media channels, and by political pundits and candidates.

But what about the reverse—freedom of speech for capitalism in a socialistic society? One need only look to North Korea, Cuba, or Venezuela for an answer to that question. Some respond by saying that these are exceptions—examples of dictator-socialism, not democratic-socialism. The difference between the two, however, is one of degree, not kind, as illustrated below.

Many universities in the US are bastions of socialistic thinking and advocates of democratic socialism. How open are they to speakers who promote democracy and capitalism? One would hope that in the US, it would not be a concern, but it is.

Ben Shapiro, a well-known political speaker and promoter of democracy and capitalism, told of his invitation to speak to the Young America's Foundation group at California State University at Los Angeles. As he approached the university, he saw "helicopters swirling overhead." Hallways and entrances were blocked by hundreds of students, some of whom were physically assaulting those who wanted to attend. Dozens of police ushered Shapiro through a back door to the auditorium.

He then said, "I put my ear to the auditorium door; it sounded like a zombie apocalypse outside. Members of the police department said that the administration had told them to stand down and allow the protestors to do whatever they pleased." He further explained that students pulled the fire alarm and pounded on the outside doors. Finally, Shapiro was ushered through back hallways and kitchens to safety.[14]

Unfortunately, this was not an isolated case. Shapiro went on to say, "At the University of Wisconsin, my speech was nearly shut down by protesters who flooded the front of the stage. At Penn State, protestors gathered outside my speech and pounded on the doors. At De Paul University, the administration threatened to arrest me if I came to campus and called out a Cook County sheriff to do the honors. At Berkeley, the administration called out hundreds of police officers to protect law-abiding citizens from the rage of violent rioters."[15]

But Ben Shapiro was certainly not alone in his experience. J. Harvie Wilkinson III, a federal judge on the Fourth Circuit Court of Appeals, said of his classmates and instructors at the Ivy League college he attended, "Many...preferred to suppress speech rather than respond to it. [My university] of all places should have stood against these trends. Instead it succumbed to them."[16]

Michael Bloomberg (founder of Bloomberg LP and former mayor of New York City) and Charles Koch (CEO of Koch Industries Inc.), certainly not political allies, but recognizing the suppression of speech on college campuses, combined to write the following:

> During college commencement season, it is traditional for speakers to offer words of advice to the graduating class. But this year the two of us—who don't see eye to eye on every issue—believe that the most urgent advice we can offer is actually to college presidents, boards, administrators and faculty.
>
> Our advice is this: *Stop stifling free speech and coddling intolerance for controversial ideas, which are crucial to a college education—as well as to human happiness and progress.*
>
> Across America, college campuses are increasingly sanctioning so-called "safe spaces," "speech codes," "trigger warnings," "microaggressions," and the withdrawal of invitations to controversial speakers. Students and professors who dare challenge this climate, or who accidentally run afoul of it, can face derision, contempt, ostracism—and sometimes even official sanctions. The examples are legion.[17]

What an exposure and condemnation of those universities who inhibit free speech. Usually, if not always, these are universities that foster a socialistic mentality.

Hayek noted, "Where freedom was concerned, the founders of socialism made no bones about their intentions. Freedom of thought they regarded as the root-evil of nineteenth-century society."[18] Benjamin Franklin, quoting from an abstract from the *London Journal*, warned about the dangers of limiting free speech: "Whoever would overthrow the Liberty of a Nation must begin by subduing the Freeness of Speech."[19]

A socialist mentality, even one espousing democratic socialism, is often hostile to free speech when it comes to opposing ideas, sometimes using force to prevent it. One might ask, "Why is this the case?" Is it because these people are intolerant of the views of others? Because they want the power associated with being the sole voice in the matter? Because they believe the First Amendment only applies to the propagation of their political philosophy? Because they do not feel confident in defending their position and thus don't want to hear an opposing argument that might prove them wrong? Or they feel guilty and do not want to hear the truth? If not any of the foregoing, then what is the answer for such anti-American behavior—such disregard for decency and free speech? If someone really cares about what is right and true, then he or she should welcome opposing arguments, knowing that such will either strengthen one's existing position or give one a more enlightened view to consider for the future.

The apostle Paul taught, "Where the Spirit of the Lord is, there is liberty" (2 Cor. 3:17). Certainly, this would include free speech—a constitutional right encouraged and fostered by capitalism. No doubt the reverse is true—where there is no liberty and free speech, the Spirit of the Lord is absent—a moral tragedy often triggered by a socialistic mentality. Capitalism is a system that not only sponsors a free market economy, but in that same spirit, a free marketplace to exchange ideas.

Capitalism Promotes Initiative, Ingenuity, and Creativity

History has demonstrated that no economic system fosters initiative, ingenuity, and creativity as does capitalism. Just consider the advancements in the world of technology as one example.

People are motivated by rewards—money and ownership being two of them. It is an inherent human characteristic. One does not have to be an economic genius to understand what will happen if socialism is adopted and excessive progressive taxes are applied against individuals, corporations, and other legal entities. With less money available for individual and corporate profits and rewards, such as dividends, bonuses, profit-sharing contributions, and the like, these businesses will appropriately take lesser risks because the results yield lesser returns. As a result, there will be a reduction in terms of initiative, creativity, ingenuity, expansion of businesses, equity fundraising, and the like. Socialism has and will continue to stifle economic growth. Capitalism has and will continue to spur it.

The United States has become the powerful economic country it is because of its people's entrepreneurial spirit. Howard Marks, a well-known American investor and author, wrote, "While there are ways in which [capitalism] can be improved, I consider it problematic when people denounce capitalism without acknowledging its benefits. It's ironic to think of politicians criticizing the capitalist system via platforms like Twitter and Facebook (accessed on their iPhones); at rallies reached via airlines and cars (perhaps employing ride-sharing services such as Uber); in meetings over a Starbucks coffee; and via cable news networks. All of these are innovations that came out of a system that encourages people to take significant risks to start companies on the premise that they'll reap the rewards of ownership if their businesses succeed."[20]

If given the option, would you choose a government-run program or a privately owned one? If you vacillate on this, just wait for your next appointment in a Social Security office. Recently, I went to apply for Part B insurance and was told the wait was two to three hours. I was unable to stay. On my way out, I happened to talk to a woman in line who had been there about two and a half hours and still believed she had a long wait ahead. I tried to make a phone appointment for another day but was told that appointments were not possible for this type of application. Accordingly, I returned at a later date with my wife, waited our turn, and was told we had successfully applied for Part B insurance. Later, my wife received her confirmation in the mail. I waited and waited, but nothing came. Finally, I called the national Social Security office and was told they did not have the ability to track the status of my application. I would have to return to the local office. Back to the local office, I went and waited my turn. Finally, after some exasperation, the governmental employee told me he could not determine the status of my application. I asked why. He replied that they were understaffed and their equipment was outdated. "Sorry," he said. "I can't do anything more. Just wait, and hopefully within sixty days, you will get further word." To rephrase an old quote: "If you love your Social Security office, you are going to love socialism."

Contrast that experience with my obtaining private insurance as a supplement to Part B governmental insurance. After one phone call, the necessary forms arrived at our home within a week. I returned them, and within ten days, confirmation was received that I was insured. No long waits, no delays, no office visits, and no excuses. Theoretically, both systems—government and private—should be equally efficient, but in practice they are not. Suffice it to say, there is nothing spiritual, nothing moral, about running an inefficient organization.

I mention these examples not because I believe government employees are ineffective but because they operate within a system that is counter to human motives or at least does not fully take full advantage of them, such as initiative, competition, and opportunity for rewards and ownership. In its quest for equality, socialism often draws people to a lower or even the lowest common denominator. It would rather have every student receive a C grade than have only some who achieve As or Bs. There must be equality at any cost.

The story of Harrison Bergeron, written by Kurt Vonnegut Jr., illustrates this "equality descent." It speaks of the year 2081 when everyone was finally equal. "Nobody was smarter than anybody else. Nobody was better looking than anyone else. Nobody was stronger or quicker than anybody else." And all this thanks to the dedicated agents of the United States Handicapper General (H-G men). One day, Harrison Bergeron, the fourteen-year-old son of George and

Hazel, was snatched away by these H-G men for plotting a suspected coup, not to be heard of again until the end of the story.

George Bergeron was exceptionally bright. To equalize his brilliance, he was required to wear a mental handicap radio in his ear that would emit sharp sounds about every twenty seconds in order to reduce his IQ level to that of the average person. His wife, Hazel, was of average intelligence and therefore needed no such device.

One day, George and Hazel were watching ballerinas on TV. None were any better than anyone else might have been. "They were burdened with sash-weights and bags of birdshot, and their faces were masked, so that no one, seeing a free and graceful gesture or a pretty face, would feel like something the cat drug in."

Suddenly, there was a news bulletin on TV. Harrison, age fourteen, had escaped from jail. He was a genius and glorious physical specimen who was heavily handicapped so he would not be better than anyone else. After all, equality, even if it resulted in mediocrity, was the hallmark and goal of society. Unexpectedly, Harrison appeared on stage. He declared, "Now watch me become what I can become."

He stripped from himself his burdensome handicaps and revealed an incredibly handsome, athletic figure. He then plucked a hideous mask from a ballerina. She was stunningly beautiful. He removed her weights, and the music began. "In an explosion of joy and grace, into the air they sprang. They reeled, whirled, swiveled, flounced, capered, gamboled, and spun." It was heavenly to behold.

Then the Handicapper General appeared on the scene. With her ten-gauge shotgun, she fired twice, and Harrison and his ballerina fell dead to the ground.[21] *The moral: excellence had to be extinguished for the sake of equality.*

And so it is with socialism. Its obsessive quest for equality dampens initiative, ingenuity, and creativity—natural human cravings. The resulting consequence is no surprise—reduced productivity. James Wilson, a Founding Father, so noted, "What belongs to no one is wasted by every one. What belongs to one man in particular is the object of his economy and care."[22]

China is a prime example of Wilson's observation. In 1978, the Chinese Communist party realized that the stagnant growth in the country's agricultural production was due in part to "certain inefficiencies of China's collective production structure." The party then introduced sweeping capitalistic reforms: "Collectivized agriculture...was replaced with a system of household farming in which the land was divided among existing households. Decisions on cropping patterns and the quantities of fertilizers and other inputs to be used are now made by each household rather than by team and brigade leaders. Peasants [were] encouraged to specialize and produce for the market rather than being forced to be self-sufficient. Comparative advantage cropping [was] encouraged by reopening rural markets."[23]

Commenting on these reforms, Howard Marks wrote, "The Chinese experience...tells the whole story in eight short years: deregulation and decontrol; free enterprise and the profit motive; increased flexibility and choice; the benefits of specialization; and the allocation of resources via the free market. The results: vastly increased production, but also greater inequality and reduced government services." And then his conclusion: "*In other words, you can't have it all. Most people lived much better because of the reforms, whereas under the prior system [communism] everyone had it the same, but most people lived far less well. Which was fairer?*"[24] China's growth was stagnant under socialism. Only when it began to adopt a market system and allow human initiative to work its magic did its economy begin to explode.

The irony is that in the end, socialism may achieve relative equality for most, but that equality results in poverty, not wealth, as witnessed by those who live in North Korea, Cuba, and Venezuela, and previously in the Soviet Union. As Haskins noted, "When the lowest-performing, laziest workers receive the same wealth as the highest-performing, hardest-working individuals, there's little, if any, motivation for most people to work as hard or harder than the most productive employee. Instead, the entire factory workforce only needs to work as hard as the least-productive person. Put simply, the entire socialist economy is a race to the bottom."[25] He then added that socialism is promoted under the delusional principle that it "will work because people will *choose* to behave in ways that seem contradictory to all of human history and nature."[26]

No wonder there was a common saying among the workers in the former USSR: "We pretend to work and the government pretends to pay us." That is the fruit of socialism—a system that inhibits initiative, ingenuity, and creativity.

Government inefficiency compared to that of private enterprise is further highlighted when one compares the financial operations of government-run businesses with related businesses in the private sector. I realize these are not perfect comparisons, and that government-run programs may address some social and policy concerns not addressed by private enterprise, but I could not find any studies that could quantify these social concerns in a way that made up for the huge gap in profitability between the two. In the course of my study, I was not surprised to learn that the US postal service ran an 8.8 billion-dollar deficit in 2019[27] and has had total losses of 78 billion since 2007. Meanwhile, FedEx, a private company, operated at a 540 million-dollar *profit* in 2019.[28] Amtrak, a government-run railroad, operated at an 881 million-dollar *loss* in 2019,[29] while Union Pacific, a private company, operated at a 5.9 billion-dollar profit.[30]

In addition to the foregoing, the US government has operated in the red for the last approximately twenty years, running up a staggering national debt in excess of $25 trillion. What private business could survive this trend? Considering these facts, one must honestly ask, "Why would anyone want to advocate the cause of socialism by encouraging more government control of industries such as the health, transportation, media, and energy sectors now largely operated by private enterprises?"

Conclusion

To put it mildly, socialism is an enemy to moral liberty, freedom of speech, efficiency, initiative, ingenuity, and creativity. It is a system that kills the golden goose but unrealistically expects the golden eggs to appear with equal or even greater frequency. On the other hand, capitalism provides a remarkable climate in which moral liberty, freedom of speech, efficiency, initiative, ingenuity, and creativity can thrive. Of course, some will use that freedom for immoral purposes, prompted by greed and unjust power, but others will use that freedom to provide desired jobs with accompanying health insurance and retirement benefits, contribute financially to those in need, and improve the world with advancements in health, science, and the like. God's plan is to allow His children the right to choose, knowing this will ultimately provide the greatest benefit to themselves and to society. This right is compatible with the basic principles of capitalism. On the other hand, socialism forces people to "do good," but in the process it destroys their freedom and thus limits their individual growth and happiness. This is the underlying principle of socialism—in direct contravention to the basic purpose for our existence.

---

1 Buick, "A Question of Definition: Socialism/Communism," worldsocialism.org.

2 See Haskins, *Socialism Is Evil*, 7.

3 Lest there be any confusion on this issue, the members of Christ's original church did share all things in common (see Acts 2:44–45; 4:32), but this was not socialism. Their contributions to the church were voluntary, not forced through a system of excessive taxation or military confiscation. Likewise, the proceeds were not distributed "equally" but according to one's needs (see Acts 2:45). The spirit of Christ's gospel is rooted in giving and sharing; the spirit of socialism in taking and forcing. Only the former produces personal and spiritual growth. Winston Churchill made this further comparison: "There is a great difference between Socialists of the Christian era and those of [today]. The Socialism of the Christian era was based on the idea that 'all mine is yours' but the Socialism of [today] is based on the idea that 'all yours is mine'" (*Never Give In!* 23–24).

4 Meacham, *The Soul of America*, 8.

5 Schlesinger, *The Birth of the Nation*, 128.

6 In Wells, *The Life and Public Services of Samuel Adams*, 1:154. James Madison added, "That is not a just government…where the property which a man has in his personal safety and personal liberty, is violated by arbitrary seizures of one class of citizens for the service of the rest" (*Selected Writings of James Madison*, 224).

7 Durant, *The Lessons of History*, 20; emphasis added.

8 Hayek, *The Road to Serfdom*, 217.

9 But some might say that it is immoral to kill, yet did not many Americans kill in world wars in order to preserve our freedoms? Therefore, the question "Did

not this worthy end goal—to obtain freedom—justify the immoral means of killing?" It is true that God gave the general command not to kill, but He also reserved the right to direct killings in specific circumstances. For example, in Ecclesiastes, we read, "To every thing there is a season, and a time to every purpose under the heaven. A time to kill, and a time to heal; A time of war, and a time of peace" (Eccles. 3:1,3, 8). Consistent with this, did not God command the hosts of Israel to slay the wicked inhabitants of Canaan so they could occupy the promised land? Was not Goliath delivered into the hands of David to be slain? In these instances, killing was not immoral because it was done in accordance with God's will, and whatever is done in accordance with God's will is moral. To have a moral end, one must first have a moral means. Socialism fails that test because it requires a means that curtails one's individual liberty.

10 Haskins, *Socialism Is Evil*, 3, 81; emphasis in original. Myron Magnet, author and recipient of the National Humanities Medal in 2008, summarized Madison's similar observations, from *Federalist Papers* no. 10, as follows: "We have designed a government that will protect our natural rights to life, liberty, and property, Madison says. But since men, though equal in rights, have different talents and ambitions, the Constitution's protection of their freedom to employ those talents as they see fit will result in quite different—that is, unequal—outcomes. Some will be rich; some poor. That is not a flaw but a sign that the liberty we value is alive and well" (*Clarence Thomas and the Lost Constitution*, 96).

11 In Hayek, *The Road to Serfdom*, 25.

12 Hayek, *The Road to Serfdom*, 67.

13 Friedman, *Capitalism and Freedom*, 16.

14 See Shapiro, *The Right Side of History*, xx–xxi.

15 Shapiro, *The Right Side of History*, xxii.

16 Wilkinson, *All Falling Faiths*, 22, 42.

17 Bloomberg and Koch, "Why Free Speech Matters on Campus," wsj.com.

18 Hayek, *The Road to Serfdom*, 76.

19 Franklin, "*Silence Dogood*, no. 8," founders.archives.gov.

20 Marks, "Political Reality Meets Economic Reality," 12.

21 Vonnegut, "Harrison Bergeron," 7–14.

22 Wilson, *The Works of The Honourable James Wilson*, 3:195.

23 In Marks, "Growing the Pie," 3.

24 Marks, "Growing the Pie," 4; emphasis in original.

25 Haskins, *Socialism Is Evil*, 31.

26 Haskins, *Socialism Is Evil*, 37; emphasis in original.

27 United States Postal Service, *FY2019 Annual Report to Congress*, 11. In fact, the US Postal Service has operated at a loss for the last thirteen years.

28 *FedEx Corporation 2019 Annual Report*, 52.

29 National Railroad Passenger Corporation and Subsidiaries, *Consolidated Financial Statements*, 7.

30 "Union Pacific Reports Fourth Quarter and Full Year 2019 Results," up.com. The *Journal of Management Studies* concluded its study of private companies [POEs] compared to state-owned enterprises [SOE's] as follows: "Overall, POEs perform significantly better than SOEs," noting for example that POEs have a return on assets (ROA) that is about 10 percentage points higher than that of SOEs. This journal further noted that these findings "correspond well with many other studies of private versus public ownership."

CHAPTER 15

SOCIALISM PROMOTES BIG GOVERNMENT, POVERTY, SELFISHNESS, MISERY, AND A GODLESS SOCIETY

Big Government Generates Power, and Power Corrupts

The Founding Fathers advocated the least government necessary and the greatest diffusion of power possible in order to maximize our agency and protect our God-given rights. Socialism is the antithesis of this philosophy. In order to support its many socially driven programs, it naturally gravitates toward significant spending, big government, and dangerous concentrations of power.

Justice Scalia noted, "The cardinal sin of capitalism is greed; but the cardinal sin of socialism is power."[1] Senator Rand Paul addressed this concern: "The overthrow of Batista in Cuba gave us Castro. The overthrow of Somoza in Nicaragua gave us the Sandinistas. The overthrow of the czars gave us Stalin, and on and on. Each time a revolt of the 'people' promised the manna of socialism and justice. And each time the result was rule by an elite that degenerated into rule by the few or even rule by one."[2] History has demonstrated that socialism is the Trojan Horse for the would-be despot.

Socialism, of necessity, takes power from society at large and concentrates it in the hands of a few. It is a catalyst for diminished individual rights and for expanded governmental rights. There are always more social ills to correct and more governmental power needed to do the correction. It is never one and done.

And unfortunately, with increased power comes an increase in unrighteous dominion. History confirms that for most men and women, power corrupts, and socialism is a prime source of that unchecked power. In fact, power and dictatorships are best friends, as the histories of Mao Zedong of China, Joseph Stalin of the Soviet Union, Nicolás Maduro of Venezuela, and Fidel Castro of Cuba confirm.

F. A. Hayek cut through the idealism of the socialistic agenda with this revealing analysis: "What in ordinary language [of the socialist] is misleadingly called the 'economic motive' means merely the desire…for power to achieve unspecified ends."[3] And for socialism, economic equality is the cover, but power is the objective.

Lord Acton, a British historian, understood this causal relationship between power and corruption: "Power tends to corrupt, and absolute power corrupts absolutely."[4] That is why the term *democratic socialism* is an oxymoron. The more the socialism, the more the concentrated power. And the more the concentrated power, the less the democracy. Mark Levin noted, "The Founders understood that the greatest threat to liberty is an all-powerful government, where the few dictate to the many."[5] Unfortunately, this is exactly what socialism creates—bigger government, more corruption, and reduced personal liberty. Socialism puts its trust in government over the people; capitalism puts its trust in the people over government.

Ben Carson made this significant observation: "The Constitution is quite clear that the government has the right to tax in order to support its programs, but there is nothing in the Constitution to support redistribution of wealth. Some proponents of big government get around this by creating many programs and then argue that these have to be supported by taxes."[6] More and more government programs, coupled by more and more taxation, is the back door to socialism.

David Brooks, a former socialist who turned capitalist, wrote an opinion column for the *New York Times*, in which he said, "Over the past century, planned economies have produced an enormous amount of poverty and scarcity. What's worse is what happens when the political elites learn what you can do with that scarcity. They turn scarcity into corruption. When things are scarce, you have to bribe government officials to get them. Soon, everybody is bribing. Citizens soon realize the whole system is a fraud. Socialism produces economic and political inequality as the rulers turn into gangsters. A system that begins in high idealism ends in corruption, dishonesty, oppression and distrust."[7] A pretty good summary of the history of socialism.

The champions of socialism seem to fall within this sage warning of Daniel Webster: "It is hardly too strong to say, that the Constitution was made to guard the people against the dangers of good intention. There are men, in all ages…who mean to govern well, but *they mean to govern*. They promise to be kind masters; but *they mean to be masters*. They think there need be but little restraint upon themselves. The love for power may sink too deep in their own hearts."[8] In other words, beware of the benevolent socialist.

Rand Paul noted, "The socialists argue that Stalin, Hitler, Pol Pot, Chavez, Castro, and Kim are all anomalies and not the logical conclusion of socialism." Paul then quotes George Reisman, an economist, who concluded, "The inescapable inference to be drawn is that the terror actually experienced in the socialist countries was not simply the work of evil men, such as Stalin, but springs from the nature of the socialist system."[9] Socialism is a system that inherently concentrates power, and power most often breeds corruption.

Once one starts down the road of socialism, it is easy to expand its benign programs but very difficult, if not impossible, to stay the course or even reverse course. It is like the person who contemplates eating only one salted peanut, having only one drink, or smoking only one cigarette. The desire may be there, but the will power is usually lacking. Once government officials feel the rush of power by centralizing programs under government control, they usually have an insatiable desire for more and more power, and thus more and more programs. At first, it is only social security on a very small level, then universal social security for the aged, then Medicare and Medicaid, then comprehensive welfare benefits, then universal health care, then free college tuition, then control of local schools, then free government-provided child care, then confiscation of the energy sector, transportation systems, and the media, and the list never ends until all the tentacles of the government are completely wrapped around the individual citizen and his life. When all is said and done, socialism replaces parent, teacher, religious leader, personal doctor, and private entrepreneur with government. It is the illusionary panacea for all of society's ills.

Socialism is government on steroids. It has an inherent creeping quality, always seeking more power and control. And with each step forward toward supposed equality, the common man is forced a step backward in his or her individual liberty. It reminds one of the anecdotal story concerning the frog placed in a kettle of warm water. Degree by degree, the temperature is raised until the unsuspecting frog, unaware of the slight but steady changes, is boiled to death.

Likewise, degree by degree, socialism enlarges government until it stifles and eventually puts to death our individual liberties.

Part of the brilliance of the Constitution is that it enumerated certain powers for the federal government and left the rest to the states. Socialism disregards and disrupts that balance of power by vesting more and more power in the federal government and less and less power in the states. It concentrates power rather than diffusing it, and thus is in direct opposition to the basis on which the Constitution was founded.

Jamie Dimon, CEO of JP Morgan Chase, wrote a scathing rebuke of socialism and its big government mentality in his 2019 annual letter to shareholders. He shared the following concerns: "When governments control companies, economic assets (companies, lenders and so on) over time are used to further political interests—leading to inefficient companies and markets, enormous favoritism and corruption. [Socialism] would be as much a disaster for our country as it has been in the other places it's been tried."

There is "no question," Dimon wrote, "that capitalism has been the most successful economic system the world has ever seen. *It has helped billions of people out of poverty, and it has helped enhance the wealth, health and education of people around the world.* Capitalism enables competition, innovation, and choice. Private enterprise is the true engine of growth in any country." He then added, "*We shouldn't forget that true freedom and free enterprise (capitalism) are, at some point, inexorably linked.*"[10]

The big government that socialism unquestionably promotes leads to inefficiencies, cronyism, corruption, overregulation, immoral programs, and unchecked power—all in contradiction to the basic principles enshrined in the Constitution and advocated by the Founding Fathers. These are not just theoretical talking points. Brazilian President Jair Bolsonaro, in speaking to the United Nations General Assembly on September 24, 2019, said, "My country has been on the verge of socialism, which has put us in a state of widespread corruption, serious economic recession, high criminality rates and unending attacks on the family and religious values that underpin our traditions."[11]

If someone wants more government, more taxes, more regulation, more corruption, more immoral governmental programs, more widespread poverty, and more governmental intrusion into individual and family lives, then he or she should be an advocate of socialism.

Socialism Promotes Equal Poverty for the Masses

Contrary to the argument of some socialists, wealthy people do not necessitate or cause the existence of poor people. Abraham Lincoln addressed the fallacy of this argument: "Property is the fruit of labor; property is desirable; [it] is a positive good in the world. *That some should be rich shows that others may become rich, and hence is just encouragement to industry and enterprise.* Let not him who is houseless pull down the house of another, but let him work diligently and build one for himself."[12]

President Ronald Reagan taught the same principle by asking three rhetorical questions: "Since when do we in America believe that our society is made up of two diametrically opposed classes—one rich, one poor—both in a permanent state of conflict and neither able to get ahead except at the expense of the other? Since when do we in America accept this alien and discredited theory of social and class warfare? Since when do we in America endorse the politics of envy and division?"[13]

The philosophy of Lincoln and Reagan—that of democracy and capitalism—was one of lifting people up. Socialism is a philosophy of equality even if it brings people down. It reminds me of one man's observation to Howard Marks: "When a worker in Britain sees the boss drive out of the factory in his Rolls Royce, he says, 'I'd like to put a bomb under that car.' But when the worker in the U.S. sees the boss drive out of the factory in his Cadillac, he says, 'Someday I'll own a car like that.'"[14]

There seems to be a misconception that because we have wealthy people in society, they must of necessity be the cause of poor people. Senator Rand Paul addressed this assertion: "This whole...tale of a zero-sum economy where, when the rich get richer, the poor must get poorer is nothing more than fantasy. The deeper you look into the statistics the less believable the tale becomes."[15]

Contrary to the zero-sum argument, it seems that as wealth increases in a capitalistic society, poverty decreases. Of course, there are some greedy capitalists, but on the other hand, many wealthy people and corporations do much to reduce poverty through job opportunities and charitable giving. In fact, the wealthy in America are among the most generous donors in the world. If the wealthy had less wealth (due to socialism), there would be less charitable and humanitarian giving. Arthur Brooks, whose extensive research on charity was referred to earlier, noted, "Households with total wealth exceeding $1 million (about 7 percent of the American population) give about half of all charitable donations. Simply put, your local United Way [and the organizations it supports] would close down were it not for rich people in your community."[16]

But what if the wealthy are not charitable? Is socialism then justified? Even if the wealthy do not give one dime to charity, they provide jobs for the otherwise unemployed, and in many cases they provide accompanying health insurance and retirement benefits for them. They pay taxes that support government programs which provide housing, food, and health care for the impoverished. In addition, the wealthy buy goods and services that support other jobs.

However, as socialism reduces the wealth of individuals and businesses, it simultaneously reduces their growth and purchasing power. This results in reduced taxes and fewer jobs, meaning fewer provisions for health care, retirement benefits, housing, and food, often for those with the greatest needs.

Someone once defined insanity as doing the same thing over and over again but expecting different results. Cuba, North Korea, Venezuela, and the USSR are evidence that the results of socialism are repeatedly the same—greater overall poverty as a result of forced equality. Ben Shapiro noted the stark differences between North Korea, a socialistic country, and its neighbor South Korea, a capitalistic country: "The countries are divided only by an artificial political barrier; the population is ethnically identical. Yet six decades of central planning in the North has resulted in a gross domestic product (GDP) per capita of $1,214 as of 2017; in South Korea, the same period has resulted in a GDP per capita of nearly $30,000."[17]

Brazilian President Bolsonaro noted, "Venezuela, once a thriving and democratic country, undergoes today the cruelty of socialism. Socialism is working in Venezuela! Everyone is poor and has no freedom!"[18] Nikki Haley corroborated this observation: "Venezuela...was the richest country in South America when it was both democratic and capitalist. By August of 2018...Venezuela's government leaders had rejected both democracy and capitalism. The predictable result was millions of Venezuelans were hungry, sick, or dying due to a lack of basic food and medicine. Mothers picked through garbage cans to feed their children, even as Maduro refused to allow humanitarian aid into the country."[19] Haley added, "In a region where 31 percent of the people are poor, a stunning 90 percent of Venezuelans live below the poverty line."[20] Socialism had achieved its goal—equality for the masses. The only problem—everyone is equally poor.

But some politicians say, "Oh, I would implement socialism in a much different way than in Venezuela." Perhaps that is like the reasoning of the man who says, "Oh, I wouldn't drive over the cliff at ninety miles per hour. That would be foolish. Instead, I would obey the speed limit while doing so." Somehow, he missed the point. And so it is with advocates of socialism. No matter how it is implemented, it is a societal plunge to a social, economic, and spiritual demise.

The truth is, the wealthier a capitalistic country is, the less poverty it will usually experience. Robert P. Murphy, an American economist and author, wrote an article entitled "Extreme Poverty Rates Plummet Under Capitalism," in which he charts out some significant historical studies on capitalism and observes, "Yes, it's true that the rich (tend to) get richer, but the poor get richer too—especially if we look at a time span of decades or longer. Of course, there is more work to be done on this front, but the spread of market institutions…[has] gone hand-in-hand with rapid and unprecedented increases in human welfare, even for the poorest among us."[21]

Despite these positive results, some still present counterarguments to the statistically proven fact that capitalism lifts all boats—rich and poor. The primary counterargument admits that capitalism benefits the poor as well as the rich, but then opines, "Capitalism is delivering windfalls to the rich and crumbs to the poor. Yes, 'extreme' poverty is declining. But most people still have nearly nothing, and some people have everything they could dream of 1000 times over."[22] This rationale, however, greatly understates the substantial decrease in poverty in countries where capitalism thrives as confirmed in multiple statistical studies. The foregoing opinion then concludes with no solution to remedy the discrepancy between rich and poor other than to default to socialism—a system that has been tried scores of times and failed again and again.

Socialism, contrary to its claims, has the distinction of creating a wealthy elite (usually the government leaders) while at the same time increasing and equalizing the poverty level for the masses—hardly a notable achievement. Hugo Chavez, the former Venezuelan dictator, had an estimated net worth in excess of $1 billion; North Korean dictator Kim Jong-un approximately $5 billion; and Paul Biya of socialist Cameroon about $200 million. Yet all the while, the vast majority of their constituents were or are in abject poverty.[23] So much for the elimination of wealth inequality and class distinction as promised by socialists.

One must eventually ask, "If a moral goal is to reduce overall poverty, why would anyone select socialism over capitalism as a means to accomplish this end?" It is simply an inferior economic system, as history continues to demonstrate.

Capitalism certainly has its faults, but no better economic system seems to be on the horizon. Nikki Haley confirmed this conclusion: "The intellectual contest between democratic capitalism and socialist dictatorship has been over for a long time. Free minds and free markets won. History has shown where these separate paths lead. The freedom model has lifted more people out of poverty than any other system of government in the history of humankind."[24] Rand Paul echoed similar sentiments: "If your goal is to help the poor become better off, there is no more humanitarian economic system than capitalism."[25]

Socialism Promotes Selfishness and a Lack of Concern for Others

Arthur Brooks came to the following conclusion concerning income redistribution [socialism]: "For many people, the desire to donate other people's money displaces the act of giving one's own. People who favor government income redistribution are significantly less likely to behave charitably than those who do not. For many Americans, political opinions are a substitute for personal checks; but people who value economic freedom, and thus bridle against forced income redistribution, are far more charitable."[26] He then added, "Not only do many redistributive policies…displace giving, they discourage charity in recipients of redistributed income and stimulate the *opposite* of compassion."[27]

In other words, socialism spawns stinginess and personal selfishness. As noted by Justice Scalia, "The transformation of charity into legal entitlement has produced both donors without love and recipients without gratitude."[28]

Brooks shared this personal experience he had in Russia: "I was teaching a class in Moscow for Russian university students of nonprofit management. After reviewing the data on low levels of giving and volunteering in Russia, I asked the students why they believed this was so. Their answers were immediate and unanimous. 'Our parents,' one student told me, 'don't have any religion, and believe the government should provide for all of the people's basic needs.'"[29] A sad but no doubt accurate assessment.

In his first visit to the United States, Aleksandr Solzhenitsyn, the Nobel Prize-winning Russian author, observed, "The United States has long shown itself to be the most magnanimous, the most generous country in the world. Wherever there is a flood, an earthquake, a fire, a natural disaster, an epidemic, who is the first to help? The United States. Who helps the most and unselfishly? The United States."[30] What a candid admission from someone who had little to gain but perhaps a great deal to lose by making such a statement. It is true that capitalism results in greed in some, but it also results in profound generosity in many others. In other words, it preserves one's choice to do good or evil. And that is a moral good. Socialism suppresses that choice, and that is a moral evil.

Socialism, by its nature, stifles personal charity, compassion, and gratitude. That is understandable. When we replace personal charity with government, we replace intimacy with "distancy." Personal feelings of love and compassion are replaced by a mechanical check or deposit from a soulless institution. Gratitude is replaced by expectation.[31] In the process, we convert rewarding personal relationships to impersonal and dispassionate connections. In essence, we take the humanity out of humans. Timothy P. Carney so noted, "When you strengthen the vertical bonds between the state [government] and the individual, you tend to weaken the horizontal bonds between individuals. What's left is a whole that by some measures is more cohesive, but individuals who are individually all less connected to one another."[32] In other words, a society with less compassion and brotherly love for one another.

Under socialism, government's responsibility is to provide all charitable giving. As a result, the desire of others to help is lessened, perhaps even eliminated. And in the process, society ends up with benefactors who are forced to give through excessive taxation or military might and recipients who expect entitlements regardless of their individual effort or contribution to society. This robs the recipients of self-worth and initiative. It deprives them of the desire and will to confront and solve their own misfortunes. And why should they, since a magnanimous overseer, who knows much better than they, is there to define their problems and solve them? But in the process, it creates a nation of dependency.[33]

The philosophy that should serve as the foundation of a moral society—voluntarily giving from a charitable heart, a willingness to work whenever possible, and gracious and appreciative receiving—is not just undermined but obliterated by socialism. It sacrifices Judeo-Christian virtues in return for forced equality and a more calloused society.

What should be the first line of defense for the needy? Hopefully, the answer is personal compassion and charity. Unfortunately, these are relegated by socialistic policies to the back seat. As a consequence, the opportunity for spiritual growth, both by giver and receiver, is diminished.

In an effort to encourage unselfishness, President John F. Kennedy gave this inspired advice: "Ask not what your country can do for you—ask what you can do for your country."[34] Socialism turns this advice on its head. It promotes the attitude "What can I get from my country?" not "What can I give to it?" It is a philosophy that engenders selfishness and dependency.

Socialism Promotes a Victim Mentality and Misery

Socialism seems to breed a victim mentality. It invites the poor to think, *Because I am not rich like certain others, I have been cheated, taken advantage of, treated unfairly. Accordingly, the rich must be punished with exorbitant income taxes. Wealth taxes must be imposed on their net worth, and they must be derided in the public square, lest anyone else seek to get rich. They must be brought down at all cost. They must be forced to pay for their success. After all, everyone knows that they are the cause of our poverty.* Such is the argument of many a socialist.

Jordan Peterson made reference to the origin of such a nonsensical contention: "There is the dark side of it [socialism], which means everyone who has more than you got it by stealing it from you. And that really appeals to the Cain-like element of the human spirit. Everyone who has more than me got it in a manner that was corrupt and that justifies not only my envy but my actions to level the field so to speak, and to look virtuous while doing it. There is a tremendous philosophy of resentment that I think is driven now by a very pathological anti-human ethos."[35]

This victim mentality is evidence of an entitlement society. It is preoccupied with blame. It drains one of self-esteem, self-sufficiency, and the desire to work hard and get ahead. It elevates emotion over reason, self-pity over self-reliance, entitlement over hard work, and stagnation over initiative. It diminishes God as an influential force in our lives, demoralizes and desensitizes society, and subdues one's natural inclinations to rise above the mediocre. In the end, the fruit of socialism is misery. It is one of Satan's masterful strokes of genius—a time bomb wrapped in the finest of ribbon and glitter.

Brittany Hunter, a writer for the Foundation of Economic Education, and Dan Sanchez, its editor, wrote an article entitled "How Believing in Socialism Can Make You Miserable." In it they cited the following example:

> On my (Brittany's) college campus, the largest and most active club was the "Revolutionary Student Union," also known as the school's resident Marxists. One thing that struck me was how these students were not only wrong but seemed deeply unhappy. They always walked into class scowling and were always grousing, not just about the evils of capitalism, but about intractable frustrations and perceived injustices in their personal and academic lives.
>
> I often wondered if there was a connection between the dysfunction in their lives and their socialist ideology.
>
> To these young revolutionaries, every frustration in their lives was someone else's fault. If they

> weren't getting the grades they felt they deserved, some bourgeois professor was to blame. If they didn't have job prospects that matched their high regard for their own intellects, it must be the capitalist system holding them back.
>
> By shifting the blame to others, they relieved themselves of responsibility for their own problems. They wasted their time and energy complaining, wallowing in self-pity, and seeking redress, instead of taking ownership of their lives and fixing up their affairs. As a result, their frustrations only compounded.[36]

I debated whether to share the foregoing experience because one story does not a principle prove, but upon reflection, I realized that I have witnessed similar traits among many who advocate socialism. Instead of a spirit of compassion, which is often their battle cry, there is often a spirit of anger, even hostility in their voices, a tirade against the evil rich, and a constant demand to tear them down as though that will lift others up. Their solution to the concerns of society are centered in more money, higher taxes, and more government. It has become their religion. Lee Edwards, a historian and author, commented, "Why do so many of our university professors argue that socialism is a better way to peace and prosperity than capitalism? Because it is, to them, an article of faith. To admit that socialism has failed—repeatedly, consistently and abysmally—for over a century would be, for them, to deny their god."[37]

In essence, the spirit and product of socialism is one of doom and gloom. No wonder André Gide, a French author and winner of the Nobel Prize in literature, commented after visiting the old Soviet Union, "I doubt whether in any country in the world…have the mind and the spirit ever been less free, more bent, more terrorized over and indeed vassalized than in the Soviet Union."[38] Socialism (communism) had made it a bastion of misery. That, unfortunately, is the fruit of socialism in full bloom. Winston Churchill fully understood this when he said, "The inherent vice of capitalism is the unequal sharing of blessings. The inherent virtue of Socialism is the equal sharing of miseries."[39]

Socialism Promotes a Godless Society

Karl Marx wrote, "Religion is the sigh of the oppressed creature, the heart of a heartless world, and the soul of soulless conditions. It is the opium of the people."[40] Frederick Engels stated, "Communism is that stage of historical development which makes all existing religions superfluous and supersedes them."[41] When one reflects upon the tyranny of Stalin, Mao, and Pol Pot, it is easy to understand the observation of William Penn: "Men who will not be ruled by God will be ruled by tyrants."[42]

Each advance in socialism is a step toward communism—the ultimate economic and political philosophy to promote a godless society. Socialism is the very antithesis of the God-driven philosophy and resulting unalienable rights that serve as the foundation of our Declaration of Independence and Constitution. Justice Scalia observed, "I know of no country in which the churches have grown fuller as the governments have moved leftward. The churches of Europe are empty. The most religious country in the West by all standards—belief in God, church membership, church attendance—is that bastion of capitalism least diluted by socialism, the United States."[43]

Justin Haskins asked the Socialist Party of Great Britain if it were "possible for socialism to coexist with religious liberty." The response: "As socialist consciousness becomes far more widespread, this will most probably be accompanied by a growing decline in the need for religion."[44] The answer speaks volumes. Socialism, like communism, is the gateway to a godless society. It is based on the erroneous philosophy that trust in government and its programs, not God, can make you righteous and good. Once that ideology is accepted, there are no longer absolute values, no will of God to whom men must account. All morals become relative—the sure path to a decadent society. It is a path we are already dangerously pursuing at an accelerated rate.

But Doesn't Socialism Work in the Nordic Countries?

Most people are willing to admit that socialism isn't working in Cuba or North Korea or Venezuela and didn't previously work in the USSR, but many claim that democratic socialism has worked in the Nordic countries of Denmark, Norway, Sweden, and Finland. The problem with such a claim is that these countries are a far cry from the socialism of those who promote them as such. Recognizing this, the prime minister of Denmark remarked at Harvard's Kennedy School of Government, "I know that some people in the US associate the Nordic model with some sort of socialism. Therefore, I would like to make one thing clear. Denmark is far from a socialist planned economy. Denmark is a market economy."[45] When Finnish president Sauli Niinistö was asked if his country was socialist, he responded, "No, God bless."[46]

Jesse M. Plunkett, a columnist for the *Orlando Sentinel*, wrote an article highlighting the differences between socialistic countries and the Nordic countries: "The difference is simple: In one group of countries, the government progressively or aggressively seizes the means of production (actual socialism in Venezuela, Nicaragua and the Soviet Union) and in the other, free-market capitalism rules, with high, flattened taxes for everyone (the capitalistic welfare states of Scandinavia)."[47]

Not only are the Nordic countries market economies, but they differ from socialism in other critical particulars. Most businesses are privately owned, not government owned. They engage in free trade. Private health insurance is available. They do not have federally mandated minimum wage laws—a hallmark of a socialistic society."[48] In contrast to the many socialists who want to ban all private schools, the government of Sweden has a voucher system for every student who can then choose private or public school. Finland has a relatively low corporate tax rate of 20 percent, Sweden is 21.4 percent, Norway is about 23 percent, and Denmark is 24.5 percent, far less than what most socialists desire. In addition, Sweden has no inheritance tax—anathema to the socialist who wants heavy wealth taxes, particularly at death.[49]

Sweden tried socialism from about 1960 to 1980 before serious capitalistic reforms were set in motion, such as lower corporate tax rates and abolishment of the inheritance tax. Johan Norberg, Swedish author and historian, tells the consequences of such a socialist experiment: "It resulted in less work...general lack of getting the kind of education that matters. It led to entrepreneurs leaving Sweden."[50] Senator Rand Paul added, "During its socialist era, Sweden grew 1 percent slower than Europe and 2 percent slower than the United States."[51] No wonder the reforms came.

The Nordic countries do have safety nets of state health insurance and, in some cases, free tuition,[52] evidences of some socialistic policies, but the funds for these purposes come from tax money of businesses and individuals who are permitted to engage in a capitalistic free market with relatively little interference from government. Rand Paul summarized it pretty well when he said, "Today's socialists want Scandinavian socialism except it's not socialism because the state doesn't own or control most of the means of production. Today's socialists want to emulate Scandinavia's welfare state except for their high taxes on the middle class, their regressive 25 percent VAT [value-added tax], and the absence of punitive taxes on their top one percent. Confused?"[53] Yes, confused, if one fails to recognize that the Nordic countries all have market economies—the centerpiece of capitalism, not socialism.

Conclusion

Peter T. Leeson, while serving as visiting professor of economics at the University of Chicago, conducted an extensive analysis on the effects of capitalism versus socialism on a global basis. He concluded, "Citizens in countries that became more capitalist over the last quarter century became wealthier, healthier, more educated, and politically freer. Citizens in countries that became significantly less capitalist over this period endured stagnating income, shortening life spans, smaller gains in education, and increasingly oppressive political regimes. The data unequivocally evidence capitalism's superiority for development." He then added, "Capitalism isn't just the 'safer bet' for development. It's the only bet that makes any sense at all."[54]

It seems the evidence in favor of capitalism becomes even more convincing the further one goes down the road of socialism—for example, Cuba, Venezuela, and North Korea. Some argue, but those are dictatorships, not democratic socialist countries. It is true that socialistic dictators are probably worse than democratic socialists, but the underlying principles of immorality are the same. For example, one may take your money by military force, the other by excessive taxation, but in both cases, your property has been expropriated.

Some people who understand the evils of comprehensive socialism still believe that bits and pieces of socialism are acceptable, even beneficial when it comes to the social programs they promote. But the principles underlying partial socialism are the same disastrous principles underlying comprehensive socialism, just on a smaller scale. One might as well claim that one donut a day will have no effect on one's diet, or that one lie per day will not adversely affects one's integrity. Small sins are still sins, and thus adversely affect one's spiritual progress.

Despite good intentions, most if not all socialistic programs have a negative effect on the desired morals of society. Any step toward socialism, however minute, is a step that usually reduces human liberty and suppresses initiative, creativity, and ambition. It is a system that cuts across the grain of human nature. It inhibits free speech, destroys self-reliance, and diminishes charitable giving. In addition, it often promotes immoral social programs such as abortion and zero population growth and leads to a godless society. And historically, it has failed in its greatest claim for existence—the elimination of poverty. The words of George Santayana seem so appropriate: "Those who cannot remember the past are condemned to repeat it."[55]

Max Eastman was a member of the Socialist Party for ten years and the editor of two magazines with a socialistic bent. He said, "I gave my heart to Lenin more completely than I have to any other leader."[56] Eastman spent almost two years in Russia studying the Russian language and propagating socialism. Then, with a first-row seat, he realized that it was all a sham. To his credit, he candidly confessed, "It is better to be courageously humble about this and admit frankly that socialism was a mistake. An hypothesis proven false, I call it for my own pride's sake."[57] Page by page, he listed the defects he discovered, including but not limited to phony elections, a system that runs contrary to human nature, a misconception of the need for personal ownership, a disregard for facts, restriction of speech, press and assembly, restriction of movement, an unrealistic belief that material equality and freedom can coexist in a government-controlled setting, a loss of moral standards, and the loss of freedom to control one's economic choices. Is it any wonder he called his book on the subject *Reflections on the Failure of Socialism*?

President Harry Truman made this sad but no doubt accurate observation: "The next generation never learns anything from the previous one until it's brought home with a hammer. I've wondered why the next generation can't profit from the generation before but they never do until they get knocked in the head by experience."[58] Hopefully we can escape the sledgehammer of socialism in ours and future generations.

In theory, socialism may sound appealing—equality for all, an absence of poverty, and seemingly something for nothing. But practically, it *has never worked, anytime, anywhere*. It is promise rich and delivery poor. History has exposed it for what it is, and thus history is its worst enemy.

Socialism may wear a pretty mask, but underneath it is cankered in immorality. It is like a cancerous tumor, perhaps unnoticed at first, that spreads with disastrous consequences and destroys everything in its path until it is too late to recover. It will destroy society from within, cell by cell, as demonstrated by history again and again. Hopefully we can be wise enough to learn from the lessons of the past.

---

1 Scalia, *On Faith*, 125.

2 Paul, *The Case against Socialism*, 129.

3 Hayek, *The Road to Serfdom*, 125.

4 In Hill, *Lord Acton*, 300.

5 Levin, *Liberty and Tyranny*, 18.

[6] Carson, *America the Beautiful*, 77. Carson also noted, "The founding fathers of this nation were well aware of the perils associated with gigantic government programs, which is why they emphasized limited government and self-reliance" (*America the Beautiful*, 87).

[7] Brooks, "I Was Once a Socialist. That Changed," A31.

[8] Webster, *The Works of Daniel Webster*, 1:357–58.

[9] Paul, *The Case against Socialism*, 137.

[10] Dimon, "Chairman and CEO Letter to Shareholders," reports.jpmorganchase.com; emphasis added.

[11] Bolsonaro, "Statement by Mr. Jair Messias Bolsonaro," statements.unmeetings.org.

[12] Lincoln, *Complete Works*, 10:54. On another occasion, Lincoln said, "I take it that it is best for all to leave each man free to acquire property as fast as he can. Some will get wealthy. I don't believe in a law to prevent a man from getting rich; it would do more harm than good" (Lincoln, Speeches and Writings, 144).

[13] Reagan, "Remarks at a Conservative Political Action Conference Dinner," presidency.ucsb.edu.

[14] In Marks, "Growing the Pie," 7.

[15] Paul, *The Case against Socialism*, 42.

[16] Brooks, *Who Really Cares*, 77.

[17] In Shapiro, *How to Destroy America in Three Easy Steps*, 76.

[18] Bolsonaro, "Statement by Mr. Jair Messias Bolsonaro," statements.unmeetings.org.

[19] Haley, *With All Due Respect*, 209.

[20] Haley, *With All Due Respect*, 237.

[21] Murphy, "Extreme Poverty Rates Plummet under Capitalism," fee.org.

[22] Robinson, "How Inequality Statistics Can Mislead You," currentaffairs.org.

[23] Dougherty, "Ocasio-Cortez Finds Mega-Wealth Immoral," thenationalsentinel.com.

[24] Haley, *With All Due Respect*, 218.

[25] Paul, *The Case against Socialism*, 304.

[26] Brooks, *Who Really Cares*, 55.

[27] Brooks, *Who Really Cares*, 95; emphasis in original.

[28] Scalia, *On Faith*, 122–23.

[29] Brooks, *Who Really Cares*, 128.

[30] Solzhenitsyn, *Warning to the West*, 27.

[31] Religious leader, Wilford W. Andersen, spent time in Africa working with those in poverty. He made this wise observation: "The greater the distance between the giver and the receiver, the more the receiver develops a sense of entitlement" (in Dale G. Renlund, "That I Might Draw All Men unto Me," 39).

[32] Carney, *Alienated America*, 197. These were the exact sentiments of President Grover Cleveland: "Federal aid…encourages the expectation of paternal care on the part of the Government and weakens the sturdiness of our national character, while it prevents the indulgence among our people of that kindly sentiment

and conduct which strengthens the bonds of a common brotherhood" ("Veto Message," presidency.ucsb.edu).

33 Hayek concurred in this conclusion: "Independence of mind or strength of character is rarely found among those who cannot be confident that they will make their way by their own effort" (*The Road to Serfdom*, 147).

34 Kennedy, "Inaugural Address of John F Kennedy," avalon.law.yale.edu.

35 In Hunter and Sanchez, "How Believing in Socialism Can Make You Miserable," fee.org.

36 Hunter and Sanchez, "How Believing in Socialism Can Make You Miserable," fee.org.

37 Edwards, "The God That Failed…Over and Over Again," heritage.org.

38 In Edwards, "The God That Failed…Over and Over Again," heritage.org.

39 Churchill, "Demobilisation," api.parliament.uk.

40 Marx, *Critique of Hegel's "Philosophy of Right,"* 131.

41 Engels, "Draft of a Communist Confession of Faith," 110.

42 In Meacham, *American Gospel*, 224.

43 Scalia, *Scalia Speaks*, 336.

44 Haskins, *Socialism is Evil*, 82.

45 In Yglesias, "Denmark's Prime Minister Says Bernie Sanders is Wrong to Call His Country Socialist," vox.com.

46 In O'Neal, "Why Bernie Sanders is Wrong about Sweden," A13.

47 Plunkett, "Putting an End to the Venezuela vs. Sweden Debate," orlandosentinel.com.

48 See Dorfman, "Sorry Bernie Bros but Nordic Countries Are Not Socialist," forbes.com.

49 See *Wall Street Journal* editorial board, "Defining Socialism Down," A14.

50 In O'Neal, "Why Bernie Sanders Is Wrong About Sweden," A13.

51 Paul, *The Case against Socialism*, 88.

52 While tuition may be free in Sweden, Rand Paul exposed that the average Swede, nonetheless, ends up with about $19,000 in college debt while the average American ends up with about $24,000 of debt. He then explained why: "While tuition is 'free,' rent, food, and entertainment are not. Sweden also has one of the highest costs of living in the world" (*The Case Against Socialism*, 125).

53 Paul, *The Case against Socialism*, 98.

54 Leeson, "Two Cheers for Capitalism?" 227, 233.

55 Santayana, *The Life of Reason*, 284.

56 Eastman, *Reflections on the Failure of Socialism*, 11.

57 Eastman, *Reflections on the Failure of Socialism*, 48.

58 In Meacham, *The Soul of America*, 259.

CHAPTER 16

The Sacred Cement of Society—the Ultimate Solution

What Is the Greatest Challenge Facing Our Society Today?

If you were asked, "What is the greatest challenge facing our society today?" how would you respond? The economy, national security, immigration, gun control, poverty, racism, crime, national pandemics, climate change? While each of these is a valid concern and deserves attention, I do not believe any of them strikes at the heart of our greatest challenge—namely, finding a way to build stronger homes and a return to family and moral values. To put our prime focus on other challenges, rather than the family, is to strike at the leaves, not the root of the problem. It is as some have noted—to put an ambulance at the bottom of the cliff rather than a fence at the top.

Former US Attorney General William P. Barr addressed this critical issue:

> "Instead of addressing the underlying cause, we have the State in the role of alleviator of bad consequences. So the reaction to growing illegitimacy is not sexual responsibility, but abortion. The reaction to drug addiction is safe injection sites. The solution to the breakdown of the family is for the State to set itself up as the ersatz hus-

> band for single mothers and the ersatz father to their children. The call comes for more and more social programs to deal with the wreckage. *While we think we are solving problems, we are underwriting them.*"[1]

Fortunately, most religious traditions, whether Christian, Jewish, Muslim, or otherwise, place a focus on families and thus are striking at the root of our nation's problems. That focus is inherent in the religious experience.

George W. Bush wrote about the life of his father, who had served as director of the CIA, US ambassador to the United Nations, and vice president and president of the United States. These were all distinguished titles, but when asked about his illustrious life, his father responded that the three greatest titles he ever held were husband, father, and grandfather. George W. Bush then observed that his father "knew exactly what is most important in life: faith and family. The world knows George Bush as a master of personal diplomacy. We know George Bush as the world's best dad."[2]

If our prime focus is family and moral values, then we will have less crime and drug abuse, less fraud and abuse, fewer divorces and lawsuits, fewer babies born out of wedlock, more ethical employees and employers, a reduction in welfare cases, less contention and hate, and a resurgence of religious values. Then we will have a solid foundation upon which to build a society entitled to God's blessings. When all is said and done, families are the building blocks of a successful society.

The colonists understood this. Arthur Schlesinger wrote, "Although colonial life was woven of many strands—English, Scotch-Irish, Dutch, French, German, and so on—all the new groups, whatever their ethnic differences, shared the common belief that the family was, in Franklin's phrase, the 'sacred cement of all societies.'"[3]

Timothy P. Carney, writing about what causes alienation among Americans, came to the same conclusion as Franklin, namely that families hold our society together: "Strong families are the necessary condition of the good life, of economic mobility, and of the

American Dream." He then added, "If you grow up in a neighborhood full of broken families, your chances of climbing the ladder are slim. If you grow up amid intact families, the American Dream is alive and well. In other words, the single most important factor in the upward mobility of a child is the strength of families in the community."[4]

As important as many issues are, no political policy transcends the need to strengthen families and their moral values. Weak families with weak morals are at the root of a nation's problems. On the other hand, strong families with strong morals are the sacred cement that binds us together as a nation. Alexis de Tocqueville noted this truth when he visited America: "There is certainly no country in the world where the tie of marriage is so much respected as in America, or where conjugal happiness is more highly or worthily appreciated. In Europe almost all the disturbances of society arise from the irregularities of domestic life."[5]

No government program or policy can compensate for lack of strong families and moral values. There is no adequate substitute or replacement for them. To believe and act otherwise is to build our national hopes and aspirations on a foundation of sand, like the house of the foolish man in the parable of Christ: "The rain descended, and the floods came, and the winds blew, and beat upon that house; and it fell: and great was the fall of it" (Matt. 7:27).

Sometimes great truths are learned from "the mouth of babes" (Ps. 8:2). I once saw a film entitled *Strengthening the Home*. In it, a young mother, tired from the toils of the day, is hurriedly canning apricots before they spoil. Two of her little children appear in their pajamas and ask her to say prayers with them. Anxious not to be disturbed, she invites them to go and say their own prayers just for tonight.

One of them looks up at her and says, "But, Mommy, what is more important—prayers or apricots?" We might well ask, "What is more important than families and moral values?"

It always seems counterintuitive to me when people who can't govern their own families nonetheless want to govern a city. Or people who can't govern a city want to govern a state or nation. The Bible addressed this paradox. Speaking about the qualifications needed for a bishop (leader) of a congregation, it reads: "If a man know not how to rule his own house, how shall he take care of the church of God?" (1 Tim. 3:5). The principle is clear—if someone can't govern the small things, how can he or she possibly take care of the bigger things?

If strong families and moral values are the foundation of a successful nation, then a key question arises, "How can we as individuals and as a nation best strengthen families?"

The Role of Spouses

Just as the family is the foundation of a nation, so a husband and wife (or a single parent) are the foundations of a happy home. A loving husband and wife provide the ideal environment in which the endowments that are God-given to men and women can best complement each other and thus best nurture a morally grounded family. This is one reason traditional families should be emphasized and promoted by society and governments at every opportunity.

Traditional marriage has always been God's plan for the population and survival of the human race. Accordingly, marriage is a sacred covenant, not only between a man and woman but also with God. In this regard, the apostle Paul noted, "Neither is the man without the woman, neither the woman without the man, in the Lord" (1 Cor. 11:11). In other words, marriage was meant to be a divinely blessed triumvirate.

Because of the divine nature of marriage, each spouse has the duty to do all within his or her power to make it work. For years as an attorney, I represented a well-respected cardiologist from India. On one occasion, while traveling some distance together, I asked him if arranged marriages were still common in India. He replied in the affirmative. I then asked him if his marriage was arranged. He responded, "Kind of." He said, "I was in medical school and liked a young lady who was also a student. In my culture, we couldn't date, so I asked my friend to ask her if she would like my father to speak to her father about marriage. She said she would. Thereafter we were married."

I then asked if most marriages were arranged in India. He responded, "Yes." I further asked if couples could get divorces if they were unhappy. He replied in the negative.

I then asked, "Are these couples who are the product of arranged marriages happy?"

To my surprise, he responded, "Most are."

Finally, I asked, "Why is that?" He then gave this revealing answer: "Because they know they have no other alternative, so they make it work." The point of this story is not to endorse arranged or forced marriages but teach the principle that at the foundation of every marriage should be a rocklike, unyielding commitment to make it work—to love and be true to each other, even in difficult times (see Eph. 5:23, 25, 33).

Unfortunately, there exist many fair-weather partners who, at the slightest provocation, abandon their commitments to spouse and children and in the process destroy the nuclear family—the basic building block of society. In addition, the adoption of "no-fault divorce in every state has made marriage more of a *contingent* relationship"[6] than a permanent one. This is not to say that some divorces are not justified, for certainly some are, but rather to emphasize that great effort should be taken to keep one's marriage commitment and make it work wherever reasonably possible.

Tom Brokaw was a famous television journalist and author of the best-selling book *The Greatest Generation*, a tribute to those of the World War II generation. In the book, he highlights common men and women during that era who were true heroes in terms of their courage, their service, and their devotion to family. In the course of doing so, Brokaw noted, "It was the last generation in which, broadly speaking, marriage was a commitment and divorce was not an option." He then made this remarkable observation: "I can't remember one of my parents' friends who was divorced."[7] That statement caused me to reflect upon my parents and their friends (and they had many), and likewise I could not think of one of them who was divorced. Brokaw goes on to quote one of these heroic spouses, who, after many years of marriage, expressed a sentiment shared by others of that generation: "Expectations were different. We had a higher regard for marriage. You just didn't divorce."[8] That generation understood that marriage is among the most sacred and binding of covenants ever made by a man and woman.

I am reminded of the story of a fanatical sports fan who never missed watching a football game on TV. One day, while watching yet another game, his wife, unhappy, entered the room and said, "Bill, you love football more than you love me."

"That's true," he said, "but I love you more than I love basketball."

There is a tragic humor in that story. Some love their sports or hobbies or shopping or career or smart phones more than they love their spouse. Husbands and wives, however, who put God first and their spouse next will invite a divine influence into their relationship that will make it more rewarding than if they put their spouse before God. For more than fifty years of a marvelous marriage, my wife and I have found that to be true.

President Jimmy Carter spoke of his wife's influence for good on him: "There's nothing that gives me more pleasure, even as President of the United States, than to have [my wife] come to me in the evening, when I'm tired and concerned and worried, and put her arms around my neck and give me a kiss."[9]

There is no escaping it—traditional marriage between a man and a woman as part of the nuclear family is the foundation of a moral and happy society. Arthur Brooks noted from his studies on family and charity, "Married people are generally a lot happier than unmarried people."[10] That should be no surprise because God has commanded marriage between a man and woman, sanctioned it and blessed it.

The Role of Parents—The Prime Moral Teachers of Their Children

Years ago, my father, an attorney, defended a young man who was facing multiple criminal charges. At the time, the young man's father was a member of the Supreme Court of the State of California. During the sentencing phase, the judge, in a tone of great condescension, asked, "How could you, the son of a Supreme Court Justice, bring such dishonor upon your father—he who upholds and administers the very laws you have chosen to violate?"

There was a moment of tense silence. The boy responded, "Your Honor, I never knew my father." The tenor of the courtroom instantly changed. The judge was reminded of a sad truth—that to be a good Supreme Court justice does not necessarily make one a good father.

In contrast, Justice Scalia's son paid this tribute shortly after his father's passing: "We have been thrilled to read and hear the many words of praise and admiration for him, his intellect, his writings, his speeches, his influence, and so on. But more important to us—and to him—is that he was Dad. He was the father that God gave us for the great adventure of family life. Sure, he forgot our names at times or mixed them up; but there *are* nine of us. He loved us, and sought to show that love, and sought to share the blessing of the faith he treasured. That's the greatest wealth that parents can bestow, and right now we're particularly grateful for it."[11] What a tribute to a brilliant, accomplished man who was first and foremost a husband and father.

At some point, we will all die. When that moment comes, our life will be viewed in perspective as never before. Such a thought brings to mind the sobering quip: "No one on his death bed ever wished he had spent more time at the office." It is a stark reminder that our families and faith should be our prime priorities in life.

One Christian leader summarized this same sentiment as follows: "The most important…work you will ever do will be within the walls of your own homes."[12] There is no adequate substitute for being a conscientious parent. If careers have taken priority, business or hobbies become paramount, then as some have said: "Our ladders are leaning against the wrong wall." As one of my friends put it, "Our families deserve our prime time, not our leftover time."

Of course, mothers and fathers are equally important in the child-raising process, but Arthur Brooks shared these chilling statistics when the father is absent from the home: "Children who grow up without fathers are more likely to fail in school or drop out before graduating from high school, to have emotional or psychological problems, to engage in early sexual activity, to become pregnant, and to have problems with drugs and alcohol. Seventy percent of juvenile delinquents currently in custody were raised without their biological fathers. Young men in this group are seven times more likely to end up in prison than those from stable families."[13]

Parents not only have the responsibility to spend time with their children—but quality time. They are to be their children's prime moral teachers. Ben Shapiro understood this need. He wrote, "If we wish for our civilization to survive...we must be willing to teach our children. We must make of our children messengers for the truths that *matter.*"[14]

William P. Barr is in agreement: "For anyone who has a religious faith, by far the most important part of exercising that faith is the teaching of that religion to our children. The passing on of the faith. There is no greater gift we can give our children and no greater expression of love."[15]

In the book of Deuteronomy, the Lord gave commandments (moral mandates) and then instructed parents that it is their responsibility to teach these commandments to their children: "And thou shalt teach them diligently unto thy children, and shalt talk of them when thou sittest in thine house, and when thou walkest by the way, and when thou liest down, and when thou risest up" (Deut. 6:7). God made it clear that the duty to teach moral values was not a casual, occasional occurrence but a sacred daily responsibility. The New Testament also emphasized this parental duty to teach moral values: "Bring them [your children] up in the nurture and admonition of the Lord" (Eph. 6:4).

We now live in a society where it is often more glamorous and more revered for women to enter the workforce than to be full-time mothers. Personally, I am so grateful for a mother who sent me off to school and was there when I got home—for a mother who taught me refinement, a love for learning, a strong work ethic, the need for moral responsibility, the value of prayer, and a love of God and country. She did the same for my five siblings. No nanny, schoolteacher, day school, or media source could possibly replace her personal, love-filled training and example. My wife did the same for our six children. She used her God-given endowments to be a mother of superior capabilities. I have the highest respect and reverence for mothers who are able and willing to stay at home and unselfishly do what some consider to be the mundane—raise a family in righteousness. When all is said and done, I believe they make the greatest contribution to society. Their results are not measured in net profits or GNP but in character development and moral excellence—the true measures of a great nation. Likewise, I have the highest respect for those mothers and fathers who must work to support their families but give whatever balance of time they possibly can to them and to those who work to fulfill an academic, creative, or other bona fide need, but who do so without neglecting their first and foremost responsibilities as parents.

Elizabeth Shine wrote an article in the *Wall Street Journal* entitled "Coming to Appreciate Stay-at-Home Moms." She said, "I'm not a mother, and at 48 I'm unlikely to become one. As a global management professional, I've lived and traveled all over the world." Then she revealed that her world fell apart. Due to "a perfect storm of issues," she said, "I resigned from my job, and entered a period of physical, financial, emotional and spiritual hell. Friends fell away like fall leaves off a tree—effortlessly. A sad, hard truth I had to face was that the friends who disappeared were mirror images of myself—single, professional, ambitious women."

She then observed that her lifelines proved to be stay-at-home mothers. "In short, this small group of seven full-time mothers… breathed life back into me and helped me find the wherewithal to face my legal and financial challenges. It was a natural extension of what they did every day for their own families. They pour out their time and love—in an often unsung and unnoticed way that really matters and changes lives." Shine then added, "All these women were successful professionals before they married and had children. All chose to stay at home and, as one put it, 'invest in the most important corporation—my family.' Another said she realized she was 'outsourcing my life, including my family, and I didn't like to think where that might lead.' She gave up her role at a Fortune 50 company. Their career sacrifices gave their families solid foundations and emotional security."

Shine concluded her article with this observation: "This Mother's Day, let's recognize the full-time, stay-at-home mothers who have chosen to be the CEO of their own families, rather than sporadic parents and scattered employees."[16]

I believe that women, especially mothers, have a talent and capacity, greater than any other, to foster moral values in their children, and that there is no greater responsibility or honor in life than to raise a righteous family. The apostle Paul, in recounting the "unfeigned faith" of Timothy, observed that this faith had originated from his grandmother Lois and his mother, Eunice (see 2 Tim. 1:5). It is such a faith that so many mothers have instilled in the hearts of their children. Likewise, we have many single women who greatly contribute to the moral values of society in their roles as teachers, religious instructors, child-care providers, community and business leaders, and in many other capacities.

At some point, each of us will face our Maker at the final judgment. It is a sobering thought to contemplate the questions that might be asked by a Being who can see with perfect transparency our every thought. At that moment in time, there will be no deceit, no cover-up, no excuses. What we really are will be exposed in all its glory or infamy. I doubt the line of questioning will be along the following lines:

"What was your net worth when you died? What was your highest three-year average salary? Did you work for a Fortune 500 company? And if not, why not? What was your occupational title? How many times did you appear on cable news? How many followers did you have on Twitter?" Perhaps, instead, the line of questioning will be more along the following lines: "Were you a man or woman of integrity? Did you honestly seek God's will and strive to follow it, even when it was not popular to do so? Were you loyal and true to your spouse? Did you personally take the time to teach your children a love of God and country? And if not, why not? Was your family more important to you than your career or hobbies? Did you serve your fellow man? And if so, how?" I believe that these questions of eternal import will focus on our individual character and how we magnified our God-given responsibilities as spouses, parents, and servants of God. As distant as that day may seem, it will come with certainty to us all.

As a support to families, not a replacement of them, our education system should build character and teach moral values as the foundation of all learning. Unfortunately, in many cases, our education system has not only abandoned this responsibility but taught moral relativism instead. As a consequence, it is all the more essential for parents to exemplify and teach moral truths to their children, including the truths upon which our Founding Fathers established this nation.

In the days of the prophet Joshua, the Israelites needed to make a choice between the true God of Israel and various gods worshipped by others in the land.

Today, those competing gods come in many forms such as fame, money, pleasure, and self-indulgence. They manifest themselves in those who think they are too intelligent to believe in God—who have become their own gods, their own self-proclaimed reservoirs of moral truth. With competing gods seeking the Israelites' allegiance, Joshua gave this inspired counsel to his people: "Choose you this day whom ye will serve…but as for me and my house, we will serve the Lord" (Josh. 24:15). One can imagine what the strength of this nation might be, its moral fiber and receptivity to God's directing hand, if all households would make a choice like Joshua's—to serve the God of the land. Fortunately, we can make that choice, one household at a time. And in that process, we become in reality one nation under God.

The Role of Government in Strengthening Families

It is not enough for government to be neutral in family matters. It can and should play a vital role in strengthening spousal relations, parenting, and moral values. It can encourage these by way of national media campaigns and by the policies and programs it adopts—emphasizing the need for kind and loyal spouses. In addition, government can demonstrate how parents can spend quality time with their children and how they can become their prime teachers of moral values—particularly inculcating within their children virtues such as integrity, respect for others, hard work, and a love for

God. It can elevate the role of devoted spouses and parents, who, in truth, are the superheroes of our society. It can encourage educational institutions to have a curriculum that focuses on character development, family unity, moral values, and an understanding and respect for our Founding Fathers and country. It can adopt as a litmus test that legislation be designed to strengthen the family and moral values, and that no legislation be passed that would harm the family unit in any way. Most people have enough good in them that they will respond positively to inspired suggestions and reminders that will help them fulfil their divine roles as spouses and parents.

The story "The Great Stone Face," written by Nathaniel Hawthorne, is the account of a young boy, Ernest, who daily admires and studies the natural stone image of what appears to be a noble man's face engraved on a nearby mountainside. There is a prophecy that a native son from Ernest's village will one day be in the likeness of the Great Stone Face. The prophecy further states that he will be "the greatest and noblest personage of his time."[17] Ernest longs to meet that man.

Some powerful and well-known native sons return to the village, and for the moment, the villagers are fooled into thinking that each is the one who resembles the natural stone image. But soon, time and better judgment reveal their error.

Years pass, and young Ernest approaches the sunset of life. He has become a lay preacher, and many come to hear his simple but profound wisdom forged from a life of goodness.

Ernest, in his continued search for the man in the likeness of the stone image, invites a famous poet, long ago born in the village to visit him. Surely, he thought, this man of inspiration must be the one to fulfill the prophecy. The poet did come. He and Ernest had a day of uplifting conversation. Ernest noted some resemblance with the Great Stone Face, but, disappointed, realized this was not the one in the exact image of its likeness. Evening came and the poet accompanied Ernest to one of his sunset sermons to be delivered at the base of the mountainside where the Great Stone Face could best be viewed. Hawthorne then describes the scene as Ernest reached the climax of his sermon: "At that moment, in sympathy with a thought which he was about to utter, the face of Ernest assumed a grandeur of expression, so imbued with benevolence, that the poet, by an irresistible impulse, threw his arms aloft and shouted, 'Behold! Behold! Ernest is himself the likeness of the Great Stone Face!' Then all the people looked and saw that what the deep-sighted poet said was true. The prophecy was fulfilled."[18]

The Great Stone Face is the story of every man and woman, namely, that we become like those things that we habitually love and admire. If government will first and foremost promote the family unit in its policies and programs—if its leaders will ask, "How can this program, this expenditure strengthen the family?"—then likewise many individuals, spouses, and parents will first and foremost love, admire, and promote the family unit in their personal lives. And what will be the consequence? Families will become strong and united, and thus once again serve as the sacred cement that binds our nation.

---

1 Barr, "Remarks to the Law School and the de Nicola Center for Ethics and Culture," justice.gov; emphasis added.
2 Bush, *41: A Portrait of My Father*, 258.
3 Schlesinger, *The Birth of a Nation*, 17.
4 Carney, *Alienated America*, 13, 84–85.
5 DeTocqueville, *Democracy in America*, 1:285.
6 Carney, *Alienated America*, 188; emphasis in original.
7 Brokaw, *The Greatest Generation*, 231.
8 Brokaw, *The Greatest Generation*, 249.
9 Carter, "Remarks at Mormon Church Ceremonies Honoring Family Unity," presidency.ucsb.edu.
10 Brooks, *Who Really Cares*, 104.
11 In Scalia, *On Faith*, 217–18.
12 Lee, *The Teachings of Harold B. Lee*, 280.
13 Brooks, *Who Really Cares*, 107.
14 Shapiro, *The Right Side of History*, 214; emphasis in original.
15 Barr, "Remarks to the Law School and the de Nicola Center for Ethics and Culture," justice.gov.
16 Shine, "Coming to Appreciate Stay-at-Home Moms," wsj.com.
17 Hawthorne, *The Great Stone Face*, 7.
18 Hawthorne, *The Great Stone Face*, 30.

CHAPTER 17

WHAT ELSE CAN BE DONE TO PRESERVE OUR MORAL VALUES?

This book has addressed some of the complex issues confronting us as Americans, God's will on those matters, and actions that might be taken to preserve the moral values on which this nation was built. Among those are the need to foster religious freedom in the public as well as private sector, to protect the unborn, resist a zero population mentality, combat the spread of socialism, and perhaps, most important, promote the nuclear family and faith in God as the centerpiece of society. Following are some additional actions that might be pursued to enhance our moral values and thus preserve our Constitution and related liberties.

The Role of Education in Building a Moral Society

The prime purpose of education is not raw learning. It is not the three Rs. It is not grades, as necessary as they may be. This is not to underestimate their importance but rather to put their importance in perspective. The central purpose of education is to build character—moral integrity—men and women who will be true to their word, who will be loyal to their spouse, who will be honest in their business dealings, who will honor and cherish the principles upon which this nation was built, and who will use the knowledge they gain to further God's purposes. The purpose of education is not only to think well but to live well. When education fulfills this purpose, it will help produce a moral people—an essential element for our Constitution to work. But without this moral underpinning, we are left to the fate spoken of by Paul the apostle: "The wisdom of this world is foolishness with God" (1 Cor. 3:19).

William P. Barr noted a key example of the world's wisdom: "Many states are adopting curriculum that is incompatible with traditional religious principles. [For example,] the Orange County Board of Education in California issued an opinion that 'parents who disagree with the instructional materials related to gender, gender identity, gender expression and sexual orientation may not excuse their children from this instruction.'" Mike Huckabee, former governor of Arkansas, noted another example of secular coercion—"an absolutely mind-boggling situation at a school in the San Francisco Bay Area that focused on one of the nation's founding documents. Fifth-grade teacher Steven Williams was prevented from passing out copies of the Declaration of Independence because it made a reference to God."[1] And secularists complain about religion being forced on them? In truth, nothing less than secular religion is being forced on believers in many schools every day. Unfortunately, many schools have become bastions of indoctrination rather than centers of instruction.

Likewise, in many schools there is a dearth of learning about the actual history of the United States. The acclaimed historian Catherine Drinker Bowen noted, "Considering the immense amount of literature on the subject, it is surprising how little the average American knows about the making of our Constitution."[2]

Unfortunately, there are many in the educational system who would rather advance the theories of man than the true and tested ideals of God and the Founding Fathers, who would rather create a secular nation than a spiritual one, who prefer revisionist history to actual history as a way to advance their personal philosophies, and who teach that the ends are justified by the means, whatever those means may be. In addition, there are those who attempt to shut down debate on any view that is contrary to their own, via safe zones, alleged microagressions, and violent protests to stifle free speech. Just as we have politicians on one hand and statesmen on the other, so too we have, in the classrooms of America, political activists on one hand and moral teachers on the other.

The Founding Fathers and many other national leaders felt strongly about the need for teachers who would focus on moral values. Samuel Adams described the mission of educators as keeping alive the "moral Sense" of children.[3] Abigail Adams counseled her son, "Great Learning and superior abilities, should you ever possess them, will be of little value and small Estimation, unless Virtue, Honour, Truth and integrity are added to them."[4]

Samuel Adams further observed, "*As Piety, Religion and Morality have a happy influence on the minds of men, in their public as well as private transactions*, you will not think it unseasonable…to bring to your remembrance the great importance of *encouraging our University, town schools, and other seminaries of education*, that our children and youth while they are engaged in the pursuit of useful science, *may have their minds impressed with a strong sense of the duties they owe to their God, their instructors, and each other*, so that when they arrive to a state of manhood, and take a part in any public transactions, their hearts having been deeply impressed in the course of their education with the moral feelings—such feelings may continue and have their due weight through the whole of their future lives."[5] What a powerful injunction, from a Founding Father, to teach God and morals in our public schools!

One might ask, "Why has this injunction been lost on so many of our school administrators and teachers?" Years ago, I was asked to speak on Veteran's Day at a public school in my hometown, but a caution came from the teacher extending the invitation: "I've been asked to instruct you that you should not say anything about God in your talk." I thought, *How does anyone talk about the origin, establishment, or preservation of America without mentioning God? One might as well talk about cooking without mentioning food, or gardening without mentioning plants. The focal point of America is God!* No wonder that the Supreme Court, in a unanimous decision authored by Justice Joseph Story, declared, "Why may not the Bible…be read and taught as a divine revelation in the college—its general precepts expounded, its evidences explained, and its glorious principles of morality inculcated? Where can the purest principles of morality be learned so clearly or so perfectly as from the New Testament?"[6] How far we have strayed from this counsel.

Noah Webster, an American lexicographer and political writer, sometimes referred to as the father of American Scholarship and Education, added, "The *virtues* of men are of more consequence to society than their *abilities*; and for this reason, the *heart* should be cultivated with more assiduity than the *head*."[7]

These leaders realized that education is much more about integrity than information. Nonetheless, many teachers and students have lost their moral compass. When our daughter was in high school, one of her friends was taking a test and noticed one of her classmates cheating. As their eyes made contact, the classmate shrugged her shoulders and mouthed the words, "I need the grade." Somehow this young lady lost her sense of priorities. She let grades take precedence over morality. She lost focus on what should be the chief aim of education—to build character.

Why do so many schools produce students that can't pass a basic English or math test? Are the students just incapable of doing so? I don't believe so. Are the teachers incompetent? I doubt that. But perhaps their focus is wrong. If teachers would spend more time building character, then students would have an increased desire to learn. But without that desire, teachers are hammering on cold steel. As character is developed, there comes an inherent desire to be a better person—to be more learned, more serviceable to one's fellow man, and more Christlike. Character development is at the root of a successful educational system. When we learn that and teach that, we will produce students who are both learned and wise, students who recognize the need to improve this country but still love it for all the goodness it portrays and the ideals for which it stands, and students who are aware of the ways of the world but submissive to the ways of God. Then we will have a truly educated people, not just an informed people.

Voting for Men and Women of God

An elected official is unlikely to have heaven's blessing in the political arena if he or she does not believe in God or has only a half-hearted commitment to that belief. Such people will be tempted to follow their own standard of morality, their own powers of reason, rather than deferring to God's will. Accordingly, who we vote for as our elected officials is of monumental consequence. Fortunately, the Bible gives us this guideline for choosing our leaders: "Thou shalt provide out of all the people able men, such as fear God, men of truth…to be rulers" (Exod. 18:21).

Noah Webster gave this helpful counsel with regards to voting: "When you become entitled to exercise the right of voting for public officers, let it be impressed on your mind that God commands you to choose for rulers, *just men who will rule in the fear of God.* The preservation of a republican government depends on the faithful discharge of this duty. If a republican government fails to secure public prosperity and happiness, it must be because the citizens neglect the divine commands, and elect bad men to make and administer the laws."[8] We should encourage men and women to run for office who will discharge their duty to the electorate by seeking the same divine guidance that Washington, Adams, Lincoln, and so many of our other national heroes have sought.

The Spirit of Patriotism

Patriotism and moral values seem to be closely connected. In 1976, the two hundredth anniversary of this country, I recall reading of an American tourist who traveled to England and found that, like the United States, Great Britain was commemorating the anniversary with shows, musicals, and displays that centered on the Revolutionary War. At one such display, the tour guide led the guests from room to room, focusing on British victories and British heroes. Finally, sensing the American patriot was somewhat annoyed, she said, "Don't worry, in the end the Americans win."

Of course, they did win, but that victory and others securing and preserving our freedoms did not come cheap. It cost the life and blood and devotion of some of the best men and women who ever walked the earth.

So that we will not forget the incredible sacrifices of those patriots who gave their tomorrows that we might have our todays, the country has established Memorial Day, Veterans' Day, the Tomb of the Unknown Soldier, and the seemingly unending white crosses of Arlington Cemetery. As a young college student, I visited Arlington Cemetery. It dawned on me that many, if not most, crosses represented a young man or woman, about my age, who had made the ultimate sacrifice for our country. There came over me an intense respect and appreciation for these valiant youth. I knew I was on sacred ground. I knew I was looking at the cost of freedom. These were true patriots. It was one of those moments in life I will never forget.

In most of the famous battles in history—such as the Battle at Concord or Gettysburg or D-Day or Iwo Jima—the result came down to individual boys and girls who put their all on the sacrificial altar to protect the ideals set forth in the Declaration of Independence and Constitution. How grateful we should be for them and for the many others who protected and advanced the freedoms we now enjoy—such as the Founding Fathers, Abraham Lincoln, Susan B. Anthony, Rosa Parks, General Dwight. D. Eisenhower, Martin Luther King Jr., and numerous statesmen throughout the ages.

Our national flag is a physical reminder that our freedom was won and maintained at a terrible cost. As we honor our flag, we honor those who defended the freedoms and moral values for which it stands.

In his book *Flags of Our Fathers*, James Bradley tells of his father, John Henry Bradley, who was one of about eighty thousand Americans who fought in the intense battle on the island of Iwo Jima in World War II. Approximately twenty thousand enemy soldiers were hidden below ground in sophisticated tunnels that crisscrossed the island and which rendered the enemy all but invisible. The battle ground out over thirty-six days in February and March 1945. It claimed 25,851 US casualties, including nearly seven thousand dead. Most of the twenty thousand Japanese soldiers fought to the death. There were more medals of valor awarded for that battle than any other in the history of the US. Near the climax of that battle, six Marines fought their way to the island's highest peak, Suribachi, in the midst of machine-gun and mortar fire. There they planted the American flag. That event has now been immortalized in picture and in monument.[9] Why? Because that American flag and the sacrifice surrounding it stood for liberty and justice and courage—the very ideals on which this country was founded.

James Bradley said his father would never speak of his experience on Iwo Jima, other than to say, "Son, the real heroes of Iwo Jima were the guys who didn't come back." And in truth, there were many soldiers who never did come back. After his father passed away, Bradley found a letter that his father had saved. It had been mailed from Iwo Jima on February 26, 1945: "You know all about our battle out here. I was with the victorious [company] who reached the top of Mount Suribachi first. I had a little to do with raising the American flag and it was the happiest moment of my life."[10] John Henry Bradley was just one of many patriots who loved the American flag and the ideals for which it stands.

Time has passed, and sometimes we forget what the flag stands for. For ten years, I attended almost every football game at Glendale High School, as I watched our four sons play. The games always began with "The Star-Spangled Banner." I would look at the youth in the stands and on the field. Many were respectful with their hands over their hearts, joining in the singing of that great national anthem as they focused on the flag. But others were nudging their friends, joking and jostling while the song was being sung. I have often thought, *What good are courses in American history and civics, what good is it to be able to name the battles and generals of past wars, if we do not feel the passion and spirit of patriotism in our veins?* There are certain moments in life that aren't funny; they aren't casual. They deserve and require our better selves. They deserve our highest respect, reverence, and gratitude. And some of these include our respect for our flag and national anthem. Parents and schools can help instill this passion of patriotism in the hearts of our children.

The ancient orator Pericles once spoke at the funeral services of young men who had given their lives in the heat of battle. He observed that words are inadequate to honor great deeds: "The worth which had displayed itself in deeds," he said, "would be sufficiently rewarded by honours also shown by deeds"[11] We best honor those who founded this nation and sacrificed their lives protecting its ideals when our deeds likewise protect and promote those same ideals, when our patriotism is reflected in our love for country and flag and all they stand for.

Can One Person Make a Difference?

If there is any doubt in your mind about the difference one person can make, then you need to hear the story of Gregory Watson, as told by Justice Neil Gorsuch. In 1982, Watson was a nineteen-year-old attending the University of Texas. He was required to write a research paper for his government class. As he was reviewing books on the Constitution, he learned that in addition to the Bill of Rights, James Madison had proposed an amendment to the Constitution that had been ratified by a few states but not by three-quarters of the states necessary to adopt it. The amendment read: "No law, varying the compensation for the services of the Senators and Representatives, shall take effect, until an election of Representatives shall have intervened." Justice Gorsuch noted, "In other words, Congress can't vote itself an immediate pay raise, only one for the next Congress, so the people have a chance in an intervening election to pass judgment on the idea and their representatives who supported it."

Watson was intrigued by the amendment and wrote a paper that the amendment could still be ratified. The professor wasn't persuaded. She gave him a C grade.

Watson wanted to prove his professor wrong, and so he commenced a letter-writing campaign to members of Congress, asking them to pursue this amendment with their state legislatures. As you might imagine, most failed to respond or wrote negative replies. But a senator from Maine pursued the idea, and in 1983, the state ratified the amendment. That gave Watson the incentive to press forward at an expedited pace.

The rest of the story is in Justice Gorsuch's own words: "[Watson] began writing letters to every state legislator he thought might help. Before long, his campaign started to pick up steam with several states ratifying the amendment every year. Finally, in 1992—a decade after writing that fateful paper—the requisite three-quarters of states ratified the amendment, so more than two hundred years after Madison wrote it, the Twenty-seventh Amendment finally passed. And about that C? The professor came around. On March 1, 2017 [35 years after Watson wrote his paper], she filed paperwork to officially change Watson's grade to an A."[12] This story teaches two great truths. First, one person committed to a cause can make a substantial difference. And second, there is no excuse for judicial activism based on the premise that the Constitution, as a practical matter, cannot be amended.

Conclusion

During World War II, a young soldier named Neal A. Maxwell was on a US battleship about to be deployed as part of an invading land force. As he looked around at the other battleships in the bay and the mighty US artillery and equipment in the distance, he thought, *I am proud to be part of an army so vast and powerful as this.* Shortly thereafter, the soldiers in his company landed on the shore and marched ahead, soon out of sight of his battleship. They eventually walked past the heavy artillery and yet farther, beyond the small artillery, until they were in the front lines of battle. At night, Maxwell dug his foxhole. About ten feet away on either side of him were other soldiers digging their foxholes. He then realized that for this ten-foot plot of ground, he was the American Army. What had seemed so vast and powerful had narrowed down to him. For this plot of ground, he was it—America's defender and protector.

Like the patriots of old, we, too, have our ten-foot plot of ground for which we are the American Army, the American patriot.

It may be in our homes as we teach our children correct values. It may be in the classroom or at work as we stand up for moral principles. Every time we are honorable, every time we pray for our nation's leaders, every time we vote, every time we pledge allegiance to the flag with sincerity, every time we seek to honor and promote the intent of the Founding Fathers, and every time we submit our will to God's will regardless of opposing secular pressure, we are a patriot, and we honor those who have gone before.

---

1 In Huckabee and Feazel, *America Great*, 90.

2 Bowen, *Miracle at Philadelphia*, xiii.

3 Adams, *The Writings of Samuel Adams*, 3:237.

4 In Bennett, *Our Sacred Honor*, 219; spelling modernized.

5 Adams, *The Writings of Samuel Adams*, 4:401–2.

6 *Vidal v. Girard's Executors*, 43 US 127, 200 (1844).

7 In Bennett, *Our Sacred Honor*, 267; emphasis in original. And de Tocqueville observed, "The first duty which is at this time imposed upon those who direct our affairs is to educate the democracy; to warm its faith, if that be possible; to purify its morals" (*Democracy in America*, xiii).

8 Webster, *History of the United States*, 336–37.

9 James Bradley's father participated in a flag raising on that day but evidently not in the one that became the famous photograph. See Schmidt, "Flags of Our Fathers' Author Now Doubts His Father Was in Iwo Jima Photo," A1.

10 Bradley, *Flags of Our Fathers*, 328–29.

11 In Thucydides, *The History of the Peloponnesian War*, 120.

12 Gorsuch, *The Republic, If You Can Keep It*, 30.

CHAPTER 18

WHERE ARE THE STATESMEN OF YESTERDAY?

We have many politicians today representing all parties, but unfortunately few statesmen. There is a world of difference between the two. Politicians are generally motivated by power, fame, and money. On the other hand, statesmen are principally motivated by loyalty to country, service, and God. George Washington, Benjamin Franklin, John Adams, Thomas Jefferson, James Madison, and Abraham Lincoln were statesmen. While not perfect, they were men of integrity and morals. They could not be bought at any price. Their allegiance was not to a party but to the nation, not to men but to God.

Hopefully, our current elected officials will aspire not only to be politicians but to be much more—even statesmen. Fortunately, we have some who are striving to do just that. Following are some observations about the differences between politicians and statesmen.

Party Over Nation

Politicians are myopic. They vote the party line regardless of its justifiable nature. They are committed to fight all other parties and leaders regardless of any good they might propose or do. Their priority is party power over national interests. In essence, they are no more than political puppets whose strings are pulled by party leaders.

Unfortunately, this mentality often fosters divisiveness and a lack of love and respect for country.

On the other hand, statesmen look for good ideas wherever they may be found. They acknowledge that other people and parties may have worthy ideas and thus strive to work harmoniously with them to promote those ideas. Their loyalty is to nation over party. They are more concerned about doing right than receiving credit. They are true patriots who can find good even in their adversaries. They promote harmony and unity. They love this nation, they salute the flag and treat it with reverence, they are obedient to the laws of this nation, and they are not afraid to make constructive criticism, but underlying that criticism is an undergirding appreciation for this nation and the ideals for which it stands. Perhaps no greater tribute could be paid a statesman in this regard than that given by Congressman Joshua Giddings to his fellow Congressman at the time, John Quincy Adams: "[He] belongs to no local district, no political party, but to the nation and to the people."[1] What a tribute to someone who was loyal to nation over party.

Governance by Polls

Politicians are often driven by opinion polls rather than moral truths. If 51 percent of the public are in favor of abortion or same-sex marriage, they are ready to jump on the bandwagon, regardless of God's word on the subject. This reminds me of the man and his small son who stopped at an isolated cornfield on a remote country road and eyed the delicious corn beyond the fence. The father, after looking in front of him, behind him, to the left of him, and to the right of him, started to climb the fence and take some ears of corn. His son looked at him and said reproachfully, "Dad, you forgot to look up."[2] Politicians would rather look around them for man's endorsement than look up for God's approval. In truth, the polls have become their God.

Statesmen, on the other hand, make their decisions based on moral principle, regardless of how the polls read. They have the backbone and resiliency to stand alone if necessary. They will not sacrifice principle for polls or character for contributions. They are men and women of God first and of politics second.

Reason over Name-Calling

Politicians are often name-callers. Their vocabulary is filled with words such as *bigot*, *racist*, *homophobe*, *xenophobe*—words that have no probative value, no evidentiary weight in and of themselves. They have abandoned facts, reason, and civility for invective. Why? Because they usually lack the facts or reason to make a compelling argument. They speak in sweeping generalizations, condemnations, and platitudes that have little convincing power but great divisive consequences. It is a reflection of political, social, and intellectual immaturity. Such diatribe pours salt on the wounds that inflict our society. In essence, anger and pejoratives have become their currency in the marketplace of debate. One such example was noted by Luke Goodrich: "Some local governments have already declared various forms of Christianity *fides non grata*—like when San Francisco issued a formal resolution calling the Catholic Church's teaching on adoption and homosexuality 'hateful,' 'insulting,' 'callous,' and 'discriminatory' and urging Catholics to 'defy' it."[3] One might ask, "Does such language heal or inflame, solve the problem or exacerbate it?"

On the other hand, statesmen are political physicians who pour oil on our wounds. They can reason without arguing, discuss without debasing, give respect without yielding. They can express passion without diminishing their powers of reason and civility. Benjamin Franklin shared this counsel as to why he was such a successful statesman:

> I made it a rule to forbear all direct contradiction to the sentiments of others, and all positive assertion of my own. I even forbid myself...the use of every word or expression in the language that imported a fixed opinion, such as *certainly*, *undoubtedly*, etc., and I adopted, instead of them, *I conceive*, *I apprehend*, or *I imagine* a thing to be

> so or so; or it *so appears to me at present*. When another asserted something that I thought an error, I denied myself the pleasure of contradicting him abruptly, and of showing immediately some absurdity in his proposition; and in answering I began by observing that in certain cases or circumstances his opinion would be right, but in the present case there *appeared* or *seemed* to me some difference, etc. I soon found the advantage of this change in my manner; the conversations I engaged in went on more pleasantly. The modest way in which I proposed my opinions procured them a readier reception and less contradiction; I had less mortification when I was found to be in the wrong, and I more easily prevailed with others to give up their mistakes and join with me when I happened to be in the right.
>
> And this mode, while I at first put on with some violence to natural inclination, became at length so easy, and so habitual to me, that perhaps for these fifty years past no one has ever heard a dogmatic expression escape me. And to this habit (after my character of integrity) I think it principally owing that I had early so much weight with my fellow-citizens when I proposed new institutions, or alterations in the old, and so much influence in public councils when I became a member; for I was but a bad speaker, never eloquent, subject to much hesitation in my choice of words, hardly correct in language, and yet I generally carried my points.[4]

Oh, that we could have statesmen like this!

Motivation versus Inspiration

Politicians have the power to motivate—usually toward the acquisition of wealth, power, pleasure, and fame. Moral considerations, however, are often secondary. Sometimes this motivation is achieved through rhetoric that appeals to carnal desires, other times through force. Certainly Hitler, Stalin, and Genghis Khan had these motivational powers. Theirs was a horizontal leadership that motivated people to action, but it did not make the people better.

We have many such politicians today who can motivate, but statesmen do much more. They also have the power to inspire—to make people better. It is a vertical leadership that lifts people up. Who can read the lives of Washington and Lincoln and ponder their messages without wanting to be a better person? Statesmen, both by their exemplary lives and words, inspire us to be the best within us—to live in accordance with our conscience, to be morally responsible beings.

Their Word Is Their Bond

Politicians say what is expedient. They make unintended or ill-informed promises that will generate for them the most votes, alter the facts to justify their position, and falsely or irresponsibly speak ill of an opponent to make themselves look better. For them, expediency is the primary goal; truth is secondary. In many cases, they are modern day Pinocchios. The white lies and whoppers are almost epidemic in their ranks and are reaching alarming proportions. Even obvious and blatant mistakes are dismissed with excuses and blame for others.

How refreshing it is to hear a statesman who tells it like it really is, who candidly admits mistakes without excuse, who does not embellish the facts or withhold critical information, and who only makes promises intended to be kept—whose word is his or her bond.

For a number of years, I represented a retired attorney named Larry Beilenson, a Harvard graduate. He was one of the most brilliant men I had ever met and a man of exacting integrity—a refreshing combination of traits. For years, he served as the personal attorney for Ronald Reagan when he was in the entertainment field. Later, he served as one of his political advisors.

On one occasion, about three days before the end of the year, Mr. Beilenson was negotiating the purchase of a large supply of equipment. It would give him a tax write-off and a good return on his investment, but he needed to conclude the transaction before December 31. The other party called back to say that there was not enough time to draft and prepare the necessary documents before year-end. I will never forget the instructions that Mr. Beilenson then gave me: "Tell them that they have my word. It is better than a written contract." And then he added, almost parenthetically, "If I were bound only to a written contract, I might find a loophole, but there are no loopholes in my word." Similarly, there are no loopholes in the words of a statesman.

Political Correctness Over Factual and Moral Accuracy

Politicians are often obsessive about being politically correct more than factually and morally accurate. Of course, one needs to be sensitive about the feelings of others, but needless to say, we have now reached extremes that can degrade our way of life and dilute our nation's moral values. For example, in some cases, the words *Happy Holidays* may be used to undermine the spirit and meaning of *Merry Christmas*—to remove the focus of the day from a religious holiday to a secular one. In fact, political correctness is often used as a stealth approach to eliminate God from the public sector, to convert us from a nation under God to a nation without God.

The list of politically correct terms is spewed forth almost ad nauseum, such as the term *guest* for a prisoner, "a person creative with the facts" for *liar*, or "morally different" for *dishonest.* And often the word *tolerance* is used as a political shield to mask one's endorsement of immoral behavior.

In this regard, Michael Bloomberg and Charles Koch have noted that a major university "considers statements such as 'America is the land of opportunity' and 'everyone can succeed in this society, if they work hard enough' to be microaggressions that faculty should avoid."[5] In many cases, political correctness has become a form of political nonsense—or even worse, political coercion. Often it is an attempt to limit free speech in order to require conformance to one's political agenda.

The ripples of political correctness seemingly have no rational end. Our daughter-in-law posted this message on Halloween: "My kids were too afraid to dress up since our schools have all these stupid restrictions on what they can and can't wear. You know, no micro aggressions and victimizing groups. No Hawaiian leis. Really?!" She then added, "Meanwhile we had a shooting in [our hometown] last night. Fires, shootings, power outages for days, earthquakes. And we're worried about wearing leis to school on Halloween?"

In response, our daughter texted, "I wanted to wear a beautiful Chinese dress that one of my [Chinese] students sent me. [She was] so excited for me to wear it. But my kids told me some people would say it was offensive." How tragically ironic.

Our daughter doesn't wear a Chinese dress given to her by a Chinese student who was excited for her to wear it because some politically correct people, probably not of Chinese descent, might be offended that our daughter is disrespecting the Chinese culture. In truth, she would be honoring it, but this is where political correctness has taken us. In many cases, it is nothing less than a form of immoral coercion and absurdity. Hopefully, we can speak up and be a voice that helps return us to some sanity in the near future.

Ben Carson addressed this very issue: "The ability to think and speak freely was one of the major tenets upon which this nation was established, and I suspect that the founding fathers would turn over in their graves if they could see how such tenets are being violated on a regular basis today by people adhering to political correctness."[6]

Some have become so absorbed with political correctness that any meaningful discussion on a given subject is stifled for the many who do not feel comfortable acquiescing to their unilateral language demands. In many cases, advocates of political correctness have elevated form over substance and in so doing missed the heart of the issue. They have placed ideology over facts and in the process permitted the ends to justify the means, however immoral the means may be. As a consequence, their tactics are often centered in shame, coercion, and sometimes even violence rather than logic, facts, and kindly persuasion.

By contrast, statesmen are unwilling to sacrifice the means for the ends. With due respect, but with absolute truthfulness, statesmen call it as it really is—terrorism is still terrorism, a lie is still a lie, sin is still sin, and God is still God, whether or not acknowledged by the secularists. The Savior, the most respectful and thoughtful of all beings, knew there was a time to call out the scribes and Pharisees for what they really were—"hypocrites," "blind guides," "fools," "whited sepulchers…full of dead men's bones"—all within the course of one scathing sermon (see Matt. 23). Imagine what this sermon might score on the scale of political correctness, but political correctness was not His end goal. Rather, His message was intended to rebuke these hypocrites for the religious imposters they were, and in addition serve as a spiritual wakeup call for the apathetic by warning them of the foolish and evil traditions being championed by their leaders. There would be no mistake, no ambiguity, about the Savior's feelings on the subject. The unvarnished truth was at the heart of His ministry, coupled with perfect compassion, which compassion also included perfect candor when necessary.

Unfortunately, political correctness is frequently at odds with this philosophy. It often acts as a spiritual anesthetic that numbs our moral senses and distorts our perspective of the world as it really is.

Self-Restraint over Spending—the Need for a Balanced Budget

Politicians are shortsighted when it comes to fiscal responsibility. They believe their political credit card is magical—that somehow it has unlimited purchasing power with no payment date in sight. As a consequence, politicians have little, if any, economic self-restraint. The national debt has vanished from their radar screen. This is evidenced by the fact that our national debt is now over $25 trillion, about $70,000 for every man, woman, and child in the US.

Politicians want to win votes by promising funds for pet local and national projects, with little regard to cost and consequence.

Below are some of the projects for which our tax dollars have been spent in the past few years, as reported by Open the Books in a paid advertisement set forth in the *Wall Street Journal*:

- Testing shrimp on treadmills (2007)—$1.3 million
- Preparing religions for discovery of extraterrestrial life (2017)—$1.1 million
- Federal funding into the fifty worst junior and community colleges (2017–2018)—$923.5 million
- Virtual reality to teach children in China how to cross the street (2016)—$183,750
- Costs seven cents to make a nickel (2019)—$150 million
- Mobile app for sex diary (2016)—$1 million
- Study: Are Physician Trainees Racist? (2016)—$932,741
- Dancing with fifteen-foot fish (2016)—$10,000
- Feminist porn book and other titles (2016)—$55,000
- Cigar taste test (2016)—$114,375
- Mistaken and improper Medicare payments (2004–2019)—$306.6 billion.[7]

At some point, we need to exercise the common sense and good judgment to say that enough is enough and to ask some critical questions: "Is it worth going into debt for these expenditures? Will these expenditures secure our country, help eliminate poverty, promote character in education, and most of all strengthen moral values and the family? And finally, who is responsible for making these decisions, and what should be the consequences for doing so?"

Seemingly oblivious to this massive misspending and growing national debt, politicians nonetheless promise free abortions, free health care, expanded welfare, free college tuition, free preschool care, cancellation of all student loans, reparations, government monthly stipends for all, and the list goes on and on.

Regardless of the merits of such programs, the costs of these are often highly unrealistic and would plunge the nation into further debt. Sometimes we need to put our foot down and say, "We can't afford it even though it may be a good cause." Perhaps we forget that a balanced budget is also a good cause, even a necessary and moral cause. Otherwise we selfishly shift the economic burden from our generation to that of our children and grandchildren.

Like any household budget, the federal budget needs priorities and fiscal restraint. But unfortunately, there is no desire or will to balance the budget by politicians. The philosophy of living within one's means is considered old-fashioned. But debt has its day of reckoning. If politicians ran their own households like this, they would be in bankruptcy. But somehow, they don't believe the same principles apply to government. Author and speaker Bill Federer noted, "Our founders were willing to sacrifice their prosperity for their posterity. Today, we're sacrificing our posterity for prosperity and saddling our kids with an unpayable debt, so we can maintain our standard of living."[8]

Statesmen, on the other hand, exercise economic self-restraint. Washington observed that we should avoid "the accumulation of debt, not only by shunning occasions of expense, but by vigorous exertions in time of peace to discharge the debts which unavoidable wars may have occasioned."[9] Jefferson was in accord: "I…place economy among the first and most important…virtues, and public debt as the greatest of the dangers to be feared."[10] On another occasion, he said, "To preserve [our] independence, we must not let our rulers load us with perpetual debt."[11] These Founding Fathers were echoing the fiscal doctrine taught in the Bible: "Owe no man any thing" (Rom. 13:8).

Statesmen have long-range vision. They see the consequences of mounting debt and are willing to exercise self-restraint in an effort to live within their means. They promote a balanced budget with provident spending even though it may cost them some political points in the short run.

Wise as Serpents but Harmless as Doves

Some politicians portray the moral person as politically naïve, impractical, oblivious to the real world where the rubber meets the road. Their logic, however, is similar to the reasoning of those who claim that unless you have sinned, you cannot truly understand temptation. C. S. Lewis exposed the fallacy of such an argument:

> A silly idea is current that good people do not know what temptation means. This is an obvious lie. Only those who try to resist temptation know how strong it is. After all, you find out the strength of the German army by fighting it, not by giving in.
>
> You find out the strength of a wind by trying to walk against it, not by lying down. A man who gives in to temptation after five minutes simply does not know what it would have been like an hour later. That is why bad people, in one sense, know very little about badness. They have lived a sheltered life by always giving in. We never find out the strength of the evil impulse inside us until we try to fight it: and Christ, because He was the only man who never yielded to temptation, is also the only man who knows to the full what temptation means—the only complete realist.[12]

In like manner, the moral person is the ultimate realist. No one better understands peer pressure than he because he has resisted it at its extremes. No one better understands the temptation of money because he has never succumbed at any price. And no one knows better the lure of worldly power and fame because he has never surrendered to its seductive appeal.

Jesus Christ, who advocated the pursuit of moral perfection, was also a pragmatist. He was willing to render "unto Caesar the things which are Caesar's, and unto God the things which are God's" (Matt. 22:21). He was willing to allow the people to live the lesser Law of Moses, for a time, as a stepping-stone to prepare them for the higher Law of Christ, or as Paul said, as a "schoolmaster to bring [them] unto Christ" (Gal. 3:24).

Statesmen are not naïve. To the contrary, they are "wise as serpents, and harmless as doves" (Matt. 10:16). They understand the need on occasion to make political compromises—to temporarily settle for less than the desired goal as a stepping-stone to achieving the ultimate end.

The Founding Fathers understood this principle. The Constitution initially failed to abolish slavery. That was a terrible outcome but better than the alternative—the failure to adopt a Constitution that would unite the independent states and give them the flexibility to address that issue in the future. In fact, John Adams wrote, "My opinion against it [slavery] has always been known."[13] Fortunately, this compromise made possible the Thirteenth, Fourteenth, and Fifteenth Amendments, which corrected the inequality and injustice imposed upon slaves. In this regard, Jon Meacham noted: "The perfect should not be the enemy of the good. Compromise is the oxygen of democracy."[14]

Statesmen are moral and wise, practical and visionary. They are shrewd and politically savvy but never underhanded or devious. They have high ideals and expectations, both for themselves and those they govern. They seek the highest moral ground possible under the existing circumstances. Morality, meaning God's will, is always their priority. This is the principle that governs their decision-making process. This is what distinguishes them from the pure politician and helps them be "wise as serpents, and harmless as doves."

Advocates of a Victim Mentality

Many politicians perpetuate a victim mentality—a philosophy that people can't rise above their circumstances without government intervention. In the process, such politicians often promote public dependency, the dole, a disincentive to work, an attitude of complaining, and socialistic principles. In truth, it is a ruse to gain power.

I am not a Jew, but I have a great respect for them as a people. They have been bitterly persecuted throughout history, yet I have seldom met a Jew who espouses a victim mentality. They seem to be non-complainers about their unfair treatment in life and instead take the necessary steps to rise above their afflictions. They remind me of the poetic words my oldest brother often quoted:

> "Said John, Fight on, my merry men all,
> I am little wounded but am not slain,
> I will lay me down and bleed a-while,
> Then I'll rise and fight again."[15]

Politicians tend to take the fight out of people. They mistake compassion for a government dole, and in the process, food stamps and welfare become a way of life rather than a temporary waystation to productive work. On the other hand, statesmen champion a fighting spirit—the human spirit. Their spirit of true compassion is to give only what is necessary to help people help themselves, to get them back on their feet, to restore self-dependency and dignity. In many ways, it is a harder road in the short run, but in the long run it is always more successful. The politicians' methodology is a stopgap measure; the statesmen's methodology—a permanent solution.

The Savior demonstrated this principle again and again. He raised Lazarus from the dead but would not remove the stone from the cave where he lay or unwrap the linen about his body, because others could do that (see John 11:38–44). He raised the daughter of Jairus from the dead but did not provide the needed food for her because others had the capacity to do so (see Mark 5:35–43). He provided what was genuinely needed without ever sacrificing the principle of self-reliance. He realized that this was the most compassionate approach of all—let people do everything they can on their own even though it may require some substantial effort.

Integrity Is the Foundation of One's Character

Politicians always have a purchase price—money, fame, pleasure, or power.

Their character and vote are for sale if the price is right. Statesmen cannot be bought for any price. David McCullough summarized it well: "History teaches that character counts. Character above all."[16]

The classic play *A Man for All Seasons* illustrates this principle. It is the story of Sir Thomas More who distinguished himself as a scholar, a lawyer, an ambassador, and finally, as Lord Chancellor of England. He was a man of absolute integrity. The play opens with these words of Sir Richard Rich: "Every man has his price! In money too or pleasure, titles, women, bricks and mortar. There is always something." That is the theme of the play. It is also a recurring theme of politics: is there a man or woman who cannot be bought, whose integrity is beyond price?

As the play unfolds, King Henry VIII desires to divorce Queen Catherine and marry Anne Boleyn, but there is a catch. Divorce was forbidden by the Catholic Church. So the king, not to be thwarted in his desires, demands that his subjects take an oath to support him in his divorce. But there is a further problem. Sir Thomas More, who is loved and admired by the common people, is a holdout. His conscience will not let him sign the oath. He is unwilling to submit, even at the king's personal request. Then come the tests—his friends apply their personal charm and pressure, but he will not yield. He is stripped of his wealth, his position, and his family, but he will not sign. Finally, he is falsely tried for his life, but still he will not succumb. They had taken from him his money, his political power, his friends, his family, and they would yet take from him his life, but they could not take from him his integrity. It was not for sale at any price.

At the climax of the play, Sir Thomas More is being falsely tried for treason. Sir Richard Rich commits the perjury necessary to convict him. As Sir Richard exits the courtroom, More asks him, "That is a chain of office you are wearing. What [is it]?"

Someone in the courtroom then explains, "Sir Richard Rich is appointed Attorney-General for Wales."

More then looks into Rich's face with great disdain and retorts, "For Wales? Why, Richard, it profits a man nothing to give his soul for the whole world. But for Wales!"[17]

Yet how many politicians have sold their souls for "Wales" or a large contribution or media exposure or position?

Names such as Thomas More, George Washington, Abraham Lincoln, William Wilberforce, and John and Abigail Adams are revered icons of integrity. They are like spiritual magnets. As we read about their lives, we are drawn to their higher way.

Integrity is at the heart and core of all statesmen. It is the foundation of their lives and political service. Shakespeare understood the inseparability of integrity and all other virtues: "Mine honor is my life; both grow in one; Take honor from me, and my life is done."[18]

Integrity is a purity of mind and heart that knows no deception, no excuses, no rationalization, and no coloring of the facts. It is an absolute honesty with one's self, with God, and with others. It is the courage to do what is right regardless of consequence or inconvenience. Even if God blinked or looked the other way for a moment, it would be choosing the right, not merely because God desires it but because one's character demands it. Politicians feign this quality; statesmen exude it.

Some years ago, my business partner and I needed to terminate an employee. After some discussions, we reached a settlement to compensate him for his past services. I felt the settlement was more than fair, but nonetheless there were some strained relationships as a result of the negotiations. That night, I felt a gloom come over me. I tried to dispel it by reasoning within myself that I had been fair, but the feeling would not leave. Then this impression came: "It's not enough to be fair. You must also strive to be Christlike." In like manner, integrity is not just adherence to the legal code but to the higher moral code. It is as Abraham Lincoln suggested—living in accord with "the better angels of our nature."[19] Statesmen live this higher law.

Conclusion

It seems that we live in a day and age when we have a plethora of politicians but a dearth of statesmen. But being optimistic, I believe there is a rising generation of men and women who want to rebuild this country on a foundation of integrity and moral values as envisioned by our Founding Fathers—who believe in our country's divine origin and destiny, who are capable of being our future statesmen. And in so doing, like Washington and Lincoln, will be instruments in God's hand to bless this nation.

---

1 In McCullough, *The American Spirit*, 162.

2 See Hanks, in Conference Report, Oct. 1968, 116.

3 Goodrich, *Free to Believe*, 159.

4 *The Autobiography of Benjamin Franklin*, 228–30; spelling modernized; emphasis in original.

5 Bloomberg and Koch, "Why Free Speech Matters on Campus," wsj.com.

6 Carson, *America the Beautiful*, 10.

7 Open the Books, "100 Examples of Federal Taxpayer Abuse," A11.

8 In Newcombe, "Warnings from the Founding Fathers on Our Reckless National Spending and Debt," christianpost.com.

9 Washington, "Washington's Farewell Address," avalon.yale.law.edu.

10 Jefferson, "Thomas Jefferson to William Plummer," founders.archives.gov.

11 Jefferson, "Proposals to Revise the Virginia Constitution," founders.archives.gov.

12 Lewis, *Mere Christianity*, 109–10.

13 Adams, "From John Adams to George Churchman," founders.archives.gov.

14 Meacham, *The Soul of America*, 259.

15 "Johnnie Armstrong's Last Good-Night," 359.

16 McCullough, *The American Spirit*, 58.

17 Bolt, *A Man for All Seasons*, 95.

18 Shakespeare, *"King Richard II,"* act 1, scene 1, lines 181–82.

19 Lincoln, "First Inaugural Address of Abraham Lincoln," avalon.law.yale.edu.

CHAPTER 19

Where Do We Go from Here?

Summary

What truths has history and the spirit revealed to us about the discovery, establishment, and preservation of America that are crucial to an understanding of our nation's origin and destiny?

Columbus was inspired by God.

Columbus, an imperfect but good man, was inspired by God to discover the Americas. Why? So God could raise up a nation founded upon divine principles that would (1) maximize the opportunities for freedom and growth of His children, particularly religious freedom; (2) establish a people who would follow Him as the God of the land; and (3) be a beacon on the hill for other nations to follow.

The Founding Fathers were raised up and inspired by God.

In order to accomplish these goals, God raised our remarkable Founding Fathers to be instruments in His hands in establishing this nation. As part of their mission, they drafted the divinely inspired Declaration of Independence and Constitution. Repeatedly, these chosen men attested to the providential aid they received in these endeavors.

Our nation's charter documents depend upon a moral and religious people.

The Founding Fathers recognized that the charter documents of our nation, inspired as they were, would be of no consequence unless we were a moral people.

They further acknowledged that morality was dependent upon religion, and thus the need to encourage religion in general, without establishing a national religion. This was necessary since religion was the prime source for learning and living moral principles. Accordingly, many religious practices and symbols in public places were endorsed by the Founding Fathers and others of our national heroes.

Morality is a reflection of God's will.

The Founding Fathers understood that the morality of which they spoke did not originate from some sort of vague self-enlightenment (also known as moral relativism) but was a reflection of God's will, hence our need to seek and obey His will on matters affecting the nation's well-being.

Originalism helps us best understand God's will as set forth in the Constitution.

This raises the question of whether or not there is a preferred method of interpreting the Constitution that will help us discover and implement the will of God. Originalism, also known as strict constructionism, seems to best accomplish this goal because its objective is not to interpret the Constitution in light of current popular opinions but to remain true to the original intent of the Founding Fathers, who diligently sought the will of God in their draftsmanship.

God has expressed His will on critical moral issues facing our nation today.

Because God loves us as His children, He has given us His will and wisdom, even commandments, on critical moral issues confronting our nation. He has spoken clearly and repeatedly against abortion and same-sex expression. He has stressed the importance of traditional marriage between a man and a woman and of the nuclear family as the centerpiece of society. The doctrine of zero population growth is in clear opposition to His command to multiply and replenish (fill) the earth. The principles of socialism restrict individual liberty and promote a Godless society; hence, they are in direct opposition to God's will. Furthermore, God expects us to be good stewards of the environment and to protect and beautify it.

Once we know God's will on these matters, we have the responsibility to do all within our power to promote His will, even if it is contrary to our own prejudices and beliefs. If we do so as a people, then we are entitled to be recipients of that divine entreaty—God bless America. Those divine blessings come in many ways—through heavenly protection, peace, prosperity, happiness, and enjoyment of God's spirit in our individual and community lives.

What Can We Do to Invite God's Blessings on Us and Our Nation?

The Lord had a vision for this country which He planted in the hearts and minds of the Founding Fathers and many other inspired leaders, whom God sent here at a predetermined time and place to fulfill that vision. To their credit, they honored and magnified their divinely appointed missions at great cost to themselves and their families. Abigail Adams, speaking of her family, said, "I wonder if future generations will ever know what we have suffered in their behalf."[1]

David McCullough addressed this same concern:

> The laws we live by, the freedoms we enjoy, the institutions that we take for granted—and we should never take for granted—are all the work of others who went before us. And to be indifferent to that isn't just to be ignorant, it's to be rude.
>
> And ingratitude is a shabby failing.

> [Our way of life is] not just a birthright, it is something that others struggled and strived for, often suffered for, often were defeated for and died for, for the next generation, for us.[2]

The Founding Fathers left us a legacy of liberty, unequalled in the annals of history, and of faith in God that made it workable. May we never forget or fail to appreciate their sacrifice and contribution. It was monumental.

I love America. I honor and respect our Founding Fathers and many national heroes who made incredible sacrifices to establish and preserve the liberties we so abundantly enjoy. I revere the flag and all it stands for. I cherish the times I can pledge allegiance or sing the "The Star-Spangled Banner" or "God Bless America." There is a sacred spirit that accompanies these symbols and activities because they are indeed divinely inspired. I acknowledge and express gratitude for God's merciful hand in the origin and destiny of our nation.

It is now our choice and America's choice to continue the legacy of our Founding Fathers or to cast it aside, to place our trust in the wisdom of the world or the wisdom of God. Hopefully each of us might declare, "As for me and my house, we will serve the Lord" (Josh. 24:15). In conclusion I paraphrase a quote attributed to both Edmund Burke and John Stuart Mill: "All that is necessary for evil to triumph over good is for enough good men and women to do nothing." Hopefully, the choice of every good man and woman, and America's choice as a country, will be to become a nation under God, not a nation without God. Then we will be entitled to the promise of the psalmist: "Blessed is the nation whose God is the Lord" (Ps. 33:12).

---

1 McCullough, *The American Spirit*, 87.
2 McCullough, *The American Spirit*, 107.

BIBLIOGRAPHY

Abbott, Brianna. "Genetics Tied to Same-Sex Behavior." *Wall Street Journal*, August 30, 2019.

Abernathy, Ralph David. *And the Walls Came Tumbling Down: An Autobiography*, 1989.

Abington School District v. Schempp, 374 U.S. 203 (1963).

Adams, Abigail. "Abigail Adams to John Adams." November 5, 1775. founders.archives.gov/documents/Adams/04-01-02-0212.

Adams, John. "From John Adams to Benjamin Rush." April 18, 1808. founders.archives.gov/documents/Adams/99-02-02-5238.

______. "From John Adams to George Churchman." January 24, 1801. founders.archives.gov/documents/Adams/99-02-02-4766.

______. "From John Adams to Massachusetts Militia." October 11, 1798. founders.archives.gov/documents/Adams/99-02-02-3102.

______. "From John Adams to Thomas Jefferson." April 19, 1817. founders.archives.gov/documents/Adams/99-02-02-6744.

______. "From John Adams to Thomas Jefferson." December 21, 1819. founders.archives.gov/documents/Adams/99-02-02-7287.

______. "From John Adams to Thomas Jefferson." June 28, 1813. founders.archives.gov/documents/Adams/99-02-02-6077.

______. "From John Adams to William Stephens Smith." December 26, 1787. founders.archives.gov/documents/Adams/99-02-02-0298.

Adams, Samuel. *The Writings of Samuel Adams.* Edited by Harry Alonzo Cushing. Vol. 1, 3, and 4. 1904, 1907–8.

"American Baptist Resolution Concerning Abortion and Ministry in the Local Church." March 1994. religiousinstitute.org/denom_ statements/american-baptist-resolution-concerning-abortion-and-ministry-in-the-local-church.

"An Ordinance for the Government of the Territory of the United States, North-west of the River Ohio." Library of Congress. 1787. loc.gov/item/90898154.

Andersen, Neil L. *The Divine Gift of Forgiveness.* 2019.

Aristides. *The Apology of Aristides of Behalf of the Christians.* Translated by J. Rendel Harris. 1981.

Arnold, Samuel Greene. *The Life of Patrick Henry.* 1857.

Associated Press. "Famed Scientist Dismisses Possibility of Space Travel." *Uniontown (PA) Morning Herald*, February 25, 1957.

Ballard, M. Russell. "The Lord Needs You Now!" *Ensign*, September 2015.

Barr, William P. "Remarks to the Law School and the de Nicola Center for Ethics and Culture at the University of Notre Dame." October 11, 2019. justice.gov/opa/speech/attorney-general-william-p-barr-delivers-remarks-law-school-and-de-nicola-center-ethics.

Barrett, Joseph H. *Life of Abraham Lincoln.* 1865.

Barton, David. *Original Intent: The Courts, the Constitution, and Religion.* 2011.

Bastiat, Frédéric. *The Law.* 2013.

Bednar, David A. "And Nothing Shall Offend Them." *Ensign,* November 2006.

Bennett, William J. *Our Sacred Honor: Words of Advice from the Founders in Stories, Letters, Poems, and Speeches.* 1997.

Benson, Ezra Taft. "God's Hand in Our Nation's History." Brigham Young University devotional. March 28, 1977. speeches.byu.edu/talks/ezra-taft-benson_gods-hand-nations-history.

Bercot, David W. *Will the Real Heretics Please Stand Up: A New Look at Today's Evangelical Church in the Light of Early Christianity.* 3rd ed. 1999.

Bermudez, Alejandro. "Catholics against Columbus." *Wall Street Journal,* January 25, 2019.

Bissell, Roger. "A Calm Look at Abortion Arguments." *Reason*, September 1981. reason.com/1981/09/01/a-calm-look-at-abortion-argume.

Blackstone, William. *Commentaries on the Laws of England.* 1800.
Bloomberg, Michael, and Charles Koch. "Why Free Speech Matters on Campus." *Wall Street Journal,* May 12, 2016. wsj.com/articles/why-free-speech-matters-on-campus--1463093280.
Bolsonaro, Jair. "Statement by Mr. Jair Messias Bolsonaro, President of the Federative Republic of Brazil." 74th session of the United Nations General Assembly. September 24, 2019, statements.unmeetings.org/GA74/BR_EN.pdf.
Bolt, Robert. *A Man for All Seasons: A Play of Sir Thomas More.* 1960.
Boreham, F. W. *Mountains in the Mist: Some Australian Reveries.* 1919.
Bork, Robert H. *Slouching towards Gomorrah: Modern Liberalism and American Decline.* 1996.
———. *The Tempting of America: The Political Seduction of the Law.* 1991.
Bowen, Catherine Drinker. *Miracle at Philadelphia: The Story of the Constitutional Convention, May to September 1787.* 1966.
Bowers v. Hardwick, 478 U.S. 186 (1986).
Bradley, James. *Flags of Our Fathers.* 2000.
Brands, H. W. *The First American: The Life and Times of Benjamin Franklin.* 2000.
Brokaw, Tom. *The Greatest Generation.* 2005.
Brooks, Arthur C. *Who Really Cares: The Surprising Truth about Compassionate Conservatism.*
Brooks, David. "I Was Once a Socialist." *New York Times,* December 6, 2019.
Buick, Adam. "A Question of Definition: Socialism/Communism." *Socialist Standard.* Vol. 74, no. 886 (June 1978). worldsocialism.org/spgb/socialist-standard/1970s/1978/no-886-june-1978.
Burke, Edmund. *The Works of Edmund Burke.* Rev. ed. Vol. 4. 1866.
Bush, George W. *41: A Portrait of My Father.* 2014.
Calvin, John. *Commentaries on the Four Last Books of Moses.* Translated by Charles William Bingham. Vol. 3. 1854.
Carney, Timothy P. *Alienated America: Why Some Places Thrive while Others Collapse.* 2019.

Carpenter, Francis Bicknell. *Six Months at the White House with Abraham Lincoln.* 1866.

Carson, Ben, and Candy Carson. *America the Beautiful: Rediscovering What Made This Nation Great.* 2012.

Carson, Ben. *One Nation: What We Can All Do to Save America's Future.* 2014.

Carter, Jimmy. "Remarks at Mormon Church Ceremonies Honoring Family Unity." November 27, 1978. The American Presidency Project, presidency.ucsb.edu.

Centers for Disease Control. "Abortion Surveillance—United States, 2016." cdc.gov/mmwr/volumes/68/ss/ss6811a1.htm?s_cid=ss6811a1_w.

Chase, Irah, trans. *The Constitutions of the Holy Apostles.* 1848.

Chen, Ying, and Tyler J. VanderWeele. "Associations of Religious Upbringing with Subsequent Health and Well-Being from Adolescence to Young Adulthood: An Outcome-Wide Analysis." *American Journal of Epidemiology* 187, no. 11 (November 2018): 2355–64.

Christofferson, Tom. *That We May Be One: A Gay Mormon's Perspective on Faith and Family.* 2017.

Churchill, Winston S. "Demobilisation." House of Commons debate. October 22, 1945. api.parliament.uk/historic-hansard/commons/1945/oct/22/demobilisation.

———. *Never Give In! Winston Churchill's Speeches.* Selected and edited by Winston S. Churchill. 2004.

———. *The Second World War.* Vol. 2. 1949.

Clark, J. Reuben Jr. *Stand Fast by Our Constitution.* 1962.

Cleveland, Grover. "Veto Message." February 16, 1887. The American Presidency Project. presidency.ucsb.edu/documents/veto-message-237.

Cohen, J. M., trans. *The Four Voyages of Christopher Columbus.* 1969.

Cohen, Susan A. "Abortion and Mental Health: Myths and Realities." *Guttmacher Policy Review* 9, no. 3 (Summer 2006): 8–16.

Columbus, Christopher. *The Diario of Christopher Columbus's First Voyage to America, 1492–1493.* Abstracted by Bartolomé de las Casas. Translated by Oliver Dunn and James E. Kelly Jr. 1989.

———. *The Libro de las profecías of Christopher Columbus.* Translated by Delno C. West and August Kling. 1992.

———. *Select Letters of Christopher Columbus.* Translated and edited by R. H. Major. 1847.

Commager, Henry Steele. *Freedom and Order: A Commentary on the American Political Scene.* 1966.

Congressional Record: Proceedings and Debates of the 88th Congress, First Session. Vol. 109, part 8 (May 29–June 19, 1963).

Coolidge, Ardee. "Five Promises Abortion Couldn't Keep." Care Net. October 25, 2016. care-net.org/abundant-life-blog/five-promises-abortion-couldnt-keep.

Cousins, Norman. *In God We Trust: The Religious Beliefs and Ideas of the American Founding Fathers.* 1958.

Crigger, Megan, and Laura Santhanam. "How Many Americans Have Died in U.S. Wars?" PBS News Hour. May 27, 2019. pbs.org/newshour/nation/many-americans-died-u-s-wars.

D'Anghera, Peter Martyr. *De Orbe Novo.* Translated by Francis Augusts MacNutt. Vol. 1. 1912.

De Tocqueville, Alexis. *Democracy in America.* Translated by Henry Reeve. Vol. 1. 1838.

Delaney, Carol. *Columbus and the Quest for Jerusalem: How Religion Drove the Voyages That Led to America.* 2011.

Deng, Chao. "China's Birthrate Hits a New Low." *Wall Street Journal,* January 18–19, 2020.

Dimon, Jamie. "Chairman and CEO Letter to Shareholders." JP Morgan Chase and Co. *Annual Report 2018.* reports.jpmorganchase.com/investor-relations/2018/ar-ceo-letters.htm.

Dorfman, Jeffrey. "Sorry Bernie Bros but Nordic Countries Are Not Socialist." *Forbes,* July 8, 2018. forbes.com/sites/jeffreydorfman/2018/07/08/sorry-bernie-bros-but-nordic-countries-are-not-socialist.

Dougherty, Jon. "Ocasio-Cortez Finds Mega Wealth Immoral, but Her Favorite Socialist Leaders Are All Billionaires." *The National Sentinel,* January 23, 2019. thenationalsentinel.com/2019/01/23/ocasio-cortez-finds-mega-wealth-immoral-but-her-favorite-socialist-leaders-are-all-billionaires.

Durant, Will, and Ariel Durant. *The Lessons of History.* 1968.

Durant, Will. *Caesar and Christ.* Vol. 3 of *The Story of Civilization.* 1944.

Eastman, Max. *Reflections on the Failure of Socialism.* 1955.

Edwards, Lee. "The God That Failed…Over and Over Again." The Heritage Foundation. March 18, 2019.

Ehrlich, Paul R. *The Population Bomb.* 1968.

Eisenhower, Dwight D. "Remarks Broadcast as Part of the American Legion 'Back to God' Program." February 7, 1954. The American Presidency Project. presidency.ucsb.edu/documents/remarks-broadcast-part-the-american-legion-back-god-program.

———. "Remarks Recorded for the 'Back-to-God' Program of the American Legion." February 20, 1955. The American Presidency Project. presidency.ucsb.edu/documents/remarks-recorded-for-the-back-god-program-the-american-legion.

———. "Statement to soldiers, sailors, and airmen of the Allied Expeditionary Force." June 6, 1944. catalog.archives.gov/id/186473.

Ely, John Hart. "The Wages of Crying Wolf: A Comment on *Roe v. Wade.*" *Yale Law Journal* 82, no. 5 (April 1973): 920–49.

Engel v. Vitale, 370 U.S. 421 (1962).

Engels, Friedrich. "Draft of a Communist Confession of Faith." *The Communist Manifesto*, edited and translated by L. M. Findlay. 2004.

Epperson v. Arkansas, 393 U.S. 97 (1968).

Everson v. Board of Education, 330 U.S. 1 (1947).

Faust, Jonathan. "Law in a Changing Society: A Conversation with RGB." *Stanford Politics*, February 8, 2017. stanfordpolitics.org/2017/02/08/interview-ruth-bader-ginsburg.

Federer, William J. *America's God and Country: Encyclopedia of Quotations.* 2000.

FedEx Corporation 2019 Annual Report.

Ferguson, Everett, ed. *Encyclopedia of Early Christianity.* 2nd ed. 1998.

Ferling, John. *Almost a Miracle: The American Victory in the War of Independence.* 2007.

Finer, Lawrence B., Lori F. Frohwirth, Lindsay A. Dauphinee, Susheela Singh, and Ann M. Moore. "Reasons U.S. Women Have Abortions: Quantitative and Qualitative Perspectives." *Perspectives of Sexual and Reproductive Health* 37, no. 3 (September 2005): 110–18.

Fiske, John. *The Beginnings of New England, or The Puritan Theocracy in Its Relations to Civil and Religious Liberty.* 1894.

Flexner, James Thomas. *Washington: The Indispensable Man.* 1974.

Frankl, Viktor E. *Man's Search for Meaning.* 1984.

Franklin, Benjamin. "A Comparison of the Conduct of the Ancient Jews and of the Anti-Federalists in the United States of America." In *The Works of Benjamin Franklin*, 5: 158–62. 1844.

———. "Information for Those Who Would Remove to America." In *The Works of Benjamin Franklin*, 9:432–44. 1904.

———. "Proclamation for a General Fast." Philadelphia, Pennsylvania. December 9, 1747. franklinpapers.org/framedVolumes.jsp?vol=3&page=226a.

———. "Silence Dogood, no. 8." July 9, 1722. founders.archives.gov/documents/Franklin/01-01-02-0015.

———. "To the Abbés Chalut and Arnoux." April 17, 1787. franklinpapers.org/framedVolumes.jsp.

———. *The Autobiography of Benjamin Franklin.* Edited by John Bigelow. 1868.

Friedman, Milton. *Capitalism and Freedom.* 1962.

George, Robert P. "Return All Legislative Power to Congress." *Politico.* politico.com/interactives/2019/how-to-fix-politics-in-america/gridlock/return-all-legislative-powers-to-Congress.

Gingrich, Newt. *Rediscovering God in America: Reflections on the Role of Faith in Our Nation's History and Future.* 2009.

Gladstone, William E. "Kin beyond Sea." *North American Review*, September–October 1878.

Goldeng, Eskil, Leo A. Grünfeld, and Gabriel R. G. Benito. "The Performance Differential between Private and State Owned Enterprises: The Roles of Ownership, Management and Market Structure." *Journal of Management Studies* 45, no. 7. (November 2008): 1244–73.

Goodrich, Luke. *Free to Believe: The Battle over Religious Liberty in America.* 2019.

Gorsuch, Neil. *A Republic, If You Can Keep It.* 2019.

Griswold v. Connecticut, 381 U.S. 479 (1965).

Guttmacher Institute. "Induced Abortion in the United States." September 2019. guttmacher.org/fact-sheet/induced-abortion-united-states.

Haberman, Clyde. "The Unrealized Horrors of Population Explosion." *New York Times*, May 31, 2015. nytimes.com/2015/06/01/us/the-unrealized-horrors-of-population-explosion.html.

Haley, Nikki R. *With All Due Respect: Defending America with Grit and Grace.* 2019.

Hall, Mark David. "Did America Have a Christian Founding?" The Heritage Foundation. June 7, 2011. heritage.org/political-process/report/did-america-have-christian-founding.

Hamilton, Alexander, John Jay, and James Madison. *The Federalist Papers.* Benediction Classics, 2017.

Hamilton, Alexander. "Final Version of an Opinion on the Constitutionality of an Act to Establish a Bank." February 23, 1791. founders.archives.gov/documents/Hamilton/01-08-02-0060-0003.

———. "From Alexander Hamilton to Elizabeth Hamilton." July 10, 1804. founders.archives.gov/documents/Hamilton/01-26-02-0001-0262.

———. "The Stand No. III." April 7, 1789. founders.archives.gov/documents/Hamilton/01-21-02-0233.

———. *The Farmer Refuted.* 1775.

Hanks, Marion D. In Conference Report. October 1968. 115–18.

Harvey, John T. "Why Government Should Not Be Run like a Business." *Forbes*, October 5, 2012. forbes.com/sites/johntharvey/2012/10/05/government-vs-business/#3fb8a3362a54.

Hasell, Joe, and Max Roser. "Famines." Our World in Data. December 7, 2017. ourworldindata.org/famines.

Haskins, Justin T. *Socialism Is Evil: The Moral Case against Marx's Radical Dream.* 2018.

Hausmann, Ricardo. "Does Capitalism Cause Poverty?" Project Syndicate. August 21, 2015. project-syndicate.org/commentary/does-capitalism-cause-poverty-by-ricardo-hausmann-2015-08.

Hawthorne, Nathaniel. *The Great Stone Face and Other Tales of the Great White Mountains.* 1889.

Hayek, F. A. *The Road to Serfdom.* 1944.

Heidler, David S., and Jeanne T. Heidler. *Washington's Circle: The Creation of the President.* 2015.

Hill, Roland. *Lord Acton.* 2000.

Hinckley, Clark B. *Christopher Columbus: A Man among the Gentiles.* 2014.

Holland, Rupert S. *Lafayette, We Come! The Story of How a Young Frenchman Fought for Liberty in America and How America Now Fights for Liberty in France.* 1918.

Horowitz, David. *Dark Agenda: The War to Destroy Christian America.* 2018.

Hosanna-Tabor Evangelical Lutheran Church and School v. EEOC, 565 U.S._(2012).

Huckabee, Mike, and Steve Feazel, *The Three Cs That Made America Great, Christianity, Capitalism and the Constitution.* 2020.

Hughes, Charles Evans. *Addresses and Papers of Charles Evans Hughes.* 1908.

Hunter, Brittany, and Dan Sanchez. "How Believing in Socialism Can Make You Miserable." Foundation for Economic Education. January 23, 2018. fee.org/articles/how-believing-in-socialism-can-make-you-miserable.

Irving, Washington. *The Life and Voyages of Christopher Columbus.* Vol. 1. 1892.

Jakob, Brigitta. "Performance in Strategic Sectors: A comparison of Profitability and Efficiency of State-Owned Enterprises and Private Corporations." *The Park Place Economist* 25, no. 1 (2017): 9–20.

Jay, John. *The Life of John Jay: With Selections from His Correspondence and Miscellaneous Papers.* Compiled by William Jay. Vol. 2. 1833.

Jefferson, Thomas. "From Thomas Jefferson to John Adams." October 12, 1813. founders.archives.gov/documents/Jefferson/03-06-02-0431.

———. "From Thomas Jefferson to John Dickson." March 6, 1801. founders.archives.gov/documents/Jefferson/01-33-02-0156.

———. "From Thomas Jefferson to Joseph Cabell Breckinridge." December 11, 1821. founders.archives.gov/documents/Jefferson/98-01-02-2494.

———. "From Thomas Jefferson to Martha Jefferson." December 11, 1783. founders.archives.gov/documents/Jefferson/01-06-02-0303.

———. "From Thomas Jefferson to Samuel Miller." January 23, 1808. founders.archives.gov/documents/Jefferson/99-01-02-7257.

———. "From Thomas Jefferson to William Johnson." June 12, 1823. founders.archives.gov/documents/Jefferson/98-01-02-3562.

———. "Proposals to Revise the Virginia Constitution: I. Thomas Jefferson to 'Henry Tompkinson' (Samuel Kercheval)." July 12, 1816. founders.archives.gov/documents/Jefferson/03-10-02-0128-0002.

———. "Second Inaugural Address." March 4, 1805. avalon.law.yale.edu/19th_century/jefinau2.asp.

———. "Thomas Jefferson to Walter Jones, January 2, 1814." Library of Congress. loc.gov/item/mtjbib021613.

———. "Thomas Jefferson to William Plummer." July 21, 1816. founders.archives.gov/documents/Jefferson/03-10-02-0152.

———. "To the Danbury Baptist Association." January 1, 1802. founders.archives.gov/documents/Jefferson/01-36-02-0152-0006.

———. *The Writings of Thomas Jefferson.* Edited by Albert Ellery Bergh. Vol. 15. 1904.

———. *The Writings of Thomas Jefferson.* Edited by H. A. Washington. Vol. 4. 1854.

John, J. "How a Day of Prayer Saved Britain at Dunkirk." *Premier Christianity* (blog). July 12, 2017. premierchristianity.com/Blog/How-a-day-of-prayer-saved-Britain-at-Dunkirk.

Johnson, Abby, with Cindy Lamber. *Unplanned.* 2010.

Jones, Kevin. "Critics of Columbus Day Get History Wrong, Scholar Says." *Catholic News Agency*, May 2, 2017. catholicnewsagency.com/news/critics-of-columbus-day-get-history-wrong-scholar-says-85304.

Kaye, Kelleen, Jennifer Appleton Gootman, Alison Steward Ng, and Cara Finley. *Benefits of Birth Control in America: Getting the Facts Straight.* 2014.

Kennedy, John F. "Address at a Luncheon Meeting of the National Industrial Conference Board." February 13, 1961. The American Presidency Project. presidency.ucsb.edu/documents/address-luncheon-meeting-the-national-industrial-conference-board.

______. "Inaugural Address of John F. Kennedy." January 20, 1961. avalon.law.yale.edu/20th_century/kennedy.asp.

______. "Message Greeting President Quadros of Brazil on the Occasion of His Inauguration." In *Public Papers of the Presidents of the United States: John F. Kennedy.* January 31, 1961.

______. "Proclamation 3436: National Day of Prayer, 1961." In *Code of Federal Regulations, Title 3—The President.* 1959–63.

______. "Proclamation 3438: Thanksgiving Day, 1961." In *Code of Federal Regulations, 1961 Supplement to Title 3—The President.* 1962.

Kipling, Rudyard. "Recessional." In *Barrack-Room Ballads and Other Poems.* 1889.

Knowles, Michael. "Historical Record Shows Christopher Columbus Actually Was a Great Man." *Daily Wire*, October 5, 2017. dailywire.com/news/historical-record-shows-christopher-columbus-michael-j-knowles.

Krauthammer, Charles. *The Point of It All: A Lifetime of Great Loves and Endeavors.* Edited by Daniel Krauthammer. 2018.

Kunhardt, Philip B. Jr, Philip B. Kunhardt III, and Peter W. Kunhardt. *Lincoln: An Illustrated Biography.* 1992.

Las Casas, Bartolomé de. *A Brief Account of the Destruction of the Indies.* 2014.

Las Casas, Bartolomé de. *Historia de las Indias.* Vol. 1 and 2. 1875.

______. *History of the Indies.* Translated by Andrée Collard. 1971.

Last, Jonathan V. *What to Expect When No One's Expecting: America's Coming Demographic Disaster.* 2014.
Lee v. Ashers Baking Company (2018) UKSC, case 49.
Lee, Harold B. "'Successful' Sinners." *Ensign*, July 1971.
———. *The Teachings of Harold B. Lee.* Edited by Clyde J. Williams. 1996.
Leeson, Peter T. "Two Cheers for Capitalism." *Society* 47 (2010): 227–33.
Lemon v. Kurtzman, 403 U.S. 602 (1970).
Levin, Mark R. *Liberty and Tyranny: A Conservative Manifesto.* 2009.
Lewin, Tamar. "Rape and Incest: Just 1% of All Abortions." *New York Times*, October 13, 1989.
Lewis, C. S. *Mere Christianity.* 1952.
———. *The Collected Letters of C. S. Lewis, Vol. 3: Narnia, Cambridge, and Joy, 1950–1963.* Edited by Walter Hooper. 2007.
Library of Congress. "America as a Religious Refuge: The Seventeenth Century, Part 1." *Religion and the Founding of the American Republic.* loc.gov/exhibits/religion/rel01.
LifeSite News. "US Supreme Court Okays Public School Ban on Nativity Scene while Allowing Menorah." February 21, 2007. lifesitenews.com/news/us-supreme-court-okays-public-school-ban-on-nativity-scene-while-allowing-m.
Lightfoot, Joseph Barber, trans. *The Apostolic Fathers.* 1898.
Lincoln, Abraham. "A Proclamation for a Day of Humiliation, Fasting and Prayer." Washington, DC. March 30, 1863. Library of Congress. loc.gov/resource/lprbscsm.scsm0265.
———. "First Inaugural Address of Abraham Lincoln." March 4, 1861. avalon.law.yale.edu/19th_century/lincoln1.asp.
———. "President Lincoln's Farewell Address." Springfield, Illinois. February 12, 1861. Library of Congress. loc.gov/item/scsm000845.
———. "Proclamation 103—Day of Thanksgiving, Praise, and Prayer." August 6, 1863. presidency.ucsb.edu/documents/proclamation-103-day-thanksgiving-praise-and-prayer-august-6-1863.

———. "Second Inaugural Address." March 4, 1865. Library of Congress. loc.gov/item/mal4361300.

———. *Complete Works of Abraham Lincoln.* Edited by John G. Nicolay and John Hay. Vol. 10. 1894.

———. *Speeches and Writings, 1859–1865.* 1989.

Lincoln, Abraham. *Collected works, The Abraham Lincoln Association*, ed. by Roy P. Basler, Vol. 1. 1953.

Lincoln, Charles Z., ed. *Messages from the Governors, State of New York.* Vol. 2. 1909.

Litsky, Frank, and Bruce Weber. "Roger Bannister, First Athlete to Break the 4-Minute Mile, Dies at 88." *New York Times*, March 4, 2018. nytimes.com/2018/03/04/obituaries/roger-bannister-dead.html.

Livi Bacci, Massimo. *A Concise History of World Population.* 6th ed. 2017.

Locke, John. *Two Treatises on Civil Government.* 1884.

Lowen, Linda. "Key Arguments from Both Sides of the Abortion Debate." ThoughtCo. January 2, 2020. thoughtco.com/arguments-for-and-against-abortion-3534153.

Lund, Gerald N. "The Grace and Mercy of Jesus Christ." In *Jesus Christ: Son of God, Savior.* Edited by Paul H. Peterson, Gary L. Hatch, and Laura D. Card. 2002.

Luther, Martin. *Luther's Works, Vol. 4: Lectures on Genesis Chapters 21–25.* Edited by Jaroslav Pelikan. 1986.

Madison, James. "From James Madison to Frederick Beasley." November 20, 1825. founders.archives.gov/documents/Madison/04-03-02-0663.

———. "From James Madison to Henry Lee." June 25, 1824. founders.archives.gov/documents/Madison/04-03-02-0333.

———. "From James Madison to Thomas Jefferson." October 24, 1787. founders.archives.gov/documents/Madison/01-10-02-0151.

———. "The Difficulties of the Constitutional Convention in Devising a Proper Form of Government." *Selected Federalist Papers.* Edited by Bob Blaisdell. 2001.

———. *Selected Writings of James Madison.* Edited by Ralph Ketcham. 2006.

———. *The Writings of James Madison.* Edited by Gaillard Hunt. Vol. 5. 1904.

Magnet, Myron. *Clarence Thomas and the Lost Constitution.* 2019.

Maltby, Charles. *The Life and Public Services of Abraham Lincoln.* 1884.

Mansfield, Ty, and Danielle Mansfied. "Living with Same-sex Attraction: Our Story." *LDS Living*, May 22, 2012. ldsliving.com/Living-with-Same-sex-Attraction-Our-Story/s/68799.

Mansfield, Ty. "A Seal of Living Reality." In *Voices of Hope: Latter-day Saint Perspectives on Same-Gender Attraction—an Anthology of Gospel Teachings and Personal Essays.* Compiled by Ty Mansfield. 2011.

Marchetti, Silvia. "Buying a $1 Italy Dream House Just Got Even Easier." CNN. April 18, 2019. cnn.com/travel/article/italy-one-euro-home-websites/index.html.

Marks, Howard. "Growing the Pie." Memo to Oaktree clients. April 1, 2019. oaktreecapital.com/docs/default-source/memos/growing-the-pie.pdf.

———. "Political Reality Meets Economic Reality." Memo to Oaktree clients. January 2019. oaktreecapital.com/docs/default-source/memos/political-reality-meets-economic-reality.pdf.

Marsh v. Chambers, 463 U.S. 783 (1983).

Marshall, Joey. "Are Religious People Happier, Healthier? Our New Global Study Explores This Question." Pew Research Center. January 31, 2019. pewresearch.org/fact-tank/2019/01/31/are-religious-people-happier-healthier-our-new-global-study-explores-this-question.

Marx, Karl. *Critique of Hegel's "Philosophy of Right."* Translated by Annette Jolin and Joseph O'Malley. 1977.

Mathisen, Robert R. *The Role of Religion in American Life: An Interpretive Historical Anthology.* 1982.

Maxwell, Neal A. "Sharing Insights from My Life." Brigham Young University devotional. January 12, 1999. speeches.byu.edu/talks/neal-a-maxwell/sharing-insights-life.

McCollum v. Board of Education, 333 U.S. 203 (1948).

McCorvey, Norma. "Testimony of Norma McCorvey, the Former Roe of *Roe v. Wade,* before the Subcommittee on the Constitution of the Senate Judiciary Committee." June 23, 2005. judiciary.senate.gov/imo/media/doc/McCorvey%20Testimony%20062305.pdf.

McCullough, David. *The American Spirit: Who We Are and What We Stand For.* 2017.

______. "The Glorious Cause of America." Brigham Young University forum. September 27, 2005. speeches.byu.edu/talks/david-mccullough/glorious-cause-america.

Meacham, Jon. *American Gospel: God, the Founding Fathers, and the Making of a Nation.* 2006.

______. *The Soul of America: The Battle for Our Better Angels.* 2018.

Montesquieu, *The Spirit of Laws.* Translated by Thomas Nugent. Vol. 1. 1873.

Morison, Samuel Eliot. *Admiral of the Ocean Sea: A Life of Christopher Columbus.* 1942.

Morrow, Lance. "A Reckoning with Martin Luther King." *Wall Street Journal,* June 17, 2019. wsj.com/articles/a-reckoning-with-martin-luther-king-11560813491.

Mother Teresa. "An Address at the National Prayer Breakfast." Catholic Online. February 3, 1994. catholic.org/clife/teresa/address.php.

______. *Where There Is Love, There Is God.* Edited by Brian Kolodiejchuk. 2010.

Murphy, Robert P. "Extreme Poverty Rates Plummet under Capitalism." Foundation for Economic Education. May 30, 2018. fee.org/articles/extreme-poverty-rates-plummet-under-capitalism.

National Railroad Passenger Corporation and Subsidiaries (Amtrak). *Consolidated Financial Statements.* Years Ended September 30, 2019 and 2018.

National Right to Life Committee. "State Homicide Laws That Recognize Unborn Victims." April 2, 2018. nrlc.org/federal/unbornvictims/statehomicidelaws092302.

National Right to Life Committee. *The State of Abortion in the United States.* January 2019.

Nelson, Russell M. "Abortion: An Assault on the Defenseless." *Ensign*, October 2008.

———. "Reverence for Life." *Ensign*, May 1985.

———. "Youth of the Noble Birthright: What Will You Choose?" Church Educational System devotional for young adults. September 6, 2013. churchofjesuschrist.org/broadcasts/article/ces-devotionals/2013/01/youth-of-the-noble-birthright-what-will-you-choose.

Newcombe, Jerry. "Warnings from the Founding Fathers on Our Reckless National Spending and Debt." *Christian Post*, February 15, 2018. christianpost.com/voice/warnings-from-founding-fathers-reckless-national-spending-debt.html.

Newport, Frank. "Most Americans Still Believe in God." June 29, 2016. news.gallup.com/poll/193271/americans-believe-god.aspx.

———. *God Is Alive and Well: The Future of Religion in America.* 2012.

Newton, Michael E. *Angry Mobs and Founding Fathers: The Fight for Control of the American Revolution.* 2011.

O'Neal, Adam. "Why Bernie Sanders Is Wrong about Sweden." *Wall Street Journal*, August 24–25, 2019.

Oaks, Dallin H. "The Divinely Inspired Constitution." *Ensign*, February 1992.

Obergefell v. Hodges, 576 U.S._(2015).

Open the Books. "100 Examples of Federal Taxpayer Abuse." Paid advertisement in *Wall Street Journal*, November 5, 2019.

Order Sons of Italy in America. "Columbus: Fact vs. Fiction." osia.org.

Packer, Boyd K. *Teach Ye Diligently.* 1975.

Paine, Thomas. *The Age of Reason: Part the First. Being an Investigation of True and of Fabulous Theology.* 1795.

———. *The Theological Works of Thomas Paine.* 1830.

Pannenberg, Wolfhart. "Revelation and Homosexual Experience." *Christianity Today*, November 11, 1996.

Paul, Rand. *The Case against Socialism.* 2019.

Pelowski, Alton. "Why Columbus Sailed." *Columbia*, October 9. 2015. kofc.org/en/columbia/detail/why-columbus-sailed.

Penrosa, Victor. *God's Hand in History during World War II.* 2017.

Peterson, Kyle. "The High Court's Rocky Mountain Originalist." *Wall Street Journal*, September 7–8, 2019.

Peterson, Mark E. *The Great Prologue*. 1975.

Philanthropy Roundtable. "Who Gives Most to Charity?" philanthropyroundtable.org/almanac/statistics/who-gives.

Pinckney, Charles. "A Republican." In *Essays on the Constitution of the United States*. Edited by Paul Leicester Ford. 1892.

Plunket, Jesse M. "Putting an End to the Venezuela vs. Sweden Debate." *Orlando Sentinel*, October 25, 2018. orlandosentinel.com/opinion/os-op-us-democratic-socialists-dont-get-scandinavia-20181025-story.html.

Pullella, Philip. "Pope Compares Having an Abortion to 'Hiring a Hit Man.'" Reuters, October 20, 2018. reuters.com/article/us-pope-abortion/pope-compares-having-an-abortion-to-hiring-a-hit-man-idUSKCN1MK1E7.

Rafael. *Christopher Columbus the Hero: Defending Columbus from Modern Day Revisionism*. 2017.

Reagan, Ronald. "Proclamation 5018—Year of the Bible, 1983." The American Presidency Project. presidency.ucsb.edu/documents/proclamation-5018-year-the-bible-1983.

———. "Remarks at a Ceremony Commemorating the 40th Anniversary of the Normandy Invasion, D-day." June 6, 1984. reaganfoundation.org/media/128809/normandy.pdf.

———. "Remarks at a Conservative Political Action Conference Dinner." February 26, 1982.

———. *Abortion and the Conscience of the Nation*. 2000.

Reeves, Linda S. "Worthy of Our Promised Blessings." *Ensign*, November 2015.

Reidman, Kirk. "The Gift of Hope." In *Voices of Hope: Latter-day Saint Perspectives on Same-Gender Attraction—an Anthology of Gospel Teachings and Personal Essays*. Compiled by Ty Mansfield. 2011.

Reiné, Roel, dir. *Washington*. Season 1, episode 3, "Father of His Country." Aired February 18, 2020, on History.

Renlund, Dale G. "That I Might Draw All Men unto Me." *Ensign*, May 2016.

Reynolds, Sarrah. "Becoming." In *Voices of Hope: Latter-day Saint Perspectives on Same-Gender Attraction—an Anthology of Gospel Teachings and Personal Essays.* Compiled by Ty Mansfield. 2011.

Ripple, William J., Christopher Wolf, Thomas M. Newsome, Phoebe Barnard, William R. Moomaw. "World Scientists' Warning of a Climate Emergency." *Bioscience* 70, no. 1 (January 2020): 8–12.

Roberts, Alexander and James Donaldson, eds. *The Ante-Nicene Fathers.* Vol. 2–3, 5, 7. 1885–7.

Robinson, Nathan J. "How Inequality Statistics Can Mislead You." *Current Affairs*, April 20, 2019. currentaffairs.org/2019/04/how-inequality-statistics-can-mislead-you.

Roosevelt, Franklin D. "Proclamation 2629—Thanksgiving Day, 1944." The American Presidency Project. presidency.ucsb.edu/documents/proclamation-2629-thanksgiving-day-1944.

———. "Statement on the Four Hundredth Anniversary of the Printing of the English Bible." The American Presidency Project. presidency.ucsb.edu/documents/statement-the-four-hundredth-anniversary-the-printing-the-english-bible.

———. "Text of Radio Address—Prayer on D-Day, June 6, 1944." fdrlibrary.org/d-day.

Ruse, Cathy, and Rob Schwarzwalder. "The Best Pro-Life Arguments for Secular Audiences." Family Research Council. frc.org/brochure/the-best-pro-life-arguments-for-secular-audiences.

Rush, Benjamin. "Of the Mode of Education Proper in a Republic." In *Essays, Literary, Moral and Philosophical.* 1806.

———. "To John Adams from Benjamin Rush, 20 July 1811." founders.archives.gov/documents/Adams/99-02-02-5659.

Saad, Lydia. "Record Few Americans Believe Bible Is Literal Word of God." Gallup. May 15, 2017. news.gallup.com/poll/210704/record-few-americans-believe-bible-literal-word-god.aspx.

Sandefur, Timothy. "Misquoting Federalist 78." Pacific Legal Foundation blog. Mar. 18, 2011. pacificlegal.org/misquoting-federalist-78.

Santayana, George. *The Life of Reason, or the Phases of Human Progress: Introduction and Reason in Common Sense.* 1905.

Scalia, Antonin. *On Faith: Lessons from an American Believer.* Edited by Christopher J. Scalia and Edward Whelan. 2019.

———. *Scalia Speaks: Reflections on Law, Faith, and Life Well Lived.* Edited by Christopher J. Scalia and Edward Whelan. 2017.

Schlesinger, Arthur M. *The Birth of a Nation: A Portrait of the American People on the Eve of Independence.* 1968.

Schmidt, Michael S. "'Flags of Our Fathers' Author Now Doubts His Father Was in Iwo Jima Photo." *New York Times*, May 4, 2016.

Scott, Richard G. "Temple Worship: The Source of Strength and Power in Times of Need." *Ensign*, May 2009.

Shakespeare, William. *Henry V.* 1599.

———. *King Richard II.* 1595.

Shapiro, Ben. *How to Destroy America in Three Easy Steps.* 2020.

———. *The Right Side of History: How Reason and Moral Purpose Made the West Great.* 2019.

Shine, Elizabeth. "Coming to Appreciate Stay-at-Home Moms." *Wall Street Journal*, May 10, 2019. wsj.com/articles/coming-to-appreciate-stay-at-home-moms-11557442888.

Singapore Human Resources Institute. "Singapore." apfhrm.com/docs/Singapore-Country-report.pdf.

Skousen, W. Cleon. *The 5000 Year Leap: A Miracle That Changed the World.* 1981.

Smith, Adam. *Wealth of Nations.* 1991.

Smith, Daniel Lynwood. *Into the World of the New Testament: Greco-Roman and Jewish Texts and Contexts.* 2015.

Solzhenitsyn, Aleksandr. *Warning to the West.* 1976.

Sparks, Jared. *The Life of Benjamin Franklin.* Vol. 1. 1856.

———. *The Life of Gouverneur Morris.* Vol. 3. 1832.

Stanly, John. "Funeral Oration for John Adams." *Carolina Sentinel*, July 29, 1826. founders.archives.gov/documents/Adams/99-03-02-4695.

Stenberg v. Carhart, 530 U.S. 914 (2000).

Stepman, Jarrett. "The Truth about Columbus." *The Daily Signal*, October 6, 2017. dailysignal.com/2017/10/06/the-truth-about-columbus.

Stewart, Chris, and Ted Steward. *Seven Miracles That Saved America: Why They Matter and Why We Should Have Hope.* 2009.

Stewart, Ted. Utah State University commencement address. May 6, 2017. Transcript in possession of the author.

Story, Joseph. *Commentaries on the Constitution of the United States.* Vol. 2 and 3. 1833.

Stossel, John. "Private Enterprise Does It Better." *Reason*, August 5, 2010. reason.com/2010/08/05/private-enterprise-does-it-bet.

Strong, Bryan. "Slavery and Colonialism Make Up the True Legacy of Columbus." *New York Times*, November 4, 1989.

Taylor, Bill. "What Breaking the 4-Minute Mile Taught Us about the Limits of Conventional Thinking." *Harvard Business Review*, March 9, 2018. hbr.org/2018/03/what-breaking-the-4-minute-mile-taught-us-about-the-limits-of-conventional-thinking.

Terzo, Sarah. "After an Abortion: A Look into the Recovery Room." Live Action, October 18, 2014. liveaction.org/news/after-an-abortion-a-look-into-the-recovery-room.

The American Presidency Project. presidency.ucsb.edu/documents/remarks-conservative-political-action-conference-dinner.

Thomas, Hugh. *Rivers of Gold: The Rise of the Spanish Empire, from Columbus to Magellan.* 2003.

Thompson, Floyd E. "Some Dangerous Tendencies in Government." *Constitutional Review* 6 (January–October 1922): 167–74.

Thucydides. *The History of the Peloponnesian War.* Translated by Richard Crawley. 1874.

Torricelli, Robert G., and Andrew Carroll, eds. *In Our Own Words: Extraordinary Speeches of the American Century.* 1999.

Tower, Charlemagne Jr. *The Marquis de la Fayette in the American Revolution.* Vol. 1. 2005.

Town of Greece v. Galloway, 572 U.S. (2014).

Tribe, Laurence H. "The Supreme Court, 1972 Term, Foreword: Toward a Model of Roles in the Due Process of Law." *Harvard Law Review* 1, no. 7 (1973): 1–53.

Trop v. Dulles, 356 U.S. 86 (1958).

Truman, Harry S. "Proclamation 2978: National Day of Prayer, 1952." In *Code of Federal Regulations, Title 3—The President.* 1949–53.

Tuchman, Barbara W. *The March of Folly: From Troy to Vietnam.* 2014.

Tupy, Marian L., and Gale Pooley. "How Julian Simon Won a $1,000 Bet with 'Population Bomb' Author Paul Ehrlich." Foundation for Economic Education. March 8, 2018. fee.org/articles/how-julian-simon-won-1-000-bet-with-population-bomb-author-paul-ehrlich.

UNESCO Institute for Statistics, eAtlas of Literacy, tellmaps.com/uis/literacy/#!/tellmap/-1003531175.

Union Pacific Railroads. "Union Pacific Reports Fourth Quarter and Full Year 2019 Results." January 23, 2020. up.com/media/releases/200123-4q-2019-earnings.

United States Postal Service. *FY2019 Annual Report to Congress.*

Vonnegut, Kurt. "Harrison Bergeson." In *Welcome to the Monkey House.*

Wall Street Journal editorial board. "Defining Socialism Down." *Wall Street Journal,* June 15–16, 2019.

Wallace v. Jaffree, 472 U.S. 38 (1985).

Wang, Feng, Baochang Gu, and Yong Cai. "The End of China's One-Child Policy." March 30, 2016. brookings.edu/articles/the-end-of-chinas-one-child-policy.

Warren-Adams Letters: Being Chiefly a Correspondence among John Adams, Samuel Adams, and James Warren. Vol. 1. 1917.

Washington, George. "Farewell Address, September 17, 1796." In *George Washington Papers, Series 2, Letterbooks 1799: Letterbook 24, April 3, 1793–March 3, 1797.* 1793. Manuscript/Mixed Material. loc.gov/item/mgw2.024.

______. "From George Washington to Edward Newenham." August 29, 1788. founders.archives.gov/documents/Washington/04-06-02-0436.

______. "From George Washington to Lafayette." July 25, 1785. founders.archives.gov/documents/Washington/04-03-02-0143.

______. "From George Washington to Lafayette." May 28, 1788. founders.archives.gov/documents/Washington/04-06-02-0264.

______. "George Washington to Samuel Langdon, September 28, 1789." In *George Washington Papers, Series 2, Letterbooks 1754 to 1799: Letterbook 22, Aug. 24, 1790.* Manuscript/Mixed Material. loc.gov/item/mgw2.022.

———. "Thanksgiving Proclamation, 3 October 1789." founders.archives.gov/documents/Washington/05-04-02-0091.

———. "Washington's Farewell Address 1796." avalon.law.yale.edu/18th_century/washing.asp.

———. "Washington's Inaugural Address of 1789." April 30, 1789. archives.gov/exhibits/american_originals/inaugtxt.html.

Webster, Daniel. "Extract from the Address before the Historical Society of New York, February 1852." In *The University Speaker: A Collection of Pieces Designed for College Exercises.* Compiled by William Russell. 1854.

———. *Address Delivered by the Hon. Daniel Webster in Faneuil Hall, May 22, 1852, at the Request of the City Council of Boston.* 1852.

———. *The Works of Daniel Webster.* Vol. 1. 1851.

Webster, Noah. *History of the United States.* 1832.

Wells, William V. *The Life and Public Services of Samuel Adams.* Vol. 1. 1866.

Whitelaw, Alex, comp. "Johnnie Armstrong's Last Good-Night." In *The Book of Scottish Ballads.* 1845.

Wilcox, Ella Wheeler. "Gethsemane." In *Poems of Power.* 1903.

Wilford, John Noble. "Don't Blame Columbus for All the Indians' Ills." *New York Times*, October 29, 2002. nytimes.com/2002/10/29/science/don-t-blame-columbus-for-all-the-indians-ills.

Wilkinson, J. Harvie III. *All Falling Faiths: Reflections on the Promise and Failure of the 1960s.* 2017.

Wilson, James. *The Works of James Wilson.* Edited by James DeWitt Andrews. Vol. 1. 1896.

———. *The Works of the Honorable James Wilson.* Edited by Bird Wilson. Vol. 3. 1804.

Wilson, Woodrow. "The States and the Federal Government." *North American Review*, May 1908.

Witherspoon, John. *The Works of John Witherspoon.* Vol. 5. 1804.

———. *The Works of John Witherspoon.* Vol. 7. 1815.

Wolf, William J. *The Almost Chosen People: A Study of the Religion of Abraham Lincoln.* 1959.

Wood, Genevieve. "An Expert Told Us What Draws People to Socialism." August 5, 2019. nationalinterest.org/blog/buzz/expert-told-us-what-draws-people-socialism-71456.

World Bank. "Life Expectancy at Birth, Total (Years)—Bolivia, Ecuador." 2019. data.worldbank.org/indicator/SP.DYN.LE00.IN?locations=BO-EC.

Worstall, Tim. "But Why Did Julian Simon Win the Paul Ehrlich Bet?" *Forbes*, January 13, 2013. forbes.com/sites/timworstall/2013/01/13/but-why-did-julian-simon-win-the-paul-ehrlich-bet.

Wyler, Rich. "A Mighty Change of Heart." In *Voices of Hope: Latter-day Saint Perspectives on Same-Gender Attraction—an Anthology of Gospel Teachings and Personal Essays.* Compiled by Ty Mansfield. 2011.

Yglesias, Matthew. "Denmark's Prime Minister Says Bernie Sanders Is Wrong to Call His Country Socialist." *Vox*, October 31, 2015. vox.com/2015/10/31/9650030/denmark-prime-minister-bernie-sanders.

Zielinski, Sarah. "The Tornado That Saved Washington." *Smithsonian*, August 25. 2010. smithsonianmag.com/science-nature/the-tornado-that-saved-washington-33901211.

Zorach v. Clauson, 343 U.S. 306 (1952).

INDEX

C

D

E

N

O

P

Q

R

S

Made in the USA
Coppell, TX
24 May 2023

17227458R10193